Neil Anderson's Freedom in Christ Ministries has been raised up by God to effectively combat Satan's deceptive onslaught. Neil's message on spiritual warfare is the most balanced and powerful I've discovered. I use the Steps to Freedom with others and have seen many set free.

NEY BAILEY
International Representative, Campus Crusade for Christ International

I thank God for Neil Anderson. His principled approach works as it helps people find resolution to life's problems through their identity in Christ. Read this book; better, use it. It is unusually practical, thoroughly biblical and Christ-honoring. It's been my privilege to see lives dramatically changed right before my eyes as people repent and believe using these steps as a tool.

ROB BUGH
Senior Pastor, Wheaton Bible Church
Wheaton, Illinois

Neil Anderson is an important spiritual guide in my life. He can be the same for you. I eagerly recommend this book on discipleship counseling. Neil gives us biblical, instructive, practical, powerful and useful directions for helping people become free in Christ. We can't expect maturity or productivity in any Christian if they are tempted, accused and deceived by Satan all the time. No Christian can read this book and be left unmoved or unhelped.

JOHN CHOI
Korean Ministries Director, Christian Reformed Home Missions
Grand Rapids, Michigan

I have always felt that Neil Anderson's ministry is built solidly upon Jesus Christ, both in teaching and in practical application. **Helping Others Find Freedom in Christ** may be his best "equipping work" yet for the Church of Jesus Christ! The material presented in **Helping Others Find Freedom in Christ** has had a profound and lasting impact upon the lives of thousands here in Modesto, California, including my own life. I am thrilled to see such a practical, theological sound and systematic blueprint for helping people gain and maintain their freedom in Christ.

WADE ESTES
Senior Pastor, First Baptist Church
Modesto, California

Helping Others Find Freedom in Christ is a keen tool for people to resolve questions of ineffective Christian living. I highly commend this book to believers and recommend it explicitly for pastors and spiritual leaders seeking to free disciples of Jesus Christ to their full potential.

JOHN JACKSON
Executive Minister, American Baptist Churches of the Pacific Southwest
Covina, California

Each chapter of Helping Others Find Freedom in Christ consistently confronts us with a "truth encounter" of what it means to be a follower of Jesus Christ—as a new creation in relationship with God through Christ. This book provides biblical direction for each follower of Christ to experience not only the fullness of our relationship with God, but also the opportunity to be released from the past and to settle our relationships with each other.

GORDON E. KIRK
Senior Pastor, Lake Avenue Congregational Church
Pasadena, California

Helping Others Find Freedom in Christ should be required reading for every Christian, especially for those involved in reaching cities for Christ. Neil Anderson, operating on an absolutely biblical foundation, has laid before us the steps to a truth encounter which will indeed set our people and our churches free. This book is a unique combination of Bible-centered principles illustrated by Christ-centered experiences.

ED SILVOSO
President, Harvest Evangelism, Inc
San Jose, California

Helping Others Find Freedom in Christ is the most powerful biblical counseling tool I have ever used. It's amazing to watch people in a few short hours move from the worst problems imaginable to release, freedom and new hope. What's really encouraging is that for most of them a lasting change occurs. What made things better? Not technique or counselor skill, but confrontation with Christ and "escape from the trap of the devil" (2 Timothy 2:26, *NIV*).

CHARLES MYLANDER
General Superintendent, Friends Church Southwest
Los Angeles, California

At last God has given us through Neil Anderson the counseling tool we have needed so long. Helping Others Find Freedom in Christ is the definitive manual for learning and using the "Seven Steps." Individuals can find freedom using this book. Busy pastors and ministry leaders will use this book to train laity to assist with the counseling load. Discipleship groups will find this a valuable life-changing study. I commend this wonderful volume to all who want to live free and assist others in finding Christ's freedom.

RON PHILLIPS
Senior Pastor, Central Baptist Church of Hixson
Hixson, Tennessee

In more than 20 years of pastoral counseling, I have not found a better resource for helping people resolve personal and spiritual conflicts than Neil Anderson's Steps to Freedom. I have had full confidence using Dr. Anderson's approach because it is both thoroughly biblical and theologically consistent. It has been my joy to see people who have sought relief for years without success grasp their blessed freedom—their birthright in Jesus Christ. Every pastor working with broken and bound people needs this fully transferable tool in his spiritual arsenal.

JERRY RUEB
Senior Pastor, South Delta Baptist Church
British Columbia, Canada

Helping Others Find Freedom in Christ helps people accept responsibility for their own lives, pointing them to the truth that Christ is sufficient for all of their sin and failure. It equips and enables people not only to be free in Christ but also to maintain their freedom. The book deals with both issues dealt with in James 4:7, "Submit yourselves therefore to God. Resist the devil, and he will flee from you"(KJV). It is must reading for every believer!

TOM STARR
Senior Pastor, Valley Fourth Memorial Church
Spokane, Washington

Helping Others Find Freedom in Christ places the help-giver in partnership with God. This book's strength lies in its uniquely Christian strategy. It gives scriptural step-by-step pointers to break the bondage of sin and Satan so the person can break past slavery and walk free in Christ.

ELMER L. TOWNS
Dean, School of Religion, Liberty University
Lynchburg, Virginia

HELPING OTHERS FIND FREEDOM IN CHRIST

NEIL T. ANDERSON

Regal Books
A Division of Gospel Light
Ventura, California, U.S.A.

Published by Regal Books
A Division of Gospel Light
Ventura, California, U.S.A.
Printed in U.S.A.

Regal Books is a ministry of Gospel Light, an evangelical Christian publisher dedicated to serving the local church. We believe God's vision for Gospel Light is to provide church leaders with biblical, user-friendly materials that will help them evangelize, disciple and minister to children, youth and families.

It is our prayer that this Regal Book will help you discover biblical truth for your own life and help you meet the needs of others. May God richly bless you.

For a free catalog of resources from Regal Books/Gospel Light please contact your Christian supplier or call 1-800-4-GOSPEL.

Note: All stories, poems and quotations in this publication are used by permission.

Library of Congress Cataloging-in-Publication Data
Anderson, Neil T., 1942-
    Helping others find freedom in Christ / Neil T. Anderson.
        p. cm.
    ISBN 0-8307-1740-4 (hardcover)
    1. Freedom (Theology) 2. Spiritual life—Christianity.
    3. Interpersonal relations—Religious aspects—Christianity.
    4. Pastoral counseling. I. Title.
    BT810.2.A56 1995   95-12324
    253—dc20   CIP

1 2 3 4 5 6 7 8 9 10 11 12 / 02 01 00 99 98 97 96 95

Rights for publishing this book in other languages are contracted by Gospel Literature International (GLINT). GLINT also provides technical help for the adaptation, translation and publishing of Bible study resources and books in scores of languages worldwide. For further information, contact GLINT, P.O. Box 4060, Ontario, CA 91761-1003, U.S.A., or the publisher.

CONTENTS

PART ONE

This section presents a biblical analysis of discipleship
counseling, taking into account the reality of personal and
spiritual conflicts and a person's identity in Christ.

PART TWO

This section will walk you through each of the seven Steps
involved in helping a person find freedom in Christ.

APPENDICES

ACKNOWLEDGMENTS

I want to thank my staff at Freedom in Christ Ministries. Every one of them has a servant's heart, and it has been my delight to work with them. They are putting into practice each day, all around the world, the process outlined in this book. Every person we have helped to find freedom in Christ has also contributed to this book. We have all learned much from each other.

Special thanks to Tom McGee, our director in Denver, Colorado, and to Robert and Grace Toews, who direct our ministry in Canada. They read an early version of this book and gave valuable feedback. I also appreciate one of my Talbot students, Dr. Bill Walthall, who worked on similar material for his doctoral dissertation. As always, I have enjoyed working with the team at Gospel Light; they provide a valuable service to the Body of Christ.

This book couldn't have been completed without the help of my dear friends Ron and Carole Wormser. They are my travel companions. They have led hundreds of people to freedom in Christ and have trained hundreds of others to do likewise. They have contributed heavily to this book and to my life. So my wife, Joanne, joins me in dedicating this book to them. We love you both very much.

INTRODUCTION

Is Christ the answer to people's problems? Does truth set people free? I have never been more convinced that the answer is an emphatic yes! But I'm reasonably sure that many church attenders today could not honestly answer in the affirmative from a deep inner conviction. Many will nod their heads in agreement, but most are not experiencing the abundant life that Scripture offers them. I would even venture to say that only a small percentage of born-again Christians are living free and productive lives in Christ.

When I was a young pastor, I called on a visitor to our church and had the privilege of leading her to Christ. She attended faithfully for about four months then stopped.

In a telephone conversation, I asked her why she stopped attending. She assured me that it wasn't my preaching or because of me personally. Then she said, "But I have enough problems at home already, without having to add any more from the church!"

She told me that the neighbor who invited her to church would weekly dump on her all the problems she was having in the choir. It was so discouraging to think that I was pastoring a church that was *adding* to the problems of people instead of helping them resolve their problems.

DISCOURAGED PASTORS

I have met with many discouraged pastors in the last few years. In private conversations, I asked several if they would go to their own churches if they weren't the pastor. Many have said they wouldn't. It must be hard to enthusiastically promote a product that you don't believe in yourself.

One pastor asked me how he could bring about a greater degree of fruitfulness in his ministry. I said, "First, you have to personally believe that there is no other answer than Christ."

"Maybe that's my problem," he responded. "I'm not sure I believe that anymore."

Many of these pastors aren't discouraged only about the plight of their churches. One ex-pastor shared with me, "I quit the ministry because what I was preaching wasn't even working for me, so I lost any sense of hope that it would work for others."

Bill McCartney, speaking at Promise Keepers, shared the following results of a survey that dealt with the personal and professional lives of clergy:

- 80 percent believe that pastoral ministry affects their families negatively.
- 33 percent said being in the ministry is an outright hazard to your family.
- 50 percent feel unable to meet the needs of the job.
- 90 percent feel they were inadequately trained to meet ministry demands.
- 70 percent say they have lower self-esteems now than when they started out.
- 37 percent confess having been involved in inappropriate sexual behavior with someone in the church.
- 70 percent of the pastors do not have someone they consider a close friend.
- 40 percent say they had considered leaving their pastorates in the last three months.

STRUGGLING CHRISTIANS

If church leaders are struggling this much, what must be going on in the home of the average layperson? Haven't you ever wondered why Christians aren't living more productive lives and why so many are falling into immorality?

These questions are especially puzzling in light of clear statements in Scripture that offer the assurance of victory: "In all these things we overwhelmingly conquer through Him who loved us" (Rom. 8:37). "I can do all things through Him who strengthens me" (Phil. 4:13). "Now those who belong to Christ Jesus have crucified the flesh with its passions and desires" (Gal. 5:24).

So what's wrong?

How many people do you know who were active in church at one time but then left for some reason? When you ask them to come back to church or encourage them to read their Bibles, they answer: "I tried that once, and it didn't work." Whenever I ask groups of Christian leaders if they have heard comments like that, everyone raises their hand.

Just as troubling is the vast majority of those outside the family of God who would not draw the conclusion that Christ is the answer, given the failure they see of those inside the Church. Frankly, I think the credibility of the Church is at stake. Unless you enjoy living in denial, you would have to agree with me that something is wrong.

TRUTH LIBERATES

This is not a time to live in denial and pretend that everything is okay when it isn't. The only thing a Christian ever has to admit to is the truth. The truth is not the enemy; it is a liberating friend. The Church is "the pillar and support of the truth" (1 Tim. 3:15). "Therefore, laying aside falsehood, speak truth, each one of you, with his neighbor, for we are members of one another" (Eph. 4:25). "If we walk in the light as He Himself is in the light, we have fellowship with one another, and the blood of Jesus His Son cleanses us from all sin" (1 John 1:7).

Any time we lie, or deny or seek to cover up indiscretions, we play right into the hands of the devil, who is the father of lies and the prince of darkness. Those who are caught in Satan's web "suppress the truth in unrighteousness" (Rom. 1:18). Why do they do that? Jesus explains, "This is the judgment, that the light is come into the world, and men loved the darkness rather than the light; for their deeds were evil. For everyone who does evil hates the light, and does not come to the light, lest his deeds should be exposed" (John 3:19,20).

Rest assured that God will not sit silently by. "For it is time for judgment to begin with the household of God" (1 Pet. 4:17). We are admonished to examine ourselves in the presence of communion. "For he who eats and drinks, eats and drinks judgment to himself, if he does not judge the body rightly. For this reason many among you are weak and sick, and a number sleep" (1 Cor. 11:29,30). Judgment! Discouragement! Failure!

Is there any hope? Absolutely! People all over the world are establishing their identities and finding freedom in Christ. Am I discouraged because of all the sin that seems to entangle us? No way! "Where sin increased, grace abounded all the more" (Rom. 5:20). How can anyone be discouraged when

"The law of the Spirit of life in Christ Jesus has set you free from the law of sin and of death" (8:2)? Being a child of God and living free in Christ is the birthright of every true believer in the gospel.

CRITICAL DEFICIENCIES

Several years ago, as a seminary professor, I started asking what's wrong with our Western-world orientation to ministry and Christian living. I discovered two critical deficiencies. The first is a misunderstanding of our identities in Christ. A common denominator among all those who are not living the abundant life is that they don't have any idea who they were as children of God. Scripture says, "God has sent forth the Spirit of His Son into our hearts, crying, 'Abba! Father!'" (Gal. 4:6) and "the Spirit Himself bears witness with our spirit that we are children of God" (Rom. 8:16). So why aren't more people sensing that?

It seems as though the gospel message of "Christ in you, the hope of glory" (Col. 1:27) is missing from our Christian practices and personal expe riences. Consequently, we operate out of an Old Testament law/obedience principle instead of a New Testament life/faith principle, which is possible only by the grace of God.

The result is a subtle form of Christian behaviorism that drives people into burnout or defeat. We put our confidence in programs and strategies instead of in the Lord. The "wonderful counselor" has become the educated counselor or pastor instead of the Lord who came to give us life. We have made our walks with God intellectual exercises instead of living relationships. Counseling has become more a matter of technique than an encounter with God. We operate as though we have no theology of resolution, so we just keep trying harder.

I asked one leading psychologist what the cure rate was at his clinic.

"Cure rate?" he responded. "We don't really cure anyone, we just help them cope!" How discouraging!

The second deficiency I discovered was that our Western-world orientation has all but excluded the reality of the spiritual world. When Jesus commissioned His disciples, He knew they were about to go into a less than receptive world. Jesus identified Satan as the ruler of this world (see John 16:11). John records that "the whole world lies in the power of the evil one" (1 John 5:19). Paul says that "the god of this world has blinded the minds of the unbelieving" (2 Cor. 4:4) and admonishes us to put on the armor of God. "For our struggle is not against flesh and blood, but against the rulers, against the powers, against the world forces of this darkness, against the spiritual forces of wickedness in the heavenly places" (Eph. 6:12).

Peter writes, "Be of sober spirit, be on the alert. Your adversary, the devil, prowls about like a roaring lion, seeking someone to devour" (1 Pet. 5:8). These are not optional passages that we can dismiss as though there is no such thing as a spiritual world, nor a kingdom of darkness. In the face of that reality, Jesus prays, "I do not ask Thee to take them out of the world, but to keep them from the evil one. They are not of the world, even as I am not of the world. Sanctify them in the truth; Thy word is truth" (John 17:15-17).

FACING SPIRITUAL PROBLEMS

As a pastor, I dealt with many people whom I knew had spiritual problems, but I didn't have any idea how to help them. Seminary had not prepared me to confront the reality of the spiritual world, nor did I know of any effective tools. I didn't even have a good understanding of who I was as a child of God, or why that was even necessary.

My identity was wrapped up in the things that I did. So when I was called to teach at Talbot School of Theology, I developed and offered an elective on spiritual warfare. At first it was the blind leading the blind. I felt like a first-grader teaching kindergarten students. But the class size doubled every year, and I started to see tremendous things happen in the lives of the students.

During those growing years, my ministry was confined to the campus. Frankly, I didn't want to go public until I was absolutely sure that what I was teaching was true according to the Word of God. Seminary students began to bring hurting people from their churches to see me, and I slowly learned how to help these dear people find their freedom in Christ from every conceivable problem. Over time, we were able to apply what we were learning to alcohol and drug addictions, which will be discussed in a forthcoming book dealing with recovery in Christ, sexual bondage (see *A Way of Escape*), eating disorders, panic attacks and a multitude of other problems (see *Released from Bondage*).

Eventually I wanted to find out what was happening in the lives of younger believers, because the vast majority of the adults' problems originated when they were children. So Steve Russo and I surveyed more than 1,700 students for our book, *The Seduction of Our Children*. We discovered that 71 percent of our professing Christian young people are hearing voices or struggling with bad thoughts. Do I believe that 7 out of 10 of our evangelical young people are paranoid schizophrenic or psychotic? No, I do not! But I do concur with 1 Timothy 4:1: "The Spirit clearly says that in later times some will abandon the faith and follow deceiving spirits and things taught by demons" (*NIV*). Is that happening? Yes, it's happening all over the world! Much of what is being passed off as mental illness is nothing more than a battle for the mind.

Just as troubling to me is the 74 percent of the teenagers who believe they are different from other kids—that is, Christianity works for others but it doesn't work for them! Is that true? Of course not. But if they believe they are different, it would affect the way they live their Christian lives. I have discovered that the majority of adults believe the same lie.

In the last 10 years, I have had the privilege of personally counseling hundreds of people who were struggling with their thoughts, experiencing difficulty reading their Bibles or actually hearing voices. With few exceptions, their problem was a spiritual battle for their minds. We have learned how to help these people find their freedom in Christ in about three or four hours each. In addition, thousands of people have found their freedom in Christ in conferences as we walked them through the Steps to Freedom. The purpose of this book is to explain and illustrate this process, which is now being used all over the world and in many different languages.

TRUTH SETS US FREE

The turning point for me was when I realized that what we were dealing with was best described as a "truth encounter," rather than a "power encounter." It is truth that sets us free. The battle we are fighting is primarily for our minds. Hence the necessity to take every thought captive in obedience to Christ (see 2 Cor. 10:5) and to think upon that which is true (see Phil. 4:8).

This concept certainly is not new. In the Garden of Eden, Eve was deceived and she believed a lie. Paul said, "I am afraid, lest as the serpent deceived Eve by his craftiness, your minds should be led astray from the simplicity and purity of devotion to Christ" (2 Cor. 11:3).

That is why God so dramatically intervened in the Early Church when He struck down Ananias and Sapphira in Acts 5. What was their great sin? That they gave only half of everything they owned to the church? (Pastor, don't you wish your people would sin that badly next Sunday?) Actually, their sin was keeping back half the price of the land while allowing people to think they had given it all. Most people wouldn't consider that a capital offense. After all, that was just their cunning little idea. But that isn't what Scripture says: "Ananias, why has Satan filled your heart to lie to the Holy Spirit?" (Acts 5:3). The Lord knew that if Satan could go into your churches, your homes and your marriages undetected and get you to believe a lie, he could control your lives.

Irenaeus, an Early Church father, nailed the problem when he wrote, "The devil, however, as he is the apostate angel, can only go to this length, as he did at the beginning, to deceive and lead astray the mind of man into disobeying the commandments of God, and gradually to darken the hearts." The father of lies (see John 8:44) has deceived many, and the result is discouraged pastors, fruitless churches, broken homes, defeated Christians and powerless ministries.

WE HAVE THE POWER WE NEED

Many struggle in their Christian walks and incorrectly reason that what they lack is power. Consequently, they often look for some new experiences that will give them more power. That leads only to disaster. There isn't a verse in the Bible that instructs us to seek more power. That's because we already have all the power we need to live the Christian life.

In a tragically similar fashion, many Christians are desperately trying to become something they already are. Few Christians know who they are as children of God or understand their inheritance in Christ. That is why Paul prays, "I pray that the eyes of your heart may be enlightened, so that you may know what is the hope of His calling, what are the riches of the glory of His inheritance in the saints, and what is the surpassing greatness of His power toward us who believe" (Eph. 1:18,19). My vision is to help every child of God on planet earth to realize who he or she is in Christ, so they can live free, productive lives.

James 4:7 says, "Submit therefore to God. Resist the devil and he will flee from you." I have learned the hard way that trying to resist the devil without first submitting to God results in a dogfight. That is the classic error of some deliverance ministries. On the other hand, you can submit to God and not resist the devil, therefore staying in bondage. The tragedy is that most recovery ministries don't encourage people to submit to God or resist the devil. An unidentified "higher power," with an unexplained gospel, will only result in exchanging one bondage for another and create a dependency upon some group or program instead of Christ.

I think we are locked in a paralysis of analysis. You can be considered smart by some if you can explain with great precision how people in bondage behave, and brilliant if you can explain how they got all screwed up in the first place. Would knowing that necessarily resolve their problems? No. Identifying the lies that people believe won't accomplish much if they don't know the truth or if they refuse to believe it.

There are a million ways people can go wrong, but the paths back to God aren't numerous. There are a million ways people can sin, but the way to reconciliation is the same. You could be abused in many different ways, but you would still have to forgive if you want to be free in Christ. There are hundreds of psychological models, thousands of self-help groups, and seemingly hundreds of thousands of programs, but the only answer is Christ in you, the hope of glory. He is "the way, and the truth, and the life" (John 14:6). When I finally started to realize this, I searched the Scriptures to find out what was keeping people from having a right relationship with God. All that I discovered could be synthesized into the following seven issues:

1. Counterfeit versus real;
2. Deception versus truth;
3. Bitterness versus forgiveness;
4. Rebellion versus submission;
5. Pride versus humility;
6. Bondage versus freedom;
7. Acquiescence versus renunciation.

Knowing how to resolve these issues is what constitutes the seven Steps to Freedom in Christ. Over time, I learned how to depend on God and function as a facilitator rather than an enabler or confronter. The Lord allowed me and my family to go through a period of brokenness that taught me that compassion is an essential prerequisite. I discovered that the process was far more of an encounter with God than a counseling technique. I was committed to the truth that the path back to God must be simple enough so that the simplest of His creations could enter into it. Otherwise we reduce our walks with God down to an intellectual exercise and make it available only to the intellectually gifted.

But I also learned that we dare not be simplistic. To be complete, all reality must be understood and accepted. I believe that we have a complete God and a whole gospel that deals with the total person: body, soul and spirit. I believe we live in a natural world as well as a spiritual world. I thank the Lord for medical doctors, nutritionists and physical therapists—especially those who know that a medical model is only part of the answer—who look after our physical needs. I believe that taking pills to heal our bodies is commendable, but I also believe that taking pills to heal our souls or spirits is deplorable.

DISCIPLING IN CHRIST

In this book, I am going to address what I see as the scope and limits of biblical integration. Then I will look at the theological basis for counseling in Christ. I personally prefer the concept of discipling in Christ, because I think that fits the biblical model better. The concepts are interchangeable in my own mind, but I realize that they aren't for most people because of the secularization of "Christian" counseling. I will also share my perception of the counseling/discipling process and what it takes to be the kind of counselor/discipler whom God can work through.

My dear friends Ron and Carole Wormser, who head up the counseling ministry at my conferences, helped extensively with the second half of this book. It is a practical explanation of the counseling process, the problems we typically encounter and illustrations gathered from many years of experience by all of our staff at Freedom in Christ Ministries.

I suppose every book should be able to stand alone, but you would profit greatly if you first read *Victory over the Darkness* and *The Bondage Breaker*, in that order. Each has a study guide as well as professionally taped video and audio series for group discussion, as does this book. My colleague Tom McGee and I have prepared a study guide for this book, which allows for greater instruction and personal interaction. The study guide explains how this ministry can be established in your church. It has study questions for this book and includes two important appendices. The first defines medical, psychological, cult and occult terminology. The second answers the 25 most-asked questions that our ministry receives.

FOUNDATIONAL PRINCIPLES

Five basic assumptions underscore everything that is in this book and our ministry. First, I believe that Scripture is the only reliable source for faith and practice (see 2 Tim. 3:16,17). God's Word is sufficient to establish a foundation of truth by which all other sources of knowledge can be evaluated. I will explain later that we must look at all empirical research through the grid of Scripture.

Second, I believe that all counseling and discipling concepts and procedures must be based on the finished work of Christ (see Col. 1:27-2:10). The fact that every Christian is eternally alive in Christ right now is the only basis for hope.

Third, I rely totally on the present ministry of the Holy Spirit (see John 16:7-15). If there were no Holy Spirit, there would be no Church and no power to live the Christian life. He "is the Spirit of truth" (John 14:17), and He will lead us into all truth (see 16:13). He is the One who communicates God's presence to us and leads us into the truth that will set us free.

Fourth, we are limited by the faith response of counselees (see Gal. 3:1-5). We cannot help those who don't want to be helped or will not assume their own responsibility to choose the truth. If they choose to believe a lie or live in sin, that is their choice. I respect their right to choose, but I care enough about them to let them know what the consequences of their choices will be.

Last, I believe deeply that we all need the support of the Christian community (see Heb. 10:17-25). I don't believe God ever intended us to live our lives alone. We absolutely need God, and we necessarily need each other.

I must emphasize that the Steps to Freedom do not set anybody free! The One who sets people free is Christ. What sets them free is their willingness to choose the truth, walk in the light and assume their responsibility to live righteously before God. The Steps are just tools that are no better than the one using them. Jesus is the bondage breaker and the wonderful Counselor. Anybody who is willing to get radically right with God, be dependent upon Him and put into practice the process outlined in this book will see many people come alive in Christ right before his or her very eyes. Not because it is the only right way but because it is a comprehensive way to resolve the issues that are critical between ourselves and God.

It isn't the Steps that work in people's lives; it is God. And He wants all His children to live free and spiritually productive lives. If God wants it done, it can be done.

PART ONE

This section presents a biblical analysis of discipleship counseling, taking into account the reality of personal and spiritual conflicts and a person's identity in Christ.

CHAPTER ONE

THE FOUNDATION
AND BALANCE OF LIFE

During one of my "Resolving Personal and Spiritual Conflicts" conferences, an attractive lady who appeared to have it all together confessed privately to me, "You've described me to a tee. I've struggled for years and can't break free from my problems." After many years of fruitless counseling, she had decided to admit herself to a treatment center.

I asked if I could see her first, because I knew the treatment center that had been recommended to her relied primarily on prescription drugs. The night before her admission I walked her through the Steps to Freedom. When we were done, I said, "I'm not sure you need the hospitalization program, but if you do admit yourself, write me a letter in a week and let me know how things are going." A few days later, I received this note:

> I'll let you know how I'm doing in a week or so, but I just had to share my joy while it's still fresh and new. After meeting with you Monday night, I was absolutely euphoric, and so was my husband. He was so glad to see me happy. But the best news is that I didn't wake up with nightmares or screams. Instead, I woke up with my heart singing, and the very first thought that entered my mind was "even the stones will cry out," followed by "Abba, Father." Neil, the Holy Spirit is alive in me. Praise the Lord.
>
> I'm now in this treatment center. It's been a tremendous adjustment. There are so many truly hurting people here. I just wish I could bring you here to meet with all of them and set them free, too. There's one woman in particular who appears to be evil personified. She verbally attacked me the very first day.

Thank you, Neil, for having the courage to free God's people
from the grip of the enemy. I can't begin to tell you how free I
feel, but somehow I think you know.

I wish I could say that the doctors and counselors at the secular treatment
center reinforced what the Lord had done in this dear lady, but they didn't.
Unfortunately, three hours of biblical counsel can be nullified by four weeks
of godless counsel. A decision to be submissive and dependent upon God
can be reversed by a program that encourages self-reliance and dependency
upon groups and medication.

Is there no value in secular programs? Can the Christian learn anything
from the world? Is truth restricted to biblical revelation only? Does empirical research (experimentation and observation) refute, undermine, contradict, subvert or destroy our confidence in Scripture? Is science the natural
enemy of our faith, or is it potentially an important and necessary ally? Is all
psychology a tool of the enemy, or is there a biblical psychology that must
be understood and embraced by all Christians? How do we know what is
true, real and right?

Let's try to answer these questions as we examine how theology can or
cannot be integrated with scientific and behavioral disciplines.

THE SCOPE AND LIMITS OF INTEGRATION

First, let's lay some groundwork by looking at how God reveals Himself and
His will to us. Theologians have identified from Scripture three forms of revelation:

General Revelation
This is the basic form. As Psalm 19:1 says, "The heavens are telling of the glory
of God; and their expanse is declaring the work of His hands." Romans 1:20
says, "For since the creation of the world His invisible attributes, His eternal
power and divine nature, have been clearly seen." Paul goes on to say that we
will not be excused from knowing that there is a God, because the existence,
work and nature of God can be understood by observing His created order. As
we observe creation, the "natural" response should be to worship the Creator.

However, mankind did not honor God. "They exchanged the truth of
God for a lie" (v. 25). They still wouldn't honor Him even though it led to
their own undoing: "God gave them over to degrading passions; for their
women [and men] exchanged the natural function for that which is unnat-

ural" (v. 26; see v. 27). Passages like this have led many biblical ethicists to accept the concept of "natural law." Proponents of natural law reason that God has built into the universe a sense of justice and morality. Because God created order into the universe, there is a natural way that mankind should live and behave with one another. For instance, it is unnatural for a man to be with another man sexually. God created a man to be with a woman in terms of sexuality.

The existence of a natural law can be observed by studying pagan societies that have no knowledge of God and His ways. They seem to collectively "know" or socially agree that acts such as killing, stealing and lying are wrong. Every society eventually agrees upon certain standards of right and wrong that don't stray too far from biblical morality, even though individuals fail to live up to them.

In a pagan society like ours, natural law may be the only acceptable basis for discussing moral issues in the public arena. Standing in front of an abortion clinic and proclaiming the truth from the Word of God concerning the sanctity of life will probably not be received by those who don't know the Lord. The pagan would simply respond by saying, "I don't believe in God or the Bible." Then where do you go? If done in love, such preaching would hopefully bring conviction leading to eternal life, but it will not have an immediate effect upon the laws of our land. Why? Because the Bible is not accepted in our courts of law as the standard for morality. The constitution of the United States is the basis by which the courts of our land mete out justice. But what argument does an unregenerate person have against an honest doctor or geneticist who can demonstrate on the basis of science that an unborn child is fully human at conception and is therefore guaranteed protection under the constitution?

Catholic ethicists have placed a greater emphasis on natural law than Protestants have. I personally think we need to incorporate the concept of natural law into more of our thinking. If properly understood, it will never collide with Scripture. It actually illustrates in creation what God has said in His Word. We will explore the limitations and relative value of natural law and the rational process of verification later.

Special Revelation

Special revelation refers to the written Word of God. Most Protestants limit special revelation to the 66 canonical books divided into the Old Testament (39 books) and the New Testament (27 books). The Old Testament records the creation and fall of mankind, the relationship that God had with His people based on the promises of the Abrahamic covenant (see Gen. 12:1-3), and the law of the Mosaic covenant (see Exod. 24:8). The New Testament reveals God's answer for fallen humanity by recording the life, death, burial and resurrection of our Lord Jesus Christ and how He relates to His people under the New Covenant (see Jer. 31:31f; Matt. 26:28; Heb. 10:16,17).

The Ultimate Revelation

Jesus Christ is the ultimate and final revelation of God. "In the beginning was the Word, and the Word was with God, and the Word was God" (John 1:1). He alone perfectly reveals who God is because He is God. "And the Word became flesh, and dwelt among us, and we beheld His glory, glory as of the only begotten from the Father, full of grace and truth" (v. 14). The glory of God is a manifestation of His presence. Jesus said, "If you knew Me, you would know My Father also" (8:19). "I and the Father are one" (10:30). "He who has seen Me has seen the Father" (14:9).

The Key to Understanding

These three channels of revelation are the means by which God has revealed Himself and made His will known to us. None of these channels will be understood or effective in our lives apart from the present work of the Holy Spirit. He is first and foremost "the Spirit of truth" (v. 17), and He will guide us into all truth (see 16:13). That truth will set us free (see 8:32). Fallen humanity cannot even know the liberating truth of God's Word, because "a natural man does not accept the things of the Spirit of God; for they are foolishness to him, and he cannot understand them, because they are spiritually appraised" (1 Cor. 2:14). "Even if our gospel is veiled, it is veiled to those who are perishing, in whose case the god of this world has blinded the minds of the unbelieving" (2 Cor. 4:3,4).

Fully understanding and appropriating the liberating truth of God's Word cannot be divorced from the reality of the spiritual world. The real battle on planet earth is between the kingdom of darkness and the kingdom of light. This battle of good versus evil, the Christ versus the Antichrist and the truth versus the lie is fought primarily in the minds of all humanity. Nobody is excluded. All must choose to take "every thought captive to the obedience of Christ" (10:5), and all must learn to let their minds dwell upon that which is true, honorable, right, pure and lovely (see Phil. 4:8).

How do we determine what is true, lovely and right? Many leading theologians and Christian psychologists have debated the integration of general revelation with special revelation depicted by the following diagram:

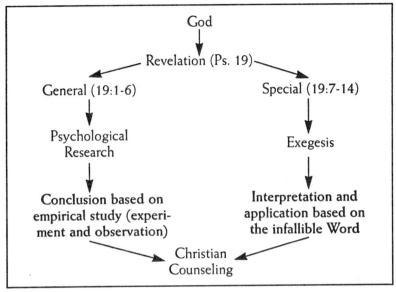

Diagram 1-A

The left side of the diagram shows the rational process of verification accomplished by observation and experimentation. It represents the scientific method of investigation, which is what higher education in our Western world is based upon. Psychological and sociological research is conducted by researchers and those who are attempting to obtain degrees at the highest levels of learning.

The right side of the diagram represents special revelation (the Bible), which is proclaimed and defended by various seminaries and schools of theology. Interpretation is accomplished by practicing exegesis (explaining) on passages of Scripture and applying principles of hermeneutics (interpretation) to better understand what God has said. Some would suggest that each side of the diagram has equal value, and the truth is ascertained by combining the two. But I, along with many other concerned Christians, believe that there are serious problems with that approach to integration. Let me offer three critical observations.

THE PRIMACY OF SPECIAL REVELATION

First, special revelation (the Bible) is authoritative, whereas general revelation (nature) is illustrative. The heavens and earth do declare and show forth the glory of God, but humanistic observations and scientific manipulations can't answer the philosophical questions of *why?* How do we explain the origin of the species, much less their purpose for being here? Without special revelation to explain life and its meaning, we have no recourse but to fall back on humanistic philosophical speculation or scientific rationalism.

Research has its place because it helps us to know "what is," and we will be more fruitful if we learn to adapt our ministries accordingly. That is the point that Paul makes in 1 Corinthians 9:19-22:

> For though I am free from all men, I have made myself a slave to all, that I might win the more. And to the Jews I became as a Jew, that I might win Jews; to those who are under the Law, as under the Law, though not being myself under the Law, that I might win those who are under the Law; to those who are without law, as without law, though not being without the law of God but under the law of Christ, that I might win those who are without law. To the weak I became weak, that I might win the weak; I have become all things to all men, that I might by all means save some.

Good ministries stay relevant by being fully informed about the societies around them and understanding what people are doing, thinking and saying. I have conducted my own research, and it has proven to be invaluable in understanding people. Without this knowledge, we will likely answer a lot of questions that nobody is asking or attempt to meet needs that nobody has.

Without compromising our message or morals, we must stay current with our society and relevant to its needs. We cannot become all things to all people without having some understanding of who they are. Although we are not of this world, we are certainly in it for a purpose. The truth of God's Word never changes, but society does because people change what they think, believe and do.

Conversely, when behavioral scientists research humanity, what they are really examining is what the Bible would call people's flesh, in the vast majority of cases. They are describing the actions and attitudes of the fallen old nature, which operates independent of God. Such research is descriptive and helpful if everyone understands its limitations. But when the result of research becomes *prescriptive* by suggesting what life and human behavior should be, it distorts the truth and becomes an enemy of the gospel.

Secular research works on the premise that we're just a product of our past. Such research makes no attempt to show the potential of the gospel, nor what a Spirit-filled life could be. We must be dependant upon the Creator and Author of life to provide the explanation of why we are here, how we should interpret what we observe and how to live meaningful lives with an expectant hope for the future. Special revelation interprets and explains natural revelation.

THE INADEQUACY OF SCIENCE TO EXPLAIN MATTERS OF FAITH

The scientific method of investigation by definition leaves out the reality of the spiritual world. God Himself doesn't submit to our methods of verification. We cannot even scientifically prove the existence of God. Metaphysics (the nature of being, or essential reality) is discussed in the philosophy departments of higher education, not the science departments. Even the Bible makes no attempt to prove the existence of God, much less the reality of the spiritual world. "Without faith it is impossible to please Him, for he who comes to God must believe that He is, and that He is a rewarder of those who seek Him" (Heb. 11:6). Rest assured that the god of this world is not going to cooperate with our research methods. He is the king of darkness and the father of lies. He operates under the cloak of deception and will not reveal himself for our benefit.

A leading Christian educator said he was mildly interested in what Freedom in Christ Ministries was doing, but he would have to have some scientific verification before he could include it in his curriculum. When he suggested that we do some research together, I said I had conducted my own research before and was open to work with him. But when I explained the limitations of what such a study could prove, he said he was no longer interested. Apparently he felt he needed research to validate revelation. We can't use research to validate revelation; revelation validates and interprets our research. Science is simply inadequate to explain matters of faith.

When the Tail Wags the Dog

Why wouldn't this educator incorporate the reality of the spiritual world into his thinking and the curriculum of a graduate-level "Christian" counseling program? Probably because of academic credibility, which in higher education is the equivalent to being politically correct. To put it bluntly, he didn't want any course listed that would threaten the school's accreditation.

It seems to me that the tail is wagging the dog. Paul would surely say, "See to it that no one takes you captive through philosophy and empty deception, according to the tradition of men, according to the elementary principles of the world, rather than according to Christ" (Col. 2:8).

In order to teach at the highest levels in our scientific Western world, you would need a research doctorate that doesn't take into consideration the reality of the spiritual world and ignores special revelation. Thus, empirical research and rationalism form the entire basis for a secular liberal arts education, from the top down. What's true, real and right is only determined by what can be seen, heard and felt through the rational process of deduction.

To graduate from the highest levels of learning in our Western world, one has to adopt a scientific method of investigation. Having been an aerospace engineer, I was familiar and comfortable with the scientific method. The method originated in the natural sciences, which are, by and large, quite precise. For instance, there are over a hundred elements listed in the periodic table of the elements. Some are man-made. If you combine them in a prescribed way under specific atmospheric pressure and temperature, you can predict with great precision what the results will be.

No Precision in Social Science

Since that precise approach works so well with chemistry, let's apply the same scientific method to the social sciences. That should produce equally precise results, right? Wrong! Any time human will is a part of the equation, the outcome cannot be predicted with any degree of accuracy or precision.

Those who receive a doctorate in the social sciences, as I have, must take classes on research methodology and statistics. You quickly learn that there cannot be any perfect research design in the social sciences because all contributing factors cannot be perfectly measured or controlled. Consequently, all results are given in degrees of probability, and correlations can only be shown to be statistically significant. There are no absolutes in sociology, psychology or anthropology. When all of our social educators come to that conclusion, it's no wonder they philosophically object to Christian absolutes.

Even though a secular society objects to absolute truth, people in the social sciences labor under the assumption that their studies and conclusions are precise and therefore authoritative. For instance, when a television news program reports that a court-appointed psychiatrist or psychologist has determined that a person is mentally stable or competent to stand trial, the public should ask, "Which court-appointed psychiatrist or psychologist? On what basis is he or she making the evaluation?" Schools of psychology vary radically from one extreme to another, and a variety of theories abound in the behavioral sciences that contradict one another.

A Broad Spectrum

At one end of the social-sciences spectrum is behavioral modification, which contends that we are little more than products of our environment. Originating with Pavlov's dogs, operant conditioning has been demonstrated with rats and pigeons for years in many schools of psychology. Assuming that mankind is just a higher form of animal, the researchers (or counselors, teachers, parents, etc.) can make a child be whatever they want just by applying the right stimulus. They do this by rewarding good behavior and punishing bad behavior.

At the other end of the behavioral-science spectrum are the personal relevance theorists and practitioners. They take a more nondirective approach to counseling, saying the answer for suffering humanity isn't found in applying external stimulus. The answer comes from within the person. The counselor should be a good listener and help people get in touch with what they are feeling. Personal relevance counselors are not supposed to force their convictions or values on the client. They employ such counseling techniques as empathy, congruence, transference, concreteness, genuineness and so on. The emphasis is on establishing trust and developing relational skills.

Somewhere between these models are gestalt therapy, cognitive therapy, reality therapy and other approaches. Which theory from this psychological smorgasbord is most correct? Are they all wrong? If there weren't some truth to what they are saying, nobody would be listening to them. If you try hard enough, you can find *some* biblical basis for any of them.

Look at behavioral modification, for instance. Doesn't the Bible teach that there will be punishment and rewards? Wouldn't that knowledge have some contribution to how we behave? For instance, spanking is a form of behavioral modification. In defense of the other end of the psychological spectrum, shouldn't we be concerned about people and demonstrate that concern by caring for them and showing empathy? Isn't the cognitive therapist somewhat right in stressing the need to think? Certainly the reality therapist isn't wrong in emphasizing the need to be responsible.

You will be deceived by the world, however, if you embrace these theories and then look for biblical passages to support them. That would be eisegesis, which is reading *into* Scripture, instead of exegesis, which is reading *from* Scripture.

WE ALL HAVE OUR GRIDS

My third concern for elevating empirical research to the same lofty heights as Scripture has to do with worldview. The rational process of verification is always interpreted through the grid of culture, education and personal experience. We can't get around it. We all interpret the world around us through this grid. We can't even think beyond our own vocabulary. Everybody sees life from his or her own perspective. Wisdom is seeing life from God's perspective.

Christians are no exception. Suppose you sensed God's call to go into full-time Christian ministry in the church where you were raised. It happened to be a good, conservative, Presbyterian church, and the pastor was a solid Calvinist and had a covenant theology. Since this man was influential in your life, you would probably ask him about seminaries. What kind of seminary do you think he would recommend? I'm reasonably sure he would recommend schools that teach covenant theology, and you would probably attend one of them. There you would learn the "correct" way to interpret Scripture and understand the world in which we live.

If the pastor in your church was a dispensationalist, what kind of seminary do you think he would recommend? One that taught dispensationalism, of course. And what if your pastor was Arminian? Anglican? Catholic? Charismatic? Evangelical? Every seminary or church has a doctrinal statement, and every professor or pastor has a theological position that he or she believes is correct, or else it wouldn't be ahdered to. So does every school of psychology and every psychologist. Every one of them and every one of us believes we are right, but are we?

The Right One Is God

No, we are not right! The only One who is right is Goa. We think we are defending the truth, but what we are actually defending is our theological position and worldview. Nobody has a perfect perspective of reality, and nobody fully knows the truth. We are not omniscient, and we all have a grid by which we interpret and evaluate life. I am not committed to *my* theology, and I'm certainly not committed to *yours*. What I am committed to is the truth. Theology is man's attempt to systematize truth. Frankly, my theology has changed over the years; what has not changed is the truth.

No one is more difficult to deal with than the person who insists he has no grid. He believes that he sees the truth perfectly, so if you disagree with him, *you* must be wrong. If that isn't taking on a god status, I don't know what is. Consequently, theology is considered divisive by some, but it isn't;

intellectual arrogance is. Solomon was more wise than we will ever be, and yet he wrote in Proverbs 3:5-7:

> Trust in the Lord with all your heart, and do not lean on your own understanding. In all your ways acknowledge Him, and He will make your paths straight. Do not be wise in your own eyes; Fear the Lord and turn away from evil.

I was raised in a Methodist church, and my wife was raised in a Lutheran church. She later converted to Catholicism. When we got married, we became Episcopalians. We found the Lord and eventually ended up in a Baptist church, where I was ordained. Later, when I taught at Talbot School of Theology, I ministered part-time in a Friends church. My wife had been taught by the Catholic church that grace is extended to the faithful through the seven sacraments. Now she was in a Friends church that didn't celebrate any of the ordinances. If baptism is an issue, nobody is safer than she is: She was sprinkled in infant baptism as a Lutheran, then again as an adult Catholic, then she went through believer's baptism by immersion as a Baptist, and finally she was "dry-cleaned" in the Friends church!

Yes, we've experienced much theological diversity, but praise God for the truth. Our theological beliefs and leanings changed, but the truth didn't.

A Matter of Perspective

When I performed premarital counseling as a pastor, I would hold up one of my hands with the palm facing toward myself. Then I'd ask the couple sitting across from me to describe in detail what they saw.

They would say, "Four fingers and a thumb."

"What else do you see?" I'd respond.

"Skin, fingernails..."

"Wait a minute," I would interject. "There are no fingernails on this hand. Are we looking at the same hand? I don't see any fingernails!"

Of course, they would look at me like I was a nut. But try it once, and you will see that from your perspective—looking at your palm—there are no fingernails. Now turn your hand slightly, and you will see fingernails. That is an illustration of a paradigm shift. Perhaps you see my point: We have a hard time coming to terms with the fact that truth has more than one dimension. It is easy to reject things outside of our own experiences.

That is why we have four Gospels. All tell about the life, death, burial and resurrection of Christ. All four are different. So which one is correct? All four were written from the authors' divinely inspired perspectives. One saw

Jesus as the Messianic King, another saw Him as the Suffering Servant, another as the Son of Man and another as the Son of God. If you want a full perspective of Christ and the truth that God revealed, then you will need to read all four Gospels, because all four tell the truth.

We even interpret Scripture from our own perspective. Let me illustrate: An intellectually gifted and committed seminary professor gave a message in chapel one day. His text was 2 Timothy 2:24,25: "The Lord's bond-servant must not be quarrelsome, but be kind to all, able to teach, patient when wronged, with gentleness correcting those who are in opposition."

After grammatically breaking down the text, he shared how we were to relate to one another in staff relationships. I about came out of my chair. This man taught hermeneutics and was a fine biblical scholar. Why didn't he finish the text? "If perhaps God may grant them repentance leading to the knowledge of the truth, and they may come to their senses and escape from the snare of the devil, having been held captive by him to do his will" (vv. 25,26).

That passage wasn't teaching how to relate to one another on a church staff. It was describing what kind of person God can work through to set a captive free. Why didn't he see that? He was an intelligent Christian man. I think it was his worldview. For him, the spiritual world was a reality in the days of Christ but apparently not now. Understand that I'm not judging him, since we all make interpretations based on our own perspective.

When I first got married, I was told that I was the head of the home, so I had to make sure that the right perspective was brought to bear on all things, which, of course, was *my* perspective. In time, I matured a bit more and began to *tolerate* the perspective of my wife, Joanne. Then I matured even more, and I began to *appreciate* Joanne's perspective. Then I matured to the point that I began to *seek out* her perspective. All along, her views and positions were as legitimate as mine; they were just different.

When my son, Karl, was little, he would sometimes fall down and scratch his knee. When that happened, I was inclined to say, "Get up. Be a man." My perspective came from my stoic, Norwegian, self-sufficient farm background. Joanne was more inclined to say, "Oh, poor baby." Which perspective was right? Which response was needed? I would say both. Now my response to Karl after 30 years of marriage is, "Get up, poor baby." Joanne's response is, "Oh, poor baby, get up." We have had that kind of effect on each other's life, and I submit to you that it is essential for healthy relationships and growth in character. We have to learn how to appreciate the other person's perspective, even to the point of seeking it out.

The following testimony illustrates how our education and worldviews form a grid by which we interpret data and evaluate events:

SILENCE

When I sit and think, I think of many things—my life, what I want to do, what I think about issues and people. I have conversations with myself inside my mind. I talk to myself and answer myself...I am my own best friend. We get along great! Sometimes I talk to myself so much during the day that I am really tired at the end of the day. But I keep myself occupied, and it helps me to think things through.

Sometimes I think of myself as two people: the one who is me every day of the week...the one I want to change. The one who has a low self-esteem and is afraid to really be herself in front of everyone. And then there's the one inside of me...the confident me who I wish would come out but for some reason won't. I call that part of me "her." She is a "she," and I refer to her as such. She is very bold, and everybody loves her; at least that's what I think would happen if I would just let her out. If I could just be myself...life would be so much easier and happier.

But until then, I talk to her inside of me. We talk about what we will do today, where we will go to eat, what we will wear, who we will talk to. Sometimes she comes up with very good ideas, and I am impressed with myself that I am so smart and clever. *If only people knew the real me*, I think, *they would really love me.* And sometimes I hear her say things to me that don't make sense. *I shouldn't really do that*, I think. *That isn't very nice. That would hurt someone. That is a stupid thing to do...*And I don't listen to her that time. But I don't mind. I like talking to her, so I continue talking.

Before you hear the rest of her story, ask yourself some questions. Is what this lady is describing "normal"? Is this self-talk? Does she have a split personality? Is she psychotic? Maybe she is struggling with multiple personalities. Is this an inner child of her past? Your education and worldview would certainly affect your diagnosis. Now let's finish her story:

One day, things changed between her and me. My life was going okay, but I wanted a closer relationship with God. I wanted to be free from the past and to be healed in my heart from the pain that I have been carrying. Someone told me I should go through something called the Steps to Freedom in Christ, and I made an appointment with a counselor. I wasn't thinking about my friend inside of me; I was thinking about me.

In the counseling session, I was asked to read some prayers and Scripture out loud. While doing this, my mind became fuzzy, and I couldn't concentrate. Most of all, when I tried to speak to her in my mind, I became confused. I couldn't hear her clearly. I became scared, my heart raced, and I became enraged inside. I shook. Where was my friend inside of me? Why all of a sudden was she mad? What was going on? What was wrong with me?

Then I found out. She wasn't my friend. She wasn't really me. She didn't want me to be friends with Jesus, and she didn't want me to get my life right with God. It didn't make sense because these were things that I wanted to do. I thought she was on my side. But I was wrong. I had to tell her to leave...out loud. Out loud? It seemed weird when I was told that she couldn't read my thoughts. But it made sense...she wasn't God, and she wasn't omnipresent. So I told her out loud to leave...and she was gone.

And there was silence. There were no more conversations going on in my mind anymore. And I missed her. I knew I shouldn't, but I did. I knew that she wasn't good for me and that God wanted me to talk to Him and not her. I struggled with the thought of not talking to her. I couldn't stand the silence...I felt alone. She tried to come back, and when she did, it scared me. She was angry and hostile. I felt betrayed. But after time, I got used to the silence. I used it to remind me to talk to God, and I did. He didn't answer like she did. I couldn't hear His voice like I could hers. But I began to love talking to Him, singing to Him. I really felt close to Him...like He cared. And after a while, I forgot about the silence.

After some time I found myself lonely again. I forgot about the silence and found myself in conversation without even realizing it. My life was in confusion, and I couldn't figure out why, until one day I had to pray. My friend who had been discipling me wanted to help me, and I wanted help. She talked to me about my rebellion and how I needed to stop living independent of Him. It was then that I heard a very loud voice inside of me say, "I AM INDEPENDENT OF GOD." It scared me. Was that me? Did I really feel that way? No, I didn't...*she* was back. Then I got angry because I had let her back. I wanted her gone, but I couldn't move and I couldn't say anything. My friend prayed with me, and I bowed my head. She told me to picture heaven with a light, the lampstands and the throne of God. I started to really see it and to feel calm again. But then the voice started yelling, "No! No! No!" So I opened my eyes and gave up. My heart became hard, and I didn't really want to give everything to God. I still wanted control. There were some things that I did not want to give up.

But inside I longed for the silence again. *How ironic,* I thought. *Something that I didn't like at first had become my freedom.* How I fought inside trying to struggle with praying to God or running away from Him. It is so easy to run, so easy to put off what I can do right now. But I didn't FEEL repentant. I didn't FEEL like letting go, even though I knew I needed to. I wondered if I would ever feel like it again.

And that is when I saw the words from the Steps to Freedom in Christ jump out at me from the page. It read, "Faith is something you decide to do, not something you feel like doing." So I did it.

And now I live in wonderful silence.

This lady's problem was, of course, spiritual in nature. Could someone with her symptoms have a neurological or chemical problem? Yes, but in too many cases, those are the only possibilities considered. Every natural option has to be explored first, and when none is found, *then* people say, "There's nothing left to do now but pray." I think the order is reversed. My Bible reads, "But seek first His kingdom and His righteousness" (Matt. 6:33). Why not go to God first?

A CALL FOR BALANCE

Our secularized Western worldview is out of balance when it comes to recognizing the reality of the spiritual world. We have been educated to believe that there is a natural explanation for everything and, therefore, a natural answer for everything. The Church will defend the miracles of the Bible but is skeptical about any miraculous presence today. We profess to believe that "Our struggle is not against flesh and blood, but against the rulers, against the powers" (Eph. 6:12), but it is not a perceived reality in our daily lives. We will even hear someone say euphemistically, "The devil had a field day last night," but when asked how the devil did it, they don't know. It becomes a cliché for explaining difficulties, or worse, an opportunity to blame something or somebody else.

As we search for biblical balance, consider the following diagram. Keep in mind that I am assuming a correct biblical understanding of God (theology), man (psychology)—the natural world and the spiritual world. And I am not pitting one against the other. I want to show what can potentially happen if one is emphasized at the expense of the other:

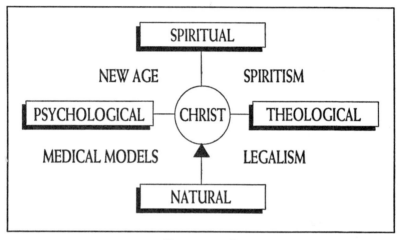

Diagram 1-B

First of all, we need to realize that the Western world has been skewed substantially toward the natural. But that has been changing dramatically in the last quarter of the twentieth century with the astonishing growth of the New Age movement.

Natural/Psychological
In the lower left quadrant you see the medical models, which have dominated the helping professions. Man and nature are the only players here, with humanism the dominant philosophy. Secular psychology entered into the Christian arena out of this quadrant, with many trying to integrate these models into Christianity. In some cases, the result is nothing more than nice Christian people doing secular counseling. Others are sincerely trying to embrace these approaches from a Christian perspective.

I don't believe the latter will be successful or balanced until two issues are thoroughly embraced. First, do you have a gospel? Does it make any difference whether the person is a Christian or not? Are we just products of our pasts, or are we products of the work of Christ on the cross? Does 2 Corinthians 5:17—"Therefore if any man is in Christ, he is a new creature; the old things passed away; behold, new things have come"—have any practical relevance to us today? Are we trying to fix our pasts, or be free from them? Does our hope lie in God, or does it lie in some technique or group? I will have more to say about that in the next chapter.

Second, does our Christian counseling take into account the reality of the spiritual world? In other words, do we have a biblical worldview? Are our struggles against flesh and blood? Are we trying to accomplish God's will without depending upon the Holy Spirit? Do our methods or concepts of helping people change if the people are Christians or not? If we are trying to help people establish their identities, find meaning in their lives and seek to meet their needs without Christ, then we need to know that is precisely the agenda of Satan on planet earth. Sobering!

Psychological/Spiritual

There is a dramatic shift of these secular models as we move upward on the left side of the diagram. Unfortunately, the spiritual reality is not Christian but demonic. In the absence of an adequate theology, demons have been renamed spirit guides, and mediums are called channelers. Humanism as a viable philosophy is waning. New Agers reason that man as only man cannot save himself, but man as god has a better chance. The New Age can be appealing. This teaching says, "You are not a sinner in need of salvation; you are a god who needs to be enlightened. You can have spiritual power and materialism." Wow!

The rise of paganism as a religious philosophy among the elite and influential in England is an interesting offshoot of the New Age in America. Adherents look at the Church with disdain because it lacks spiritual substance. The New Age, occult and ancient religions appear to offer much more spiritual reality. Power is what they want, and Satanism offers it. The lure of esoteric knowledge and power has trapped many a traveler into the web of the occult.

Spiritual/Theological

The movement upward on the right side of the diagram has also been rapid. The Holy Spirit came out of hiding in the sixties and seventies for conservative Christians, and the devil is coming out in the eighties and nineties. Much of this new awareness has been sorely needed, but distortions are evident when it becomes unbalanced. Personal needs and responsibilities are often overlooked. People are judged by others as having a "spirit of this" or a "spirit of that." In other words, if they can just get rid of that "spirit," they will be okay. Some pray and pray for *God to do something*, when *He has already done all He needs to do* for us to be free in Christ. He will not do for us what He has required *us* to do.

Theological/Natural

The lower right quadrant is diminishing, but the legalistic remnant has a tendency to drift even further to the right as it encounters people who are not interpreting Scripture correctly (i.e. like it does). The further these people remove themselves from hurting humanity, the more controlling and judgmental they get. They are the "defenders of the faith" like the Pharisees. They believe they alone are right, and if you don't agree with them, you are wrong. Their major characteristic will become evident when you try to get close to them. They won't let you. They motivate through fear and guilt. If you tried to help them understand how they got so hard and bitter, they would castigate you for psychoanalyzing them.

People in their churches are perceived as sinners in the hands of an angry God. But in truth, that's not what Christians are. We are saints in the hands of a loving God. I have never been able to understand how that simple truth is so often distorted by those who claim most vehemently the authority of Scripture. I think the Lord would say to them, "Go and learn what this means, 'I desire compassion not sacrifice,' for the goal of our instruction is love" (see Matt. 9:13; 1 Tim. 1:5).

Christ Is Central

Please don't draw the wrong conclusion from the diagram—don't think I am giving man an equal billing with God. Nothing could be further from the truth. Christ, the God-Man, is the center. We will see in chapter 3 how everything radiates from Him. What I am saying is that doctrine should never be an end in itself. If our theology is right, it should cause us to fall in love with God and man, which is the great commandment. There is a time to pray and a time to serve, a time to worship and a time to share. Prayer and worship come first. But if we say we love the Lord, then we need to care for and feed His lambs (see John 21:5-19). If we say we love the Lord, Scripture requires that we love our brother (see 1 John 4:19-21).

The previous explanation of the four different emphases in the diagram is a simple analysis of those who stray too far from the center. So who is perfectly in the center of the diagram? Only Christ! There are no perfectly balanced people, so let me add two circles to the diagram:

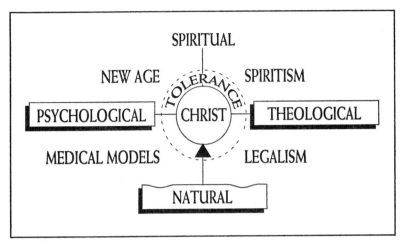

Diagram 1-C

The inner circle would constitute orthodox teaching by those who hold to the absolute authority of Scripture. If only God was interpreting His Word, the circle would be a dot. For us, it is a circle, because there will always be minor disagreements even among the most intellectually gifted theologians. No one man will ever be able to achieve omniscience.

Where you would fall on the inner circle is also affected by giftedness. Those with the gift of prophecy would probably be more oriented to the right, because they are calling for holiness; the administrators to the bottom, because they work in the world of facts and figures; those who have the gift of helps to the left because they are motivated to serve people, and so on.

The next circle indicates that, whereas our convictions may be centered on Christ, we need to exercise tolerance, up to a certain point. People are in transition and at various stages of growth.

But people outside the circle of tolerance need to renounce what they are doing and the lies they have believed. They are in bondage to those lies and to the sins they have committed. How do we help them find their freedom in Christ? Basically the answer is, "Submit therefore to God. Resist the devil and he will flee from you" (Jas. 4:7). Trying to resist the devil without first submitting to God is a dogfight. That is often the error of confrontational-type deliverance ministries. On the other hand, you can submit to God without resisting the devil and stay in bondage. The tragedy of our time is that many recovery ministries aren't doing either one.

I have a deep appreciation for medical doctors, and I thank God for what the medical profession has been able to accomplish in alleviating human suffering and sickness. I have no doubt that chemical imbalances and glandular problems plague some people, but any honest doctor would have to say that the medical model can take you only so far. The most conservative estimate you will hear from medical doctors is that 50 percent of the people they see are there because of psychosomatic reasons. That is where the Church comes in. We are the agent by which God brings about wholeness, because the Church is the pillar and support of the truth (see 1 Tim. 3:15). That truth is intended by God to set His people free!

CHAPTER TWO

CONCERNING CRITICAL ISSUES

A colleague in ministry asked if I would see a man who attends his church. The man's problems began when his 26-year-old "biker" son returned home to live with him and his wife. Within six months, the mother had been hospitalized for a "nervous breakdown," and the father had gotten himself into serious spiritual trouble.

About the time his son moved into his house, the father was awakened by something fondling his genitals. At first he thought it was his wife, but it wasn't. He made the unfortunate mistake of participating with it. Every encounter led him deeper into bondage. He even started to experience it on the way to work.

Finally, he woke up to the reality of what he was doing, but he didn't know how to make it stop. By the time he came to see me, he was trying to go to sleep at night with pictures of Jesus on his body and a Bible between his legs to protect himself!

I led him through the Steps to Freedom, and he sensed the resolution and healing. But I had to inform him that the bizarre things going on in his home would probably continue unless his son worked through his issues. The next meeting I had was with the whole family. The most mature Christian by far was the mother. After I heard the son's wild story, the mother was expecting me to back her opinion that he needed psychiatric help.

"Maybe he could use that kind of help for some issues in his life," I said, "but most of what he has described today is better understood as a spiritual conflict."

That was not what she wanted to hear. So I asked her, "Ma'am, do you believe in evolution?"

Startled, she said, "Of course not."

I continued, "You mean to tell me that you don't accept the scientific explanation for the origin of the species?" Again she assured me that she did not. Then I asked her, "Do you accept without question the psychiatric explanation of mental illness?"

"Yes, I do," she answered.

This woman saw her son's problems as psychiatric, rather than spiritual. Although she did not buy into the scientific theory of evolution, she was willing to place her complete trust in the medical-psychiatric model, while dismissing the possibility that her son's troubles were spiritual in nature.

How can a secular psychologist or psychiatrist, without the aid of divine revelation, give us an adequate understanding of who we are, why we are here, what our problems are and what the answer is? Most secular programs are like ships that pass by a person who is floating in the middle of the ocean. They throw out a life vest to keep him from sinking, but they don't have any means to save the person. Only God can do that.

DEFINING MENTAL HEALTH

According to mental health experts, you are mentally healthy if you are in touch with reality and relatively free of anxiety. That is a fair assessment, but based on this definition, you would fail on both counts if you are under a spiritual attack. Let me explain. Suppose a client tells a secular counselor that he is hearing voices or seeing things. If the counselor doesn't hear or see anything, the analysis would be that the person is not in touch. There is a good chance, however, that the one who is out of touch with reality is not the client. What the individual is hearing and seeing is very real. The problem isn't "out there," it's between the ears.

A common medical explanation for those who hear voices, have panic attacks or suffer from severe depression is, "You have a chemical imbalance or a body chemistry problem." Chances are that a prescription for medication will be given with the hope of curing the problem or eliminating the symptoms. Of course, it's true that our body chemistries can get out of balance and cause us to feel discomfort, and hormonal problems can throw our systems off. But I also believe that other legitimate questions need to be asked, such as "How can a chemical produce a personal thought?" and "How can our neurotransmitters involuntarily and randomly fire in such a way that they create thoughts that we are opposed to thinking?" Is there a natural explanation for that? I'm open and will remain open to hear any legitimate answers and explanations, because I really care for people. I want to see their problems resolved by the grace of God, but I don't think that will happen unless we take into account all reality.

When people say they hear voices, what are they actually hearing? The only way we can physically hear is to have some physical source of sound. A sound wave is a rhythmic compression of air molecules. Sound is a physical movement through the medium of air that is picked up by our eardrums, which in turn sends a signal to the brain. That is how we hear. But the "voices" that people hear are not coming from that kind of source.

In a similar fashion, when people say they see things, what are they actually seeing? The only way we can see something through our eyes is to have a light source reflecting off a material object. The spiritual world doesn't have material substance, so we cannot see a spiritual being with our natural eyes nor hear them with our ears. I have had people in my office suddenly become fearful and claim to "see" things, but I don't see anything. In fact, I don't even bother to look, because I know that there is nothing physical there to see.

The same holds true with alleged "out of body" experiences. In near-death experiences, when people supposedly see themselves lying in bed, what actually left their bodies? If the soul left the body, the person is dead. Did their eyes somehow leave their bodies, so they could look back at a corpse with empty sockets? Nothing left the body; this is all taking place in the mind. It would then fit the analogy of a dream, but not astral projection or soul travel.

There is much we don't know about mental functioning, but we do know that there is a fundamental difference between our brains and our minds. Our brains are organic matter. When we physically die, we separate from our bodies, and our brains will return to dust. At the moment we die, we will be absent from our bodies and present with the Lord. But we won't be mindless, because the mind is a part of our souls.

Let me draw an analogy. Our ability to think is similar to how a computer functions. Both have two separate components: one is the hardware, which is the actual physical computer (brain); the other is the software (mind), which programs the hardware. If the software is removed from the hardware, it would weigh the same. Likewise, if the Spirit is removed from the body, it also would remain the same weight. A computer is absolutely worthless without software, but software won't work either if the hardware shuts down.

The simple medical definition of physical death used to be the absence of vital signs. That definition is no longer acceptable because of advanced technological life support and the ability to resuscitate. Even the presence of brain waves may not be sufficient, because the mind could be gone. The biblical definition of death is separation of the soul from the body. The physical body may continue to function because of life-support systems. The lights are on, but there is nobody home.

Our society assumes that if something isn't functioning right between the ears it must be the hardware. I don't believe the primary problem is the hardware; the primary problem is the software. If a person has organic brain syndrome, or Alzheimer's disease, the brain won't function as it should. Severe brain damage, however, is relatively rare, and there is little that can be done about it. Romans 12:1,2 says we are to submit our bodies (which include our brains) to God and be transformed by the renewing of our minds. We have been programmed by the world, the flesh and the devil. Now we need to be reprogrammed by the Spirit of God. Thankfully we can, because "we have the mind of Christ" (1 Cor. 2:16).

The good news is that salvation comes with a brand-new software package. The bad news is that there's no delete button, so the old software (flesh or old nature) is still loaded into the memory and the computer is vulnerable to a virus (evil influence). We have to choose the right program and constantly check for viruses (demonic attacks).

The clear emphasis in Scripture is upon renewing our minds. The most dangerous thing we can do spiritually is to be mentally passive. Our thoughts are to be externally focused and active, never internally focused and passive. Our responsibility is to choose the truth and to think. "In evil be babes, but in your thinking be mature" (14:20). "Think so as to have sound judgment" (Rom. 12:3). "Finally, brethren, whatever is true, whatever is honorable, whatever is right, whatever is pure, whatever is lovely, whatever is of good repute, if there is any excellence and if anything worthy of praise, let your mind dwell on these things" (Phil. 4:8).

Is there a battle going on for our minds? Absolutely! Steve Russo and I surveyed 1,725 high schoolers who were attending evangelical schools or churches. Here is what we found:

- 47 percent had experienced a presence in their rooms that scared them.
- 54 percent struggled with bad thoughts about God.
- 37 percent said it was mentally hard to pray and read their Bibles.
- 70 percent had heard "voices" in their heads as if a subconscious self talked to them, or they struggled with really bad thoughts.
- 20 percent frequently entertained thoughts of suicide.

- 24 percent had impulsive thoughts to kill someone, such as "grab that knife and kill that person."
- 71 percent thought they were different from others (i.e., Christianity works for others, but it doesn't work for them).

Those percentages get worse if the subjects have dabbled with the occult, as you can read in our book, *The Seduction of Our Children*. I don't believe that the 70 percent who have heard voices are paranoid schizophrenic or psychotic. I believe what 1 Timothy 4:1 says: "The Spirit explicitly says that in later times some will fall away from the faith, paying attention to deceitful spirits and doctrines of demons." Is that happening? Yes, it's happening all over the world. It doesn't matter where I go, the problems are basically the same and the answer is always the same.

In the last 10 years, I have counseled hundreds of adults who heard voices or struggled greatly with their thought life. With only a few exceptions, the problems were spiritual. It takes us an average of three hours to help people find their freedom in Christ. Most will experience for the first time "the peace of God, which surpasses all comprehension" (Phil. 4:7).

One pastor wrote to me after reading *The Bondage Breaker*: "I have been in the pastorate for 15 years, and during that time I have struggled with three compulsive addictions: workaholism, overeating and my private thought life. Praise God for the freedom in Jesus Christ. I have just experienced this freedom and I am looking forward to enjoying it until death or Christ's return."

Why can't we detect such problems and then try to help those caught in bondages? Because I can't read your mind, and you can't read my mind. So we don't have any idea what is going on in the minds of other people unless they have the courage to share with us. In many cases they won't, because they may be labeled *mentally ill*. They will tell you about their abuses or what has happened to them, but only to the right person would they dare share what is going on inside. Are they mentally ill, or is there a battle going on for their minds? The lack of any balanced biblical contribution to the mental health professions has left them with only one conclusion: Any problem in the mind must either be psychological or neurological! Read this powerful testimony that a dear lady sent to me:

> It is by God's grace that I attended your conference. It wasn't easy getting here, as those voices in my head made me walk out halfway through the first night, and halfway out of the parking lot before the second night even started. Now I know why.

Thank you for putting all of my worst nightmares to rest, for presenting the truth about the voices in my mind. It is the first time someone has attempted to explain an aspect of "mental illness" without me having to cringe and throw up (that would have been embarrassing, since I was sitting in the front row)!

This is truly the happiest day of my life. What a relief to know that I am sane. For 30 years I have begged God to save me from the pits of hell—mental illness. He answered my prayer at your conference. All my life, I have lived with the fear that I would be crazy like the rest of my family and that I was only fooling myself that I was sane because I had been "covering up" by serving God all these years.

I was so terrified to tell anyone about the voices, that I thought about suicide instead. I shuttered at the thought of living like my mother for the rest of my life. My marriage was being destroyed by those voices, because I knew if I told my husband, he would have me locked up and committed. I would wear a one-size-fits-all white jacket for the rest of my life. I saw no way out. I had almost given in to those voices and given up on God completely.

My mother is the victim of a split personality. She tried to kill me three times that I can vividly remember. She sexually abused all of us children. I lived in tremendous fear all my life. She told us we were born to a crazy family, and we all needed psychiatrists. If you can believe it, she was the head of a Bible school based in our church, and my father traveled as an evangelist for more than 30 years. Naturally, my view of God hasn't been too clear.

I am the only member of my family who hasn't suffered from a nervous breakdown. I simply refused to. And after hearing you, I know I never will. What a relief to know that others hear those same voices. I have not been alone. I don't have to be afraid anymore. I can be free! Really free! I feel like you should send me a bill. What is funnier is that I would be happy to pay it! Thank you! You can't imagine what it feels like to get out of this prison.

I was always waking up at exactly 3:00 A.M. For years and years I have been terrified of 3:00 A.M. It is now 3:30 A.M. I woke up at exactly 3:00 A.M. and immediately checked the clock. This time there were no voices, and I started to cry. I knew it was

God. I didn't have to be afraid anymore. Thank you! It is finally over!

I believe every church can and should be able to help someone like this. I also believe that we need to equip parents to provide the instruction and protection that every child needs. If your child came into your room and said, "Mom, there's something in my room!" What would you do? The average parent would go in the room and look under the bed and in the closet, and say, "Honey, I don't see anything. Now go back to sleep." Being an adult, if you saw something in that room, would you go back to sleep? Probably not. "But I looked under the bed and in the closet, and there was nothing there," says the frustrated mother. There never was anything in the room that could be seen by the eyes; it was in the mind of the child. "Then it isn't real," argues the skeptic. Yes, it is, and it may be more real than what you see. "While we look not at the things which are seen, but at the things which are not seen; for the things which are seen are temporal, but the things which are not seen are eternal" (2 Cor. 4:18).

From God's perspective, the unseen world is more real than the world we can see with our eyes. It is like looking at a computer, and all you see is the hardware. You could look at the microcircuitry for the rest of your life and never determine what the software is. You could look at every cell in a brain under a microscope and never find out what has been stored in the memory or what the person's thoughts were. "For as he thinks within himself, so he is" (Prov. 23:7). We look at our children and all we can see is their behavior, so guess what we try to change? Their behavior! But what they do is just the result of what is going on inside.

That is the problem with labels and the classifications of mental illness. All you are doing is categorizing them according to symptoms. Someone may be diagnosed as being paranoid schizophrenic because she has irrational fears and hears voices, but what does that explain? What is *causing* the fear and the voices? Establishing causation is not an easy thing to do, but if you don't know enough to ask the right questions or take into consideration the reality of the spiritual world, you will lack an adequate answer to the problem. Medications are prescribed to alter the hardware, but there is no "smart pill" that can think for us. Taking a pill to cure the body is commendable, but taking a pill to cure the soul is deplorable.

Most people cannot identify with the problem of hearing voices, but everybody struggles with tempting and accusing thoughts. Where they are coming from is less important than what to do about them. In one sense, it doesn't matter whether the thought originated from the television set, your memory bank, your imagination or from the pit, because the answer is the same. We need to take "every thought captive to the obedience of Christ" (2 Cor. 10:5). We need to examine each thought according to the Word of God and choose the truth. Paul says, "I am afraid, lest as the serpent deceived Eve by his craftiness, your minds should be led astray from the simplicity and purity of devotion to Christ" (11:3). The way you overcome the father of lies is to choose the truth. This is certainly not a new phenomenon. Eve was deceived, and she believed a lie.

If what is being passed off as mental illness in some cases is nothing more than a battle for the mind, how can we know it? There must be some way to find out. I think there is, and that is what this book is all about. When you go to your doctor, you expect to be checked out, don't you? If the blood and urine tests came back negative, you wouldn't be upset, would you? If you are struggling with obsessive thoughts, chronic depression and anxiety attacks, wouldn't you want a safe way to check it out? If churches follow the procedure outlined in this book, you won't be labeled, judged, rejected or charged. And if your conflicts aren't resolved, go see your doctor. What do you have to lose?

The process I am describing in this book does far more than just check for some evil presence, because that alone wouldn't solve anything. The Steps to Freedom in Christ are a comprehensive, biblical way to resolve personal and spiritual conflicts by the grace of God. Then the life of Christ will be manifested in people's lives, and they will be able to be the person Christ wants them to be.

The Church has to be careful not to think that there is a "spiritual" answer for everything, in the same way that the medical profession must not assume there is a "physical" answer for everything. We need each other because we are both physical and spiritual beings who live in both a physical and a spiritual world, and God created both.

RELATIVELY FREE OF ANXIETY

Being relatively free from anxiety is the other criteria for determining mental health. In my book *Walking in the Light*, I analyzed and offered a biblical response to both fear and anxiety. Let me touch on some of the key points as they relate to our discussion.

Anxiety is a fear of the unknown, or fear without an adequate cause. The basis for anxiety is uncertainty and a lack of trust. We worry about what we treasure in our hearts (see Matt. 6:19-24), and we worry about tomorrow (see vv. 25-34), because we don't know what will happen. Scripture says, "Do not be anxious for tomorrow" (v. 34), because God will take care of you. To be anxious is to be double-minded. That is why Jesus said, "No one can serve two masters; for either he will hate the one and love the other, or he will hold to one and despise the other. You cannot serve God and mammon. For this reason I say to you, do not be anxious for your life" (vv. 24,25). A mind that is free and pure is single-focused.

James writes that if we are experiencing trials in life, we should ask the Lord in faith for wisdom. But if we are overcome by doubting thoughts, we will be overcome by the storms of life. "Let not that man expect that he will receive anything from the Lord, being a double-minded man, unstable in all his ways" (Jas. 1:7,8). God is the antidote for anxiety. Therefore, cast "all your anxiety upon Him, because He cares for you" (1 Pet. 5:7). We have to choose to trust Him and turn to Him in prayer. "Be anxious for nothing, but in everything by prayer and supplication with thanksgiving let your requests be made known to God" (Phil. 4:6).

Unlike anxiety, fear has an object. Fears are even categorized by their objects. Claustrophobia is a fear of enclosed places. Xenophobia is a fear of strangers or foreigners. Agoraphobia is a generalized fear of open spaces. In order for a fear object to be legitimate, it must have two attributes: It must be perceived as potent (having some power), and it must be imminent (present). For instance, I have a healthy fear of rattlesnakes. But as I am writing this, I sense no fear for them at all because there are none present.

To eliminate a fear object in your life, all you have to do is remove just one of those attributes. For instance, physical death is no longer a legitimate fear object for us, because God has removed one of the attributes. Although death is still imminent, it is no longer potent, because "death is swallowed up in victory" (1 Cor. 15:54). Therefore, Paul could write, "For to me, to live is Christ, and to die is gain" (Phil. 1:21). Physical life is not the ultimate value; spiritual life is. It will be heaven when our souls separate from our bodies; it will be hell if our souls are separated from God. "And do not fear those who will kill the body, but are unable to kill the soul; but rather fear Him who is able to destroy both soul and body in hell" (Matt. 10:28).

Why is "the fear of the Lord...the beginning of wisdom" (Prov. 9:10)? Because that is the one fear that expels all other fears. "You are not to fear what they fear or be in dread of it. It is the Lord of hosts whom you should regard as holy. And He shall be your fear, and He shall be your dread. Then He shall become a sanctuary" (Isa. 8:12-14). It is not a wise person who fears man, death or Satan more than God.

What two attributes of God make Him the ultimate fear object? He is omnipotent and omnipresent. No matter where you go, God is there, and His power and authority exceed all others. Fear of anything other than God is mutually exclusive from having faith in Him. "Even if you should suffer for the sake of righteousness, you are blessed. And do not fear their intimidation, and do not be troubled, but sanctify Christ as Lord in your hearts, always being ready to make a defense to everyone who asks you to give an account for the hope that is in you, yet with gentleness and reverence" (1 Pet. 3:14,15).

When I have asked Christian audiences all over the world if they have had a fearful encounter with some spiritual force, at least 50 percent have responded affirmatively. I have found it to be much higher among Christian leaders, which shouldn't be surprising. At least 35 percent of the audiences I've queried have said they had been awakened terrified. They probably felt as though they were half asleep. They may have felt a pressure on their chests or something grabbing their throats. When they tried to say something, they couldn't. Why couldn't they? Because they need to submit to God first, then they can resist the devil. Because God knows our hearts, we can always turn to Him in our minds. When we do by verbally calling upon the name of the Lord, we will be saved. I must confess that I am not a timid man, but I have felt the terror of a spiritual attack at night. In each case, I have experienced immediate victory by turning to God.

If I shared that experience with a secular doctor or counselor, it would be called an anxiety or panic attack. Why don't they call it fear, because that is what it is? Because, they can't identify the fear object. Therefore, it would better fall under the definition of anxiety. Every child of God should know what a spiritual attack is, and they should know how to deal with it.

A godly pastor used the Steps to Freedom to help the woman who wrote the following testimony:

> For the past 35 years, I have lived from one surge of adrenaline to the next. My entire life has been gripped by paralyzing fear, which seems to come from nowhere and everywhere. This fear made very little sense to me or anyone else. I invested four years of my life obtaining a degree in psychology, hoping it would enable me to understand and conquer those fears. Psychology only perpetuated my questions and insecurity. Six years of professional counseling offered little insight and no change in my level of anxiety.
>
> After two hospitalizations, trips to the emergency room, repeated EKGs, a visit to a thoracic surgeon and a battery of

other tests, my panic attacks only worsened. By the time I came to see you [the pastor], full-blown panic attacks had become a daily feature.

It has now been three weeks since I've experienced a panic attack! I have gone to the malls, church services and even made it through Sunday School with peace in my heart. I had no idea what freedom meant until now. When I came to see you, I had hoped that the truth would set me free, but now I know it has.

When you live in a constant state of anxiety, most of life passes you by, because you are physically, emotionally and mentally unable to focus on the fear that is swallowing you. I could hardly read a verse of Scripture in one sitting. It was as though someone snatched it away from my mind as soon as it had entered. Scripture was such a fog to me. I could only read verses that spoke of death and punishment. I had actually become afraid of opening my Bible. These past weeks, I have spent hours a day in the Word, and it makes sense. The fog is gone. I am amazed what I am able to hear, see, understand and retain.

Before reading *The Bondage Breaker*, I could not say "Jesus Christ" without my metabolism going berserk. I can now call upon the name of Jesus Christ with peace and confidence...and I do it regularly.

There is a major difference between fears that are developed over time and those that are essentially attacks. The latter can be dealt with at the time. For instance, an abusive husband was going to harm his wife when she was taking a shower. She verbally paraphrased 1 John 5:18, "I am a child of God. The evil one cannot touch me." He suddenly became disoriented and ran out of the house. I also heard about a doctoral student who was confronted by three thugs at a train stop. When they demanded his money, he said, "I am a child of God. The evil one cannot touch me." They said, "Oh," and walked away. A word of caution. This type of response requires some discernment, because those attacks may not have originated from the enemy. There are things in this world that should evoke a healthy fear. If this is the case, then call the police, but it never costs you anything to first call upon the Chief of all police, and we are biblically encouraged to do so.

Irrational fears that are learned over time must be unlearned, and that will take time. First, you have to separate legitimate fears, which are necessary for survival from irrational fears (phobias). Phobias either compel us to do something that is irresponsible or prevent us from doing that which is responsible. Then you need to make a commitment to not allow that fear to have any control over you, and then work out a plan to overcome it. A wise man once said, "Do the thing you fear the most, and the death of fear is certain."

Fear is a powerful motivator. Paul said, "Knowing the fear of the Lord, we persuade men" (2 Cor. 5:11). The fear of the Lord is not a negative concept, because the love of God is not out to get us; it will restore us and protect us. "There is no fear in love; but perfect love casts out fear, because fear involves punishment, and the one who fears is not perfected in love" (1 John 4:18). I don't fear that God will punish me someday. The punishment that I deserved was taken out on Christ. I fear the Lord because I will have to stand before Him someday and give an account for my life. I want Him to say, "Well done, faithful servant." That is a powerful motivation that has far-reaching ramifications for how I live my life. The fear of God is the answer to panic attacks, and the Word of God is the answer to irrational fears that we have learned in a fallen world.

BIBLICAL MENTAL HEALTH

Biblical mental health begins with a true knowledge of God and who we are as His children. You are a mentally healthy person if you know: that God loves you; that He is able and willing to meet all of your needs; that you can do all things through Christ who strengthens you; that He will never leave you nor forsake you; that He's gone before you to prepare a place for you in heaven; that there is no legitimate reason to fear death; that the guilt of your sins have been forgiven and there is no condemnation for those who are in Christ Jesus; and that you are a child of God. Or look at it this way: If the fruit of the Spirit were evident in your life, would you be a mentally healthy and balanced person? Of course you would.

But let me quickly add that the greatest determinant of mental illness is a distorted concept of God and who we are as children of God. Visit a hospital psychiatric ward and you'll see some of the most religious people you've ever met. Some of them think they're Michael the Archangel. Others think they are Gabriel. Some even think they're Jesus Christ! That's why some secular counselors have such a negative view of the Church. All their clients are religious, and many bring their Bibles with them to the hospital. The counselors wonder where they are getting all this religious junk. It is easy to see why they want to de-emphasize religion and get their clients back into "reality." In most cases, incredible thoughts have been raised up against the knowledge of God.

I'm convinced that the most important belief we must have is a true knowledge of God. That's why Paul says, "I count all things to be loss in view of the surpassing value of knowing Christ Jesus my Lord" (Phil. 3:8). The second critical belief we must have in order to be mentally healthy is a true knowledge of who we are as children of God and what our relationship is with Him. These two pillars of belief form the basis for Christian living. I could undermine your life simply be distorting either one.

Let me illustrate. In Psalm 13:1,2, David said: "How long, O Lord? Wilt Thou forget me forever? How long wilt Thou hide Thy face from me? How long shall I take counsel in my soul, having sorrow in my heart all the day?" Who is David talking to? Himself! He continues: "How long will my enemy be exalted over me?" David is locked in depression, overcome by the circumstances of life. Much of his depression is based on a wrong concept of God and his relationship with Him. Can God forget him, much less forever? No, God couldn't forget him even if He wanted to, because God is omniscient. But if you believe that He can or will, there goes your hope.

The writer of Psalm 42:5 says, "Why are you in despair, O my soul? And why have you become disturbed within me? Hope in God, for I shall again praise Him for the help of His presence." Our hope lies in God, and all depression is hopelessness that is not truly endogenous (that is, physical in origin). The same instruction is illustrated in Lamentations. Chapter 3 begins with a distorted concept of God and the author's relationship with Him. Consequently he says, "My soul has been rejected from peace; I have forgotten happiness. So I say, 'My strength has perished, and so has my hope from the Lord'" (vv. 17,18).

Out of this despair, something incredible happens: "Surely my soul remembers and is bowed down within me. This I recall to my mind, therefore I have hope. The Lord's lovingkindnesses indeed never cease, for His compassions never fail. They are new every morning; great is Thy faithfulness" (Lam. 3:20-23). His circumstances didn't change. What changed was his perception of God. That is why we are admonished to worship God, which is to ascribe to Him His divine attributes. We don't worship God because He is an egomaniac who needs His ego stroked every Sunday morning. That is paganism. God does not need us to tell Him who He is. He is fully secure within Himself. We worship God because He truly is worthy, and we must keep the divine attributes of God constantly before us. Then we will live mentally and emotionally healthy lives of obedience that are humbly dependent upon Him.

PSYCHOLOGICAL VERSUS SPIRITUAL

So when is a problem psychological and when is it spiritual? This commonly asked question presupposes a clear distinction between the psychological and the spiritual natures of mankind. I believe it creates a false dichotomy. Our problems are always psychological (to some degree) in the true sense of the term, since we are always human. There is no time when our minds, our emotions, wills, personalities and relationships are not contributing factors. Likewise, our problems are always spiritual. There is no time when God isn't here. Hebrews 1:3 says God "upholds all things by the word of His power." He is not a deistic God, who started the whole thing but now sits idly by as we struggle in our own human dilemmas. We are created in the image of God, and "God is Spirit, and those who worship Him must worship in spirit and truth" (John 4:24).

Because we are spiritual people who live in a spiritual world, the Bible gives no indication that it is ever safe to take off the armor of God. On the contrary, it says, "Therefore, take up the full armor of God, that you may be able to resist in the evil day, and having done everything, to stand firm" (Eph. 6:13). Our tendency is to polarize into psychotherapeutic ministries—which ignores the reality of the spiritual world—or jump into some kind of deliverance ministry, which ignores developmental issues and human responsibility. I don't believe either paradigm is going to be sufficient to deal with the whole person.

We cannot emphasize only one aspect of the body, soul and spirit at the expense of any other parts and have an adequate or balanced answer. We are whole people who have a whole God who has a whole answer. In our failure to address the interconnection between body, soul and spirit, we have allowed New Age philosophers to be the primary proponents of wholistic health instead of the Church.

IDENTIFYING CHRISTIAN DISCIPLESHIP/COUNSELING

I think there are two primary bases by which Christian discipleship, counseling or recovery ministries can be evaluated. First, do they have a gospel? I'm not talking about whether the helper is a Christian; I'm talking about how the gospel plays into the person's understanding of how we establish people complete in Christ. Are the people we are trying to help just products of their pasts? Or are they primarily products of the work of Christ and the cross? Is it our goal to understand or fix the past? Or does the gospel provide us the means to be free from our pasts? Is the "old self" dead and the "new self" alive? Are we still in Adam or are we in Christ? Do we have a practical understanding of the truth that "if any man is in Christ, he is a new creature; the old things passed away; behold, new things have come" (2 Cor. 5:17)? Is this pie-in-the-sky theology or is it the basis for Christian living?

The failure to understand the truth of "Christ in you, the hope of glory" (Col. 1:27) will result in a law (or principle)—obedience response to God instead of a life-faith response. The former approach tries to shape behavior according to God's standards. The counselor or discipler may explain from Scripture how the person got screwed up because of what he did or what was done to him. He is then encouraged to confess and seek God's forgiveness. The next step is to show from the Word of God how he should live his life. The person is then admonished to commit himself to do the very best he can. Lesser forms of this approach wouldn't make much use of the Bible. The counselor or discipler would use common sense, or secular theory, to root out the irresponsible behavior and encourage the individual to start living a responsible life.

Those who understand the gospel know that Christ came to give us life, and our response is to walk by faith according to what God said is true by the power of the Holy Spirit. They also know that the wonderful Counselor is God Himself, and they know that the person they are trying to help must abide in Christ in order to glorify God and bear fruit (see John 15:8). Their procedure is to help the person resolve the issues that are critical between himself and God. Once that is accomplished, the life of Christ is manifested in him, and he is able to be the person God wants him to be. The emphasis is placed on what the person believes so that he will renew his mind and walk by faith according to what God says is true. They know that apart from Christ no one can do anything (see v. 5), and that we are all inadequate without God, as stated in 2 Corinthians. 3:5,6:

> Not that we are adequate in ourselves to consider anything as coming from ourselves, but our adequacy is from God, who also made us adequate as servants of a new covenant, not of the letter, but the Spirit; for the letter kills, but the Spirit gives life.

I heard one "Christian" counselor say that people aren't ready for God. We have to help them resolve their problems first, then they will be able to go to church and worship God. In other words, God is only there to be worshiped, so we are the ones who are really going to help this person. That is either hopelessly naive or incredibly arrogant. People don't need us. They need the Lord. They may have to lean on us initially, but the whole goal is to get them to live their lives dependent upon God, not upon ourselves. To do any less is to take upon ourselves a god status, but we are incapable of giving anyone life or meeting their critical needs. Only God can do that.

I once asked a Christian counselor, "If you took Christ out of your counseling ministry, would it make a difference what you do? Do you apply the same procedure for the Christian client as the non-Christian client?" He said it probably wouldn't make much difference! Are we actually trying to help people establish their identities, determine their purposes and find meaning in life without Christ? If we are, then we need to realize that is precisely the devil's agenda on planet earth!

That leads to the second basis for evaluating whether a ministry is truly Christian: Does it have a biblical worldview that takes into account the reality of a spiritual world? Does the Bible teach that there is a kingdom of darkness and a kingdom of light? Is there a god of this world, a prince of power of the air? Do we have a practical understanding and acceptance of the fact that "our struggle is not against flesh and blood, but against the rulers, against the powers, against the world forces of this darkness, against spiritual forces of wickedness in the heavenly places" (Eph. 6:12)? Without this knowledge, we are like blindfolded warriors who don't know who our enemy is, so we strike out at ourselves and each other.

On the positive side of the spiritual world, do we understand the role of the Comforter, the Paraclete, the One who comes alongside? Do we know that He "is the Spirit of truth" (John 14:17), that He will lead us into all truth (see 16:13) and that the truth will set us free? Are we trying to be the convictor of sins, or do we let Him fulfill that role? Do we know how to live by the Spirit so we "will not carry out the desires of the flesh" (Gal. 5:16)? Do we understand the need for spiritual discernment that can only come from Him? Are we trying to provide the assurance of salvation, when "the Spirit Himself bears witness with our spirit that we are children of God" (Rom. 8:16)?

THE ROAD TO RECOVERY

In many cases, we are locked in a paralysis of analysis, because we don't know how Christ is the answer or how the truth will set us free. In some circles, you would be considered smart if you could correctly read the symptoms and assign the right label. You may be considered brilliant if you could explain with great precision why people behave the way they do because of past experiences. But how does that resolve the problem? If you were hopelessly lost in a maze, would you want a mazeologist to explain all the intricacies of your own private maze and how to survive there? Would you want a legalistic preacher to tell you what a jerk you were for getting in the maze in the first place? What would you want to know? You would want to know how to get out of the maze! You would want to know the way, the truth and the life (see John 14:6).

There are a million ways to go wrong, but the path back to God is not obscure, nor numerous. There are a million ways to sin, but the answer to sinfulness is the same. You can be abused a thousand different ways, but in each case, forgiveness is the means by which you can be free from your past. The Steps to Freedom are a path back to God. They can be summarized by one verse: "Submit therefore to God. Resist the devil and he will flee from you" (Jas. 4:7).

You will have a dogfight if you try to resist the devil without first submitting to God. You can submit to God and not resist the devil, and stay in bondage. The tragedy of our day is that most recovery ministries aren't encouraging people to do either one. No wonder we aren't seeing better results, considering all the human effort that is being put into the movement.

Ephesians 2:22 says that each Christian is a dwelling place of God in the Spirit. Unresolved personal and spiritual conflicts are like garbage in the temple that we have failed to take out, or spills that we haven't cleaned up. The mess attracts flies. Some have suggested that we should study the flight patterns of the flies and determine their order and rank. Although that may have some value, that's not the answer. We should never let the devil set the agenda, nor should we accept a "devil made me do it" attitude.

The answer is repentance, which includes taking personal responsibility for our own attitudes and actions. Most people have been unjustly treated, but we have only ourselves to blame for not taking the way out that God has provided. We have to get rid of the garbage, and that is what this book is all about. The actual step-by-step process is given in the second part of this book (chaps. 7-13). The theological and practical basis for Christ-centered ministries follows in the next chapter.

CHAPTER THREE

Discipling in Christ

An enthusiastic youth pastor had all but dragged his senior pastor to one of my advanced seminars. The pastor had been a professional counselor before he realized that his gifts were more suited for preaching and teaching.

After the conference the man said, "I really appreciated what you had to say, but tell me, don't you give any place to psychology?"

I was puzzled by his question because I had spent the bulk of the time talking about the believer's identity in Christ, our purpose and meaning in life, how strongholds have been erected in our minds, the battle for our minds, how to renew our minds, the need to acknowledge our emotions and how to heal damaged emotions by forgiving. I then related all this to marriage and family relations.

The next person I talked to was a missionary who didn't hear the previous conversation. He said, "It seems to me that what you've given us is a Christian psychology."

How could two people have such totally different perspectives? People come to a conference with their own worldviews and evaluate what they hear through the grids of their own cultures and educational backgrounds. The pastors probably said what they did because I didn't attempt to integrate what I was saying with secular psychological theory or use their jargon. My reading, research and educational background has prepared me to do that, but I haven't and I won't because my ministry is primarily to the Church. And I made the personal choice several years ago to understand who we are and how we can live productive lives based solely on the Word of God. Have we been so secularized that even a good conservative pastor couldn't recognize a Christian psychology?

WHAT IS PSYCHOLOGY?

So what is psychology? Simply put, it is a study of mankind—how people think, feel and relate. As Christians, we can't be against that. Every standard systematic theology work has a section on psychology or anthropology. What we are opposed to is a secular psychology in the same way we are opposed to a liberal theology.

"But there are bad counselors in my community who lead my people astray," said the concerned pastor. I'm sure there are, and I share this concern, but there are probably some really bad pastors in that same community. Who is doing the most damage—a secular counselor who is trying to help people without Christ, or a controlling, legalistic pastor who keeps people in bondage? The Gospels reveal that it was the latter group that upset Jesus the most. His war was not against sinners; it was against religious bigots and hypocrites.

Some ultrafundamentalist "Christians" react violently to any mention of psychology. You will feel the sting of their rejection if you talk about feelings, and judgment will come upon you if you even mention the words "self-esteem." To not acknowledge how we feel is a blatant denial of reality. Suppressing our feelings breeds emotional dishonesty and develops emotional cripples.

I would seriously question the heart of any pastor who showed no concern for the negative perception that people have of themselves. Such pastors unwittingly assist the accuser of the brethren by heaping guilt upon their congregations when, in fact, there is "no condemnation for those who are in Christ Jesus" (Rom. 8:1). These pastors would have people believe that they are sinners in the hands of an angry God instead of saints in the hands of a loving God. The main difference between the legalistic pastor and the secularized Christian counselor is that they take turns ignoring different passages of Scripture!

The secular world has done a good job of analyzing what the basic needs of humanity are. It is not so much this analysis that I disagree with; it is the answer the world offers. Stroking one another's egos and pulling ourselves up by our own bootstraps is not going to get it done. We cannot esteem ourselves without being prideful, but why should we have to since we are already Christ-esteemed?

Christ and only Christ can meet all our needs "according to His riches in glory" (Phil 4:19). The most critical needs, and the ones most wonderfully met in Christ, are the "being" needs (life itself, identity, acceptance, security and significance). I attempted to show how those needs are met by being alive in Christ in my book *Living Free in Christ*.

THE CHURCH'S ROLE IN MEETING NEEDS

I have observed two extremes in our churches concerning personal needs. One extreme is the impersonal church that ignores many needs. People come to church to hear the preacher preach and the teacher teach. In this setting, pastors see themselves as mini-theologians. They are the defenders of the faith. Some are known more for what they don't believe than what they do believe. The problem with some Protestants is that they protest rather than proclaim. They are more prepared to fight than to love. The "spiritually mature" person is the one who doesn't smoke, drink or do other bad stuff. They don't do any personal counseling and in many cases remove themselves from hurting humanity. One has to wonder whatever happened to pastoring.

The biblical art of discipleship has suffered a similar fate. It has degenerated into a curriculum-based program. In this setting, the two most important questions are: What curriculum are you using and what program are you following? How sad! Discipleship is an intensely personal experience between two or more people in the presence of Christ and centered in the Word of God. The Bible doesn't just give us a message, it gives us a method as well. One has to wonder whatever happened to discipleship.

I am deeply concerned for the churches that have strayed away from their central purposes. Parachurch ministries have been raised up to fill the gap of their deficiencies. If you want to do evangelism, join Campus Crusade for Christ. If you want to do discipleship, join the Navigators. If you really care for people, become a Christian counselor. But aren't those the primary functions of the local churches? Some would correctly say that our primary purpose is to worship God and love Him. But the necessary result of a church body that truly worships God in Spirit and in truth would be to care for and love people. Such believers would be compelled by the Holy Spirit to reach their communities for Christ and build them up in the Lord.

Seminaries must see the need to prepare the *whole person* for ministry, and not just to educate the mind. A person could graduate from most seminaries purely by answering most—not even all—of the questions correctly. You could do that and not even be a Christian. When we make knowledge or doctrine an end in itself, we distort the very purpose for which it was intended. Paul says, "The goal of our instruction is love from a pure heart and a good conscience and a sincere faith" (1 Tim. 1:5). We have a tendency to extol the virtues of the theologian and the apologist at the expense of the soul winner and lover of people. However, Scripture teaches that "he who is wise wins souls" (Prov. 11:30) and "by this all men will know that you are My disciples, if you have love for one another" (John 13:35). That is why a main scriptural requirement to be a leader in the church is godly character, and true disciples are known for the fruit they bear.

Love Is the Greatest Commandment

A Pharisee asked Jesus what was the great commandment in the law. He responded by saying, "'You shall love the Lord your God with all your heart, and with all your soul, and with all your mind.' This is the great and foremost commandment. The second is like it, 'You shall love your neighbor as yourself.' On these two commandments depend the whole Law and the Prophets" (Matt. 22:37-40). The purpose of divine revelation is to govern our relationships with God and each other. The Pharisee didn't ask what the second commandment was, but Jesus gave it anyway because He wanted to drive home the point that if we truly love God, we will also love people.

Loving people is the bottom line in ministry. People don't care how much we know until they know how much we care. Love is the greatest apology for our faith. Bitter judgment against others is the greatest denial. "If someone says, 'I love God,' and hates his brother, he is a liar; for the one who does not love his brother whom he has seen, cannot love God whom he has not seen" (1 John 4:20).

In contrast to impersonal churches, counseling is intensely personal. Most counselors work hard at developing trust. Many of them have learned to listen and have acquired skills such as accurate empathy, congruence and concreteness. Without divine revelation, however, they lack an adequate answer. Suppose a caring secular counselor is able to develop an intimate and trusting relationship with a client. After hearing the person's entire life story, the counselor explains with great precision why the client behaves the way she does. Okay, now what? Explaining pathologies or problems just leaves the individual a product of her past. The gospel allows us to be free from our past and to become brand-new creations in Christ.

We need to take seriously the words of Psalm 1:1: "How blessed is the man who does not walk in the counsel of the wicked, nor stand in the path of sinners, nor sit in the seat of scoffers!" I don't like the idea of Christians seeking the counsel of the ungodly, but they will unless we provide them with Christian counsel and show concern for their needs. If the Church functioned as God intended, people would come flocking to us. They would receive eternal life, all their sins would be forgiven, and they would be free to be all that God wants them to be. They would have a means to resolve their personal and spiritual conflicts, and all their needs would be met in Christ.

But when the Church fails to live up to its responsibility, we abdicate our roles in society. For instance, the government was the primary agency to bring an end to racism in America. I wish I could say it was the Church. In some cases the "Church" actually perpetuated the problem. Some Christians even cry "social gospel" when an attempt is made by the Church to address the ills of society. But Scripture says it is "pure and undefiled religion in the sight of our God and Father, to visit orphans and widows in their distress" (Jas. 1:27).

When we fail to meet the needs of even our own people, we unwittingly drive them out of our churches and into the hands of secular psychologists and social workers. Do we dare criticize them for what they are doing if we have not lived up to our calling?

The other extreme regarding people's personal needs can be found in a few churches that really do care. An opportunity is afforded in every church service for people to come forward to be prayed over. Spiritual leaders will anoint you with oil and pray fervently for you. The prayers are petitions for God to do something. The requests might be for healing, deliverance, wisdom or God's intervention in a personal tragedy. I appreciate the heart and concern of these leaders, but I believe God has already done all He needs to do for us to live free and victorious lives in Christ. What is often overlooked is the need for assuming personal responsibility.

Personal Responsibility

To my knowledge, only one passage specifically says what to do if we are sick or suffering—James 5:13-18. In a doctor of ministry course I teach, I have the pastors practice exegesis on this passage before they come to class. Most of their time is spent identifying the oil and what it is to be used for. Was the anointing of oil a medical practice of the day, or does it symbolize the work of the Holy Spirit? They also focus on the role of prayer, because these two functions directly relate to what their responsibilities are. I think three critical concepts in this passage are routinely overlooked, all of which relate to the sick person's responsibility.

First, the passage begins by saying, "Is anyone among you suffering? Let him pray" (v. 13). Initially, the one who is suffering is the one who should pray. Many times hurting people have come to us for prayer, and we usually oblige them. But if that is all that's done, how much do we really see as a result of our prayers? If we are honest, we would have to say, "Not much." Why don't we see more answers to our prayers? Because we cannot do another person's praying for him, just as we cannot think or believe for another person. Don't get me wrong, I believe in intercessory prayer, but not if it takes the place of the individual's responsibility to pray. We cannot have a secondary relationship with God

Previously, when I reached a stalemate in counseling, I used to stop and pray, asking the Lord for wisdom. I still do that occasionally, but I have learned it is far more effective to have the person I'm counseling pray. (In the second part of this book, when we discuss the process of taking people through the Steps to Freedom, notice that the one who prays is the one we are trying to help.) I have discovered that most people don't know how to pray or what to pray for. So what may appear to be canned prayers are simply petitions for the Holy Spirit to reveal to their hearts what they need to renounce, who they need to forgive, and so on. Paul teaches in Romans 8:26,27, "The Spirit also helps our weakness; for we do not know how to pray as we should, but the Spirit Himself intercedes for us with groanings too deep for words; and He who searches the hearts knows what the mind of the Spirit is, because He intercedes for the saints according to the will of God."

Many people have been led to believe that somebody else needs to pray for them, but when it comes to resolving personal and spiritual conflicts, the only effective prayers are the ones that come from a repentant heart. I even prefer that the individuals I'm trying to help will assume their responsibilities to test the spirits. As I was taking a young man through the Steps, he suddenly stopped and said, "This voice in my head says it wants to go to heaven with me." I encouraged him to pray, asking the Lord to reveal to his mind the true nature of that voice. What he saw or heard I don't know, but he immediately knew that the source of that thought was evil.

Second, James 5:14 says, "Is anyone among you sick? Let him call for the elders of the church." To whom does God give the responsibility to take the initiative? We are never going to see a spiritually, mentally and emotionally healthy Church unless we put responsibility back on the individual where it belongs. Caring people have a tendency to be rescuers and enablers, but we cannot assume responsibility for others. We can instruct others on how to live balanced lives by eating properly, exercising, meditating, praying and so on, but we cannot do these things for them.

Good health is not contagious, but bad health is. Physically, you cannot get healthy by simply living in the proximity of healthy people, unless you practice what they practice. But you can catch a disease just by being around another sick person. The same holds true spiritually. You cannot be a mature Christian simply by being around spiritual giants. To "catch" their maturity, you would have to choose to believe what they believe, and then practice what they do. You can, however, degenerate spiritually be being around ungodly people. "Do not be deceived: 'Bad company corrupts good morals'" (1 Cor. 15:33).

On the other hand, every legitimate Christian is somewhat codependent, in a good sense, because we are to love one another. This means that we are subject to the needs of one another. "We know love by this, that He laid down His life for us; and we ought to lay down our lives for the brethren. But whoever has the world's goods, and beholds his brother in need and closes his heart against him, how does the love of God abide in him? Little children, let us not love with word or with tongue, but in deed and truth" (1 John 3:16-18). We become codependent in a bad sense when we allow other people to exercise control over us. They often do this by motivating through guilt, confusing personal wants with legitimate needs, and determining how and when we are to satisfy their expectations.

Third, before the prayers of a righteous man can accomplish much, the hurting people are instructed to "confess your sins to one another, and pray for one another, so that you may be healed" (Jas. 5:16). Then and only then will the prayers of a righteous person be effective. Suppose you had an irresponsible son who was disobedient and dishonest with you. You had instructed him to mow the lawn, but he hadn't. Now he comes to you and asks for $20 and the keys to the car because he has a hot date. Would you give him the keys and the money? Many of us would be tempted to, but I don't think that's what God would have us do. He patiently waits until we face the truth, assume our own responsibility and repent of our self-centered ways.

Many people are sick for "psychosomatic" reasons, which at times can be little more than a euphemism for not living responsible lives according to God's instructions. God didn't create us to live our lives independent of Him. This strikes at the heart of the spiritual battle, because all temptation is an attempt to get us to live our lives independent of God. The basis for temptation is made up of legitimate needs. Satan doesn't have to look very hard, because the needs of our society are overwhelming. If we don't assume the responsibility to show how these needs are met in Christ, people will seek to have their needs met by the world. And the devil will entice them through "the lust of the flesh and the lust of the eyes and the boastful pride of life" (1 John 2:16) to live their lives independent of God.

THE BIG PICTURE OF SPIRITUALITY

Why do people choose, and in many cases prefer, to live their lives independent of God? To answer that question we need to look at the big picture, and in so doing establish what essentially must happen in order for our discipleship/counseling process to be effective. Recall that Adam and Eve were born both physically and spiritually alive. Their act of independence against the will of God caused them to lose their lives, not physically at first, but spiritually. Separated from God, they learned to live their lives independent of God.

From that time on, everyone who has entered this life has been born physically alive but spiritually dead, separated from God. Paul says we were dead (spiritually) in our trespasses and sins (see Eph. 2:1). We had neither the presence of God in our lives nor the knowledge of God's ways. So we sought to find our purpose and meaning in life in the natural world because that's all we had. Consequently, we all learned to live our lives independent of God, which is the essential characteristic of the flesh. It's this learned independence that makes the flesh (old nature) hostile to the Spirit. Why? Because the Holy Spirit, like Jesus, is totally dependent upon God the Father.

When I came into this world I was a child of Marvin Anderson. But what if Marvin Anderson had never been physically born? Would I be here? No. If my grandfather had never been here, would my dad have been here? Of course not. In reference to our physical heritage, we are all "in Adam" at the time of conception (please refer to the following "Life Line" diagram for the remainder of this discussion). In that condition, where is your life? It's in the flesh. Where else could it be? What's your identity? Who knows? Carpenter? Plumber? Engineer? Pastor? Homemaker? The natural tendency is for people to derive their identities from the things they do. Understanding the purpose and meaning in life would also be derived from the natural order of things because that is all they have.

Our Fallen Nature

The essential nature of fallen humanity is sinful because of separation from God. Paul says, "Among them we too all formerly lived in the lusts of our flesh, indulging the desires of the flesh and of the mind, and were by nature children of wrath" (v. 3). Sinful behavior is just the evidence that the natural man is separated form God. The real problem is that the natural man is dead in his trespasses and sins. The good news is that Jesus came to give us life.

Descendants of Adam naturally determine their identities by the things they do, find their purpose and meaning in life from the fallen world they live in, and are sinful by nature. If they never choose life in Christ, they will simply look forward to the inevitable consequences of sin, which is physical death. The Bible assures us there will be a final resurrection of the dead and they will stand before God at the Great White Throne. Those whose names are not written in the Lamb's Book of Life will be cast out of God's presence

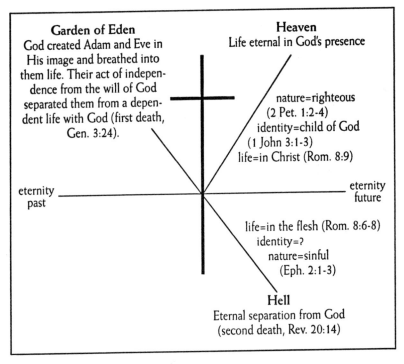

Garden of Eden
God created Adam and Eve in His image and breathed into them life. Their act of independence from the will of God separated them from a dependent life with God (first death, Gen. 3:24).

Heaven
Life eternal in God's presence

nature=righteous
(2 Pet. 1:2-4)
identity=child of God
(1 John 3:1-3)
life=in Christ (Rom. 8:9)

eternity
past

eternity
future

life=in the flesh (Rom. 8:6-8)
identity=?
nature=sinful
(Eph. 2:1-3)

Hell
Eternal separation from God
(second death, Rev. 20:14)

Diagram 3-A

a second time for all eternity, which is "the second death" (Rev. 20:14). The first death of humanity was the expulsion from God's presence in the Garden of Eden.

However, for myself—and I hope for you as well—there was an intervening period when I encountered Christ. I was transferred out of the kingdom of darkness and into "the kingdom of His beloved Son" (Col. 1:13). Likewise, I became a new creature; the old things passed away and new things came (see 2 Cor. 5:17). My life is no longer in the flesh; it's in Christ. Paul writes, "You are not in the flesh but in the Spirit, if indeed the Spirit of God dwells in you. But if anyone does not have the Spirit of Christ, he does not belong to Him" (Rom. 8:9).

Hope for the Christian

It is critically important to realize that every Christian is no longer *in* the flesh, because every child of God is *in* Christ. Does that mean that I am teaching the eradication of the sin nature at the new birth? It depends on how you define your terms. Do I believe that I am no longer in Adam, that the old man (self) is dead? Absolutely. However, since the flesh remained when I was spiritually born again, I can choose to walk according to the flesh or old nature. I still live in a physical (mortal) body, and my mind is still programmed to live independent of God. But my hope lies in the biblical fact that I am alive in Christ, and I have become a partaker of the divine nature (see 2 Pet. 1:4).

Paul writes, "You were formerly darkness, but now you are light in the Lord; walk as children of light" (Eph. 5:8). God had to do something about the basic nature of fallen humanity, and He did so by giving us life. Now that our souls/spirits are in union with God, we have become partakers of the divine nature. The only reason we can walk as children of light is because we are children of God. "But as many as received Him, to them He gave the right to become children of God" (John 1:12). "For you are all sons of God through faith in Christ Jesus" (Gal. 3:26). "See how great a love the Father has bestowed upon us, that we should be called children of God; and such we are....Beloved, now we are children of God,....And everyone who has this hope fixed on Him purifies himself" (1 John 3:1-3).

Understand that the eternal life we received is "Christ, who is our life" (Col. 3:4). This life is eternal past, present and future. Paul says, "I have been crucified with Christ; and it is no longer I who live, but Christ lives in me; and the life which I now live in the flesh I live by faith in the Son of God, who loved me, and delivered Himself up for me" (Gal. 2:20). We were not crucified with Christ in time because that happened nearly two thousand years ago. But we can literally say we have been crucified with Christ in eternity because the life of Christ is eternal. Remember that eternal life is not something we get when we die physically. "He who has the Son has the life; he who does not have the Son of God does not have the life" (1 John 5:12).

When we are born again, we become spiritually alive. Our souls/spirits are in union with God. We are "in Christ," which is one of the most repeated prepositional phrases in the New Testament. Being "in Christ" is the core theological foundation for discipleship and counseling. It is the basis for Christian living. Paul identifies every true believer with Christ:

- In His death—Romans 6:3,6; Galatians 2:20; Colossians 3:1-3;
- In His burial—Romans 6:4;
- In His resurrection—Romans 6:5,8,11;
- In His life—Romans 5:10,11;
- In His power—Ephesians 1:19,20;
- In His inheritance—Romans 8:16,17; Ephesians 1:11,12;
- In His heavenly position—Ephesians 2:4-7.

Because human life is lived according to what we believe, this essential truth of who we are in Christ is tremendously important. Our attitudes, responses and reactions to the circumstances of life are determined by our conscious or subconscious self-perceptions. No one can consistently behave in a way that is inconsistent with how he perceives himself to be. If Christians are no different inwardly from non-Christians, or if they *perceive* themselves to be no different, then life will be lived at best in a mediocre manner, with very little distinction between Christians and non-Christians. The result will be repeated defeats in the Christian life. The accuser of the brethren capitalizes by pouring on the guilt and is often assisted by self-righteous, legalistic teachers.

Paul corrects this thinking by teaching, "There is therefore now no condemnation for those who are *in Christ Jesus*. For the law of the Spirit of life *in Christ Jesus* has set you free from the law of sin and of death" (Rom. 8:1,2, emphasis added). Is the law of sin and death still operative? Yes, sin is still present, strong and appealing; and physical death is still imminent. That is why they are called laws. We can't do away with a law, but we can overcome it with a power greater than it, which is the "law of the Spirit of life in Christ Jesus."

For instance, I cannot fly because the law of gravity is greater than any power that I have. With a great deal of human effort, I can get off the ground a couple of feet for one or two seconds, but the law of gravity will quickly demonstrate its superiority. However, I can fly by getting in an airplane and putting my confidence in the pilot. As long as we live our lives in Christ by the power of the Holy Spirit with our confidence in God, we will not carry out the desires of the flesh (see Gal. 5:16-18).

Physical death is still imminent, but Jesus said, "I am the resurrection and the life; he who believes in Me shall live even if he dies" (John 11:25). In other words, we shall live spiritually even if we die physically. And sin is still powerful and appealing, but we don't have to sin. Because the "old man" has been crucified with Christ, sin's power has been broken (see Rom. 6:7,12,14). The true believer is under no obligation to serve sin. We can, by the grace of God, walk as children of light (see Eph. 5:8-11).

True Christians will come under conviction when they choose to believe the lie that their identities and purposes for life can be found in a course of action contrary to and independent of God. Returning to legalism (see Gal. 5:1,2) or license (see v. 13) will bring the believer back into bondage again. If we walk according to the flesh, we are living in violation of who we really are in Christ (see Rom. 7:16,22), and freedom must be regained through repentance (see Prov. 28:13; 1 John 1:9). Conviction is sensed when we choose to believe the lie and act differently than who we really are in Christ.

Living According to His Will

So why don't we live our lives according to who we really are? I have discovered that many people try to put the old man (self) to death, but they can't. Why not? Because he is already dead. We cannot do for ourselves what Christ has already done for us, and it is useless trying to become people we already are. We simply accept that what Christ said is true about us because of His work on the cross and then walk accordingly by faith. Salvation is not addition; it is transformation. We are regenerated, born again, new creations in Christ. Let me summarize who we are:

In Adam (1 Cor. 15:22a)		In Christ (1 Cor. 15:22b)
Old Man (Col. 3:9)	By Ancestry	New Man (Col. 3:10)
Children of Wrath (Eph. 2:1-3)	By Nature	Partaker of Divine Nature (2 Pet. 1:4)
In the Flesh (Rom. 8:8)	By Birth	In the Spirit (Rom. 8:9)
Walk After the Flesh By Choice (Rom. 8:12,13)		Walk After the Spirit (Gal. 5:16)

Does that mean we are living in sinless perfection? Absolutely not.

As 1 John 1:8 says, "If we say we that have no sin, we are deceiving ourselves, and the truth is not in us." But let me quickly point out that "having" sin and "being" sin are two totally different concepts. We can, as children of God, choose to walk according to the flesh and sin. We can also choose to believe a lie and sin, because whatever is not of faith is sin (see Rom. 14:23).

What is at stake is our loss of victory, but not our salvation. It is not so much a question of whether we can hang onto God. The real issue is that God will not let go of us. "I will never desert you, nor will I ever forsake you" (Heb. 13:5). Jesus said, "My Father, who has given them to Me, is greater than all; and no one is able to snatch them out of the Father's hand" (John 10:29). Paul says, "For I am convinced that neither death, nor life, nor angels, nor principalities, nor things present, nor things to come, nor powers, nor height, nor depth, nor any other created thing, shall be able to separate us from the love of God, which is in Christ Jesus our Lord" (Rom. 8:38,39).

Although we are secure in Christ, there is no such thing as instant maturity. It will take us the rest of our lives to renew our minds and develop the character of Christ. The first is possible because "we have the mind of Christ" (1 Cor. 2:16). The second is possible because we are "partakers of the divine nature" (2 Pet. 1:4). But I have learned from years of experience and from the Word of God that the process of growth is totally stopped or severely limited if our people do not first establish their freedom in Christ.

Paul says in Colossians 2:6,7, "As you therefore have received Christ Jesus the Lord, so walk in Him, having been firmly rooted and now being built up in Him." I believe that we have to be firmly rooted *in Him* before we can be built up *in Him*. And we can't expect people to live (walk) *in Him* as mature Christians if they have not first been built up *in Him*. We would be like cars without gas. We may look good, but we won't be able to run. In *Victory over the Darkness*, I attempted to identify spiritual, mental, emotional, volitional and relational levels of conflicts and levels of growth. Please examine diagrams 3-B and 3-C.

Are all Christians firmly rooted in Him? Hardly! I have discovered that a large majority of Christians don't have the foggiest idea who they are in Christ, and most are ignorant of their spiritual inheritance. Most think eternal life is something they get when they die; they are desperately trying to become something they already are; and they believe that who they are is determined by what they do! No wonder we are not seeing much growth even though many are trying their very best. Most of our teaching and preaching is geared to people who we think are at level three on Diagram 3-C. So if we give them good instruction on how to live the Christian life, they will do it. Level-three counseling is just good, common-sense advice based on the Word of God. We assume that they are firmly rooted and built up enough in the Lord that they will be able to do what we are telling them to do. Bad assumption!

In reference to this, let me summarize what I said on pages 54 to 57 in *Setting Your Church Free*. Luke 2:52 says, "Jesus kept increasing in wisdom and stature, and in favor with God and men." In other words, Jesus grew mentally, physically, spiritually and socially. If we want to grow in a balanced way, we need to do the same. To accomplish this, we have developed certain disciplines, as Diagram 3-D illustrates.

To discover these disciplines, we search our concordances to find everything that God has to say about marriage, parenting, rest, prayer, meditation and other relevant topics. In the process, we develop some good spokes to the Christian wheel. Tremendous books have been written about each discipline, and most of them accurately portray what God has to say about each subject. Considering all the available resources, what aren't our people doing better? Why are so few Christians living victorious and fruitful lives?

I think the spokes are not functionally connected to the hub, who is Christ. The result is a subtle form of Christian behavioralism that sounds

LEVELS OF CONFLICT

	Level I	Level II	Level III
	(Col. 2:10, NKJV) "You are complete IN Him."	(Col. 2:7) "Having been firmly rooted and now being built up IN Him."	(Col. 2:6) "You...have received Christ Jesus the Lord, so walk IN Him."
SPIRITUAL	Lack of salvation or assurance (Eph. 2:1-3)	Walking according to the flesh (Gal. 5:19-21)	Insensitive to the Holy Spirit's leading (Heb. 5:11-14)
RATIONAL	Darkened in their understanding (Eph. 4:18)	Wrong belief or philosophy of life (Col. 2:8)	Pride (1 Cor. 8:1)
EMOTIONAL	Fear (Matt. 10:26-33)	Anger (Eph. 4:31) Anxiety (1 Pet. 5:7) Depression (2 Cor. 4:1-18)	Discouragement and sorrow (Gal. 6:9)
VOLITIONAL	Rebellion (1 Tim. 1:9)	Lack of self-control, compulsive (1 Cor. 3:1-3)	Undisciplined (2 Thess. 3:7,11)
RELATIONAL	Rejection (Eph. 2:1-3)	Unforgiveness (Col. 3:13)	Selfishness (Phil. 2:1-5) (1 Cor. 10:24)

Diagram 3-B

like this: "What you are doing is wrong. You should do it this way," or "That is not the best way to do it. Here is a better way." People respond by saying, "Okay, I'll try harder!" And back comes the answer, "But you're not trying hard enough. If only you would try harder!"

LEVELS OF GROWTH

	Level I	Level II	Level III
	(Col. 2:10, NKJV) "You are complete IN Him."	(Col. 2:7) "Having been firmly rooted and now being built up IN Him."	(Col. 2:6) "You...have received Christ Jesus the Lord, so walk IN Him."
SPIRITUAL	Child of God (1 John 3:1-3) (1 John 5:11-13)	Walking according to the Spirit (Gal. 5:22,23)	Led by the Holy Spirit (Rom. 8:14)
RATIONAL	Renewed mind (Rom. 12:2) (Eph. 4:23)	Handling accurately the word of truth (2 Tim. 2:15)	Adequate, equipped for every good work (2 Tim. 3:16,17)
EMOTIONAL	Free (Gal. 5:1)	Joy Peace Patience (Gal. 5:22)	Contentment (Phil. 4:11)
VOLITIONAL	Submissive (Rom. 13:1,2)	Self-control (Gal. 5:23)	Disciplined (1 Tim. 4:7,8)
RELATIONAL	Acceptance (Rom. 5:8) (Rom 15:7)	Forgiveness (Eph. 4:32)	Devoted to one another in brotherly love (Rom. 12:10) (Phil. 2:1-5)

Diagram 3-C

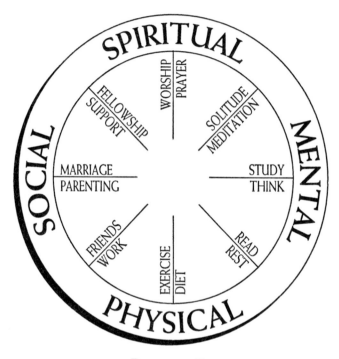

Diagram 3-D

The try-harder methodology causes people to be driven instead of called. Some have managed to progress from negative legalism ("don't do this and don't do that") to positive legalism ("do this and do that"). The farther we are from the hub, the harder we try, until something snaps. Burnout or rebellion are the only possible consequences of Christian behavioralism.

Jesus said, "By this is My Father glorified, that you bear much fruit, and so prove to be My disciples" (John 15:8). We read that passage and conclude that we have to bear fruit. No you don't. What you have to do is abide in Christ. If you abide in Christ, you will bear fruit. Bearing fruit is evidence of the fact that you are abiding in Christ. Some Christians try to bear fruit without abiding in Christ, and they can't. Why not? Because Jesus said, "I am the vine, you are the branches; he who abides in Me, and I in him, he bears much fruit; for apart from Me you can do nothing" (v. 5). He didn't say we would be handicapped without Him, or that we wouldn't be as effective without Him. He said that without Him we "can do nothing."

We haven't taught our people to abide in Christ, and we haven't helped them to be firmly rooted in Him. Self-help programs are actually counter-productive to the process. Those who are closest to the hub are sweet-spirited and gentle people. They seem to bear fruit with little effort. They are living testimonies of the Beatitudes (see Matt. 5:3-12). Those farthest from the hub become judgmental and legalistic. They are often the "big wheels" who run over and intimidate others. They insist that they are right, and ironically, they may be right in a legalistic and moralistic sense. Using Scripture, they can prove their points and show you how you ought to behave. They know what is right and what is wrong. They have captured the letter of the law, which kills, but not the Spirit, which gives life (see 2 Cor. 3:6). They often use their theology as a smoke screen to keep every-body else on the defensive and from getting too close to them. Any effort to get through their carefully erected barriers to their inner men will be rebuffed. Their insecurities result in withdrawal or passivity, or they become sick controllers.

Most of these people have never had any bonding relationships, and they are not free in Christ. I hurt for these people, but I hurt even more for their families and congregations. Those around the controllers are the victims, and unless they are set free in Christ, they will continue the cycle of abuse. Many books have been written about these dysfunctional families, and recently, several good books have been published about churches that abuse. Many of these books are excellent and if applied in the right order, they can help greatly. Let me explain.

SAVING THE FAMILY

Prior to the 1960s, most seminaries had strong departments of evangelism and discipleship. Instruction on marriage and the family was given little attention. In the 1950s, families that went to church together usually stayed together. The 1960s brought a social revolution like we had never seen before. The Vietnam War, the civil rights movement, free sex and drugs threw our country into chaos and wreaked havoc with our families. Consequently, the Church went into high gear to save this God-ordained institution. Seminaries developed programs and offered degrees in marriage, child and family counseling. The ministerial faculty in pastoral care was slowly replaced by clinical psychologists. Most, if not all, of them were edu-cated in secular schools, because in those days Christian schools did not offer doctoral degrees in psychology. Evangelism and discipleship took a back seat because the other needs were so overwhelming.

Some of our largest parachurch ministries and radio programs are now geared to the family. More Christian books by far are sold to this market than any other because it is the number one felt need in America. Never in the history of the Christian faith has such an effort been made to save the family. With all that concerted effort, what's the result? Have marriages become stronger? Have families become more united? Are children doing better? What is wrong?

I recall my New Testament professors pointing out that Paul generally organized his Epistles this way: The first half is theological and the second half is practical or applicational. So when we go to our concordances to find out how we are to function as marriage partners or parents, we end up in the second half of Paul's Epistles. If you were only concerned about the family, then you would probably address only those practical passages. What do the first half of Paul's Epistles do? They establish you in Christ.

I believe that if we help people understand and enter into the first half of Paul's Epistles, they will instinctively follow the instruction in the second half. That would be the "natural" thing for children of God to do, if they are established free in Christ and filled with the Holy Spirit. But trying to get people to behave as Christians and to act right in their own strength when they don't know who they are in Christ will prove to be fruitless in most situations.

Is anything wrong with the many good programs and books that are available to help us? No, most are good spokes and when applied in the right order, they will provide sound advice reflecting good insight. That is what makes the problem I am addressing so subtle, because the programs and strategies can be very good and biblical. The problem is, we put our confidence in programs and in strategies instead of in Christ. If God is in it, any program will work. If God isn't in it, no program will work. But if God is in it, a good program will be more fruitful than a bad program.

Most people's problems are not primarily external, which could be resolved by learning to behave better. They are internal and resolved by being established in Christ, choosing to believe the truth and walking accordingly by faith. It is not what goes into a man that defiles him; it is what comes out (see Matt. 15:11). When we help two people get radically right with God, their marriage comes together, then their family comes together, then the community comes together, and then the world. I have seen marital conflicts resolved and stay resolved through internal change, but never through external or behavioral changes alone. We spend too much time trying to change behavior and not enough time trying to change what people believe about God and themselves. If we first establish them complete in Christ, then all those good spokes will work and become a vital part of the Christian wheel, as the following diagram illustrates:

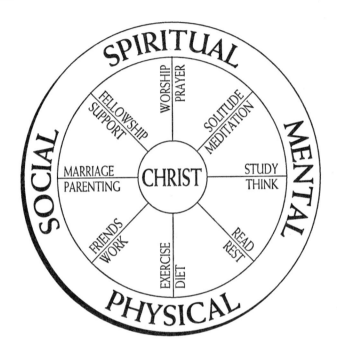

Diagram 3-E

Families are critical to this discussion because God primarily works in our lives through committed relationships. I believe He does this for two reasons. First, we may be able to deceive people outside of our homes for a little while, but we can't at home. Our children and our spouses will see right through us. I wish I could say the public and private lives of all our Christian leaders were consistent, but sadly, that is not so in too many cases. Somewhere in their Christian journeys, they started to live their lives before man rather than before God.

Second, a marriage is supposed to be a committed relationship. Rather than run away from the pressures of marriage and family, God intends for us to hang in there and grow up. The pressure cooker of the home is where we learn to love one another, forgive one another and bear with one another. With this in mind, look at the order of Scripture in the book of Colossians:

Chapter One: Transferred into the kingdom of His beloved Son in whom we have redemption, the forgiveness of sins.

Chapter Two: We are established in Christ, and the devil is defeated.

Chapter Three: We are to set our minds on the things above, put off the old man and put on the new man.

Then notice what Paul addresses: First our identities in Christ (3:11), then our characters (vv. 12-17), then the family (vv. 18-21) and then work (vv. 22-25). You can see the same order in the other Epistles of Paul and John. When we get that order right in our ministries, we will see the fruit of our labors.

One other dimension needs to be added to the growth process of level one (firmly rooted in Him), level two (now being built up in Him) and level three (now walking in Him) in diagram 3-C. In 1 John 2:12-14, the author identifies little children (level one), young men (level two) and fathers (level three). Little children of the faith have their sins forgiven. In other words, they have overcome the penalty of sin. Twice John identifies the young men of the faith as those who have overcome the evil one. That is, they have overcome the power of sin. Can we leave out John's contribution and successfully bring our people to the full maturity of Christ? I don't think so.

Our first concern in discipleship/counseling is to get people connected to God. He is the wonderful Counselor, the giver of life and the power to live it. That is the primary purpose of the Steps to Freedom, to resolve the issues that are critical between ourselves and God. Once people are firmly rooted in Him, watch them grow by the grace of God. Now let's turn our attention to the type of person God can work through in order to accomplish this.

CHAPTER FOUR

Counseling
in Christ

About halfway through each semester of the seminary class I taught on pastoral counseling, I asked the students to take out blank sheets of paper. On their sheets of paper, they were to each write down the most negative and damaging aspect about their lives—the last thing they would ever share with anybody, or the one thing they wished nobody would find out about them!

Can you imagine the thoughts going through their minds? *Why does he want us to do this? What is he going to do with this information? There is no way I'm going to write that down on a piece of paper!* Most were probably considering the possibility of putting down the fourth or fifth most offensive thing, but certainly not the first!

I waited a minute until the level of anxiety was unbearable. Then I would tell them to stop, because I really didn't want them to expose themselves on paper. I just wanted them to experience one time in their lives what it must feel like to have to face that prospect.

Put yourself in their shoes. Suppose some deep dark, horrible secret was eating away at you, and you just couldn't live with it any longer. You knew you needed some help to resolve the issue. If another person was going to help you, would that person need to know that horrible secret? Of course that person would, or he or she wouldn't be able to help you resolve it.

After the high blood pressure and the heart palpitations had decreased in my counseling class, I told the students, "What I do want you to put down on that piece of paper is this: What kind of a person would it take for you to share the worst possible thing about yourself? I don't want a name. I want one dominant characteristic. What would this person have to be or not be, do or not do. What is the one big issue for you?" After they thought about it for a moment, I had all the members of the class share their most important issues while I listed them on the board. I have discovered that what is a huge issue for one person may not even be considered by another. The typical responses are: confidentiality, loving, godly, kind, nonjudgmental, compassionate, accepting, patient, understanding and able to help.

Then I had the students look at the list and ask whom those characteristics describe. They always come up with the same answer. It is God! Herein lies the core issue of Christ-centered counseling, which prompted me to challenge the class by asking, "If you haven't before, would you now commit yourself to become that kind of a person?" If we don't become that kind of person, we will never hear other people's stories, because nobody will want to share problems with us. Consequently, we end up dealing with the symptoms and not the root causes. If we don't hear the whole story, we don't know the unresolved conflicts or unbiblical beliefs that are at the root of other people's bondages and irresponsible behaviors.

One irate pastor looked me in the eye and said, "We don't have these kind of problems in our church, and I'll tell you why, because I preach the truth around here." He may, in fact, proclaim the Word of God. What he doesn't realize, however, is that not one person in his church would ever share personal problems with him because of his bombastic and judgmental ways! Proverbs 23:7 says, "For as he thinks within himself, so he is." What do we observe in others? The "so he is." So we try to change the "so he is." But we have to back up a notch and find out what is going on inside of the other person. What the person is doing is just a result of what he is thinking and choosing to believe.

NOTHING IS HIDDEN FROM GOD

A man in a church I pastored years ago made a lunch appointment with a counselor friend to talk about a problem he had. Three times they had lunch together, but the man couldn't muster the courage to talk about his pornography addiction and bondage to lust. So he discussed his symptoms of apathy toward the church and disinterest in his wife.

Eventually, he confided in me. I suppose he couldn't hold it in any longer because he was about to be exposed for doing something inappropriate with his daughter. And I suspect he finally sought help when the fear of getting caught and the subsequent consequences were greater than the shame of sharing his problem with his pastor.

Let's face it—it would be difficult to share all the dirt in our lives with a stranger, a friend or a pastor. Consequently, many people live with unresolved issues they are too embarrassed to talk about. They fear being exposed and are scared to death that someone may find out what is really going on inside.

Does God know what has happened to them, what they did, how they think and feel? Should there be any doubt? Listen to Hebrews 4:13: "There is no creature hidden from His sight, but all things are open and laid bare to the eyes of Him with whom we have to do." I would suspect, however, that most people are more concerned about what *others* think and know than what God thinks and knows. Our spiritual lives are headed for ruin when we start living our lives before mankind rather than before God. When the prophet Samuel confronted Saul, the king finally confessed, saying, "I have sinned; I have indeed transgressed the command of the Lord and your words, because I feared the people and listened to their voice" (1 Sam. 15:24).

Paul said, "For am I now seeking the favor of men, or of God? Or am I striving to please men? If I were still striving to please men, I would not be a bond-servant of Christ" (Gal. 1:10). Think about it for a moment. If you are a man pleaser, to whom are you a bond servant? Don't play for the grandstand. Play for the coach. That truth alone will liberate many.

One lady couldn't hold in her secrets any longer and dumped years of frustration and defeat on me. The next day, I got a call from her. She said, "I feel terrible that I shared all that stuff with you. What do you think of me?"

I said, "Well, I thank you for sharing that with me. That's the only means by which I can love you and help you."

There was a slight pause, and then she said, "Oh! Well then, I have a lot more to tell you."

LEARNING TO BE TRUSTWORTHY

When I first went to seminary, my counseling professor challenged us to work on just one area of our lives. I chose marital communication, because I thought it was safe and I thought I had pretty well worked all of that out with my wife. When I shared my decision with Joanne, I was expecting something like, "Oh, that's great! Yes, let's work on our communication." But she didn't respond that way. In fact, she seemed a little concerned.

Two weeks later, Joanne and I were talking about the prayer group she was meeting with once a week. Most of the ladies were married to men who weren't saved. In reality, the group was more of a pity-party. They were always complaining about their marital relationships and how their husbands were treating them. So I asked Joanne, "Are they sharing this with their husbands?"

"No, I'm sure they're not," she said.

"Well, Joanne, how in the world can they expect their husbands to meet their needs if they don't know what they are?"

When she didn't answer right away, I asked Joanne if she was sharing anything about us in the group.

Reluctantly, Joanne confessed that she had, in fact, shared some concerns about our relationship with her prayer group. My first response was, "Well, what's wrong with you? Why didn't you tell me? I share everything with you."

Dear reader, that was a painful night, for I found out what wasn't wrong with Joanne and what was wrong with me. Why wasn't I the kind of person with whom she would feel free to share? Apparently, she couldn't trust me. Ironically, I thought trustworthiness was my strongest attribute. I thought, *You could count on good ol' Neil Anderson!*

You may be wondering why she couldn't trust me. Was it because I couldn't keep the information confidential? No, that wasn't the issue. It was how I responded to the information she shared with me. My nature was to give her two reasons she shouldn't feel that way and three things she ought to start doing.

We made a commitment to each other that night. She agreed not to share with others about our relationship unless she first shared with me. My commitment was to learn how to truly listen and not give unsolicited advice and opinions. I told her I didn't want to be that kind of a husband or pastor. So I asked her to hold me accountable.

So for the next several years, Joanne would preface her statements with, "Now I'm going to share something with you, but don't give me two reasons why I shouldn't feel that way and three things I ought to start doing."

Then I would say, "Come on, Joanne, don't you trust me yet?"

But when she started to share something personal with me, guess what was going through my mind? Two reasons she shouldn't feel that way and three things she ought to start doing! It's incredible! Many of us in the Western world are wired that way. Instead of learning to listen, we immediately want to give advice. Of course, at times giving advice is appropriate. But as Proverbs 18:13 says, "He who gives an answer before he hears, it is folly and shame to him."

A mother once asked me, "Why won't my teenager talk to me? I know she's struggling at school."

I asked her, "Do you really want to know?"

"Of course," she said.

I knew her well enough to say, "She probably thinks she can't trust you."
She was surprised by my answer and said, "What do you mean she can't trust me? Of course, she can trust me. I'm her mother."

I said, "Let me illustrate: Suppose your teenager came home from school and said, 'Mom, my best friend is smoking pot.' What would you do?"

She had to think long and hard about her response.

Let me ask you the same question. How do you think the average parent would respond? I'm sure many would fight to keep from overreacting, but most would have some strong advice, especially concerning that friend.

Finally, this mother said that, yes, she would tell her daughter to stop hanging around with that friend.

I said, "Exactly! That's why she won't share it with you."

"Well, what would you do?" she asked.

A person never knows how he would respond at any moment of crisis, but I don't think I would respond that way. At least I hope I wouldn't. And why not?

First of all, I wouldn't have any idea what the real problem was. I haven't heard the whole story. Did her friend try drugs once, or has she been taking drugs for months or years? Does she plan to continue, or was it a one-time bad experience?

Wouldn't it be better to say something like, "Honey, I'm really sorry to hear that. Can we talk about it?" You need to realize that there's a very good chance that the one smoking pot is sitting right in front of you. When she finds out your reaction, that's the end of the story. She won't share any more with you unless she is absolutely desperate. Every parent and pastor needs to realize this.

When people have the courage to share something intimate, what are they looking for initially? Acceptance and affirmation. If you confess to God, what do you get? Acceptance and affirmation.

> For we do not have a high priest who cannot sympathize with our weaknesses, but one who has been tempted in all things as we are, yet without sin. Let us therefore draw near with confidence to the throne of grace, that we may receive mercy and may find grace to help in time of need (Heb. 4:15,16).

In *Living Free in Christ*, I tell the story of a lady in my church who was clinically depressed. My wife suggested to her that she make an appointment to see me for counseling.

She responded, "Neil? He's always up!"

Now if you were down, what kind of person would you want to see? Somebody who is up? If you were sick, would you seek out the most sickly, emaciated, wasted, sniffling, wheezing doctor in town and ask him his secret for good health? Of course you wouldn't, but that isn't the initial problem. This depressed lady was questioning whether I could understand or was capable of giving mercy.

Many people do not see the Church as a house of mercy, and in too many cases, they are right. They may receive more mercy and less judgment in a secular 12-step program or the local bar than they do in our churches. But the problem is these places have no grace to help in times of need. The people are accepted for who they are, and they are encouraged to depend upon the group and work the program, or drown their sorrows in a bottle of booze. The Church has the grace to help in time of need, but won't be given the opportunity if it cannot withhold judgment and be merciful. Jesus said, "Be merciful, just as your Father is merciful. And do not judge and you will not be judged; and do not condemn, and you will not be condemned; pardon, and you will be pardoned" (Luke 6:36,37).

I initially went to seminary to learn the right answers so I could give good advice. Unfortunately, I learned all kinds of answers to questions that nobody was asking. I even thought I had arrived as a person. It doesn't take many years of ministry to correct that kind of thinking! Peter said you have to "sanctify Christ as Lord in your hearts, always being ready to make a defense to everyone who asks you to give an account for the hope that is in you, yet with gentleness and reverence" (1 Pet. 3:15). We cannot impart to others what we do not possess. We cannot be instruments in God's hand to bring freedom to others if we are in bondage ourselves. Christ has to first be the Lord of our lives. Then we have to be able to share with others the hope that lies within us, and learn to do it in gentleness and reverence.

THE KIND OF PERSON GOD USES

The one definitive passage that describes the person God can work through is 2 Timothy 2:24-26:

> The Lord's bond-servant must not be quarrelsome, but be kind to all, able to teach, patient when wronged, with gentleness correcting those who are in opposition, if perhaps God may grant repentance leading to the knowledge of the truth, and they may

come to their senses and escape from the snare of the devil, having been held captive by him to do his will.

First of all, we have to be the Lord's bond servant. This ministry requires total dependence upon the Lord. He is the one who grants repentance. We don't set anybody free. Only God can do that. The temptation is to lean on our own understanding instead of acknowledging God in all our ways (see Prov. 3:5,6). Most programs focus on learning counseling techniques and developing personal skills to help others. That is commendable, but please know that if God isn't in it, no technique will work regardless of how well the person exercises his or her skills. Remember, all temptation is an attempt to get us to live our lives independent of God. I do believe that if God is in it, a good technique and good personal skills will bear more fruit than a poor technique and poor personal skills.

Second, the Lord's bond servant must not be quarrelsome. Have you ever noticed that some people enjoy arguing for argument's sake. I have come to realize that arguing is nothing but a smoke screen to keep people on the defensive and at a distance. In my early years of ministry, I was pretty good at winning arguments, but over time I realized that I seldom, if ever, won any converts by winning arguments. The poet says, "A man convinced against his will is of the same opinion still." A little maturity and experience in ministry taught me how to avoid arguments. Listen to the wisdom of Solomon, "A fool does not delight in understanding, but only in revealing his own mind" (Prov. 18:2). I certainly don't want to spend my time enabling the fool.

Maintaining control and focus in counseling is a critical skill to learn. If you let a deceived person determine the direction of the counseling session, you will go down a thousand and one rabbit trails. Listen to Paul's advice and warnings:

> Instruct certain men not to teach strange doctrines, nor to pay attention to myths and endless genealogies, which give rise to mere speculation rather than furthering the administration of God which is by faith (1 Tim. 1:3,4).
>
> For some men, straying from these things, have turned aside to fruitless discussion (v. 6).
>
> Avoid worldly and empty chatter, for it will lead to further ungodliness, and their talk will spread like gangrene (2 Tim. 2:16,17).

Third, the Lord's bond servant must be kind. When Jesus was criticized for dining with sinners, He responded by saying, "It is not those who are healthy who need a physician, but those who are sick. But go and learn what this means, 'I desire compassion, and not sacrifice'" (Matt. 9:12,13). Compassion is the Hebrew word *hesed*, which is translated in the Old Testament as lovingkindness. We need to learn what that means, because compassion is the one prerequisite for ministry. In dealing with hurting people, one ounce of criticism or one ounce of rejection is all that is needed to torpedo the ministry.

Fourth, the Lord's bond servant must be able to teach. There is no substitute for knowing the Word of God. We are up against the father of lies, and we can stand against him not by research, nor by reasoning, but by revelation. As Jesus was about to go to the Father and leave behind His disciples, He prayed in the High Priestly Prayer, "I do not ask Thee to take them out of the world, but to keep them from the evil one....Sanctify them in the truth; Thy word is truth" (John 17:15,17). Paul admonishes us, "Be diligent to present yourself approved to God as a workman who does not need to be ashamed, handling accurately the word of truth" (2 Tim. 2:15).

We have to know the truth because it is the truth that sets captives free (see John 8:32). Look again at our passage. When God grants repentance, it leads to a knowledge of the truth. The Holy Spirit is "the Spirit of truth" (14:17), and "He will guide you into all the truth" (16:13). That truth will set us and our counselees free. People are in bondage to the lies they believe, and we have to be able to share the truth with them. Some of the more common lies are: *God doesn't love me; I'm different from others; I could never do that; This isn't going to work; I will never get out of this;* and *God won't help me.*

Fifth, the Lord's bond servant must be patient when wronged. Some don't want to hear the truth even if it is shared in love. Some don't want to get well. Others want you to fix them. They don't like it when you honestly tell them the truth—that you can't fix them, because only God can, and He can if they will assume their responsibilities. There are many rewards in helping people, but there are also many risks. I say take the risk because people are in tremendous need.

Patience is a necessary virtue in counseling. Helping people resolve their personal and spiritual conflicts and find freedom in Christ is not a timed exercise. How the counseling profession ever came up with 50-minute weekly sessions I have no idea. The process is not based on a theology of resolution. You can't resolve anything in 50-minute time slots. If I open a wound, I close it in the same session no matter how long it takes.

I strongly recommend that you take people through the Steps to Freedom in one session. I usually schedule appointments for a whole morning or an afternoon. Severe cases such as satanic ritual abuse (SRA) will often be scheduled for a whole day. I know what you are thinking, especially if you are a busy pastor: *I can't afford to give that amount of time.* If you give just 50 minutes and don't resolve anything, how many more 50-minute slots do you think you will give the person in the next several months or years? Have you ever noticed that when we don't have enough time to do it right, we always seem to find the time to do it over again!

That raises an important issue. Busy pastors who have other responsibilities cannot do this by themselves. They will be overwhelmed by the needs in their congregation. They have to see the wisdom of Ephesians 4:11,12: "He gave some as apostles, and some as prophets, and some as evangelists, and some as pastors and teachers, for the equipping of the saints for the work of service, to the building up of the body of Christ."

Our role as Christian leaders is to equip the saints (not sinners, incidentally) so they can do the work of ministry. Why? Because there are not enough professionals in this country to meet the needs of even 5 percent of our population. The good news is that many saints in our congregations can help others. All they have to do is to be equipped (which is what Freedom in Christ Ministries is committed to doing) and meet the requirements of 2 Timothy 2:24-26. The vast majority of people who are successfully using our material around the world are laypeople That has to be the case or we will not get the job done.

Sixth, the Lord's bond servant must be gentle. The only time Jesus ever described Himself was in Matthew 11:29: "I am gentle and humble in heart." If a person was mighty in God's Spirit, how would it be manifested? I believe it would be in gentleness. We cannot run roughshod over people and push too fast for resolution. If you get ahead of God's timing, you will lose people. We never have the right to violate the fruit of the Spirit, which includes gentleness. If whatever we do cannot be done in love, it is better to leave it undone. If whatever we say cannot be said in love, it is better left unsaid.

I have asked several ladies groups, "If you had to choose between strong masculinity or kindness in a man, which would you choose?" Without hesitation, they all say kindness. Proverbs 19:22 says, "What is desirable in a man is his kindness." Let me say it again: Compassion, kindness, patience and gentleness are essential prerequisites for helping others find their freedom in Christ.

Finally, the Lord's bond servant must be committed to the truth and know without question that God and only God can grant repentance that leads to a knowledge of the truth. People are being held captive by Satan to do his will. Only God can bring them to their senses so they can escape the snare of the devil.

We start every counseling session by declaring ourselves dependent upon Him, for apart from Christ we can do nothing. Using the Steps to Freedom is not a counseling technique; it is an encounter with God. We simply must get God back into the center of our lives and ministries.

A NEW APPROACH TO CHRISTIAN COUNSELING

What I am suggesting is an entirely different approach to Christian counseling. The Christian community adopted many of its present methodologies from clinical psychology and techniques of psychotherapy. They are devoid of God and the gospel. Let me give a very generalized summary of the standard approach to Christian counseling.

Counselors learn the skills of congruence, genuineness, concreteness, immediacy, accurate empathy and so on, and guide the discussion through such techniques as probing, challenging and, if necessary, confronting. The initial objective is to develop a trusting relationship so the counselee will share all the necessary information about himself and what has happened. Then the counselor explains why the person is having difficulty and helps him construct a plan to live a responsible life.

Many conservative Christian counselors who adopt this approach would add the need to repent of sins and commit to God. Some reject outright any association with secular counseling techniques and anything that sounds "psychological." They adopt a much more confrontational approach, which calls for repentance. The theory is that people have sinned, so they need to confess that sin and commit themselves to walk in obedience.

I struggle with this simplistic approach. It is based on an Old Testament law/principle concept, which calls for obedience, as opposed to a New Testament life concept, which calls for us to respond by faith according to what God said is true and then walk accordingly by the power of the Holy Spirit. Proponents of this approach don't understand the battle for the mind. As well, some dismiss the reality of the spiritual world by saying that Christians can't have spiritual problems, and they don't seem to understand the need for compassion.

Those who just tell people in bondage to confess their sins and ask for forgiveness need to realize that most of them have probably been doing that for the last 10 years. We better have a more complete answer than that. Such legalistic approaches overlook many critical issues clearly taught in Scripture, such as your identity in Christ and the need to forgive *from your heart*.

The Common Approach to Counseling

The typical approach to counseling is a common-sense, pull-yourself-up-by-your-own-bootstraps approach. Christian counselors or pastors will see some positive results if they are doing level-three counseling; that is, if the counselee is already firmly rooted and mature enough in Christ to do what he or she should be doing. Many people are helped by simply having objective people listen to them and bring clarity to their issues. Most counselors are capable of helping them get in touch with reality and suggesting responsible courses of action. There is value in that, because a problem well stated is usually half solved.

I have had people drop by my office just to talk. They often come to their own conclusions in the process of sharing their stories. They get up to leave and say, "Thanks, Neil, you've helped me a lot." I didn't do anything other than listen and maybe ask some clarifying questions. And in all likelihood, they will do the right thing *if* they are free in Christ.

One of the problems of the classic approach is that it takes so long to get out the stories, and after weeks of sharing all the pain and frustration without any resolution, people often feel even more like dirt balls. The Christian counselor starts from a totally different perspective. We can, and should, convey the truth: Beloved, now you are a child of God (see 1 John 3:2). We have the privilege to start with the assurance of victory in Christ.

I have seen the list of who we are in Christ from my book *Living Free in Christ* plastered on desks, refrigerators, mirrors and dressers. People are starved for acceptance and affirmation. Life has beat them up, and others have put them down. Just telling them who they are in Christ doesn't set them free, but it gives them hope. The person who is accepted and affirmed will voluntarily be accountable to the authority figure. But when the authority figure demands accountability without acceptance and affirmation, he will never get it.

Jane's Emotional Catharsis

A pastor asked if I would counsel his exceptionally gifted daughter. From the time she was little, she had been on the platform of churches singing like few others could. She also was exceptionally attractive, but when I heard her sing the first time, I couldn't look at her. Something was radically wrong. She was failing in school and suffering from a pathetic self-image. All her life, she received strokes for her ability to sing and for her physical beauty. The performance treadmill she was on had finally caught up with her.

I knew where we had to start. She had no idea who she was as a child of God, and her relationship with the Lord was totally based on her ability to perform. I asked her what would happen if she lost her looks and her ability to sing. She couldn't answer.

After several weeks of meeting together, a remarkable event took place. Her parents went out of town for the weekend and she had to stay home to look after her younger brother and cousins. She resented that, and on Friday evening, she got drunk. I don't know how I found that out even to this day.

The next week in my office, we had this conversation:

> *Neil:* How did your weekend go?
> *Jane:* Fine!
> *Neil:* The whole weekend went well?
> *Jane:* Yes.
> *Neil:* Friday night went well?
> *Jane:* (There was a pause before she finally answered.) Yes.
> *Neil:* Jane, I want you to know that I would not purposefully inquire about what you have or have not done, but I happen to know that Friday night did not go well. What I want you to know is that it doesn't make any difference how I see you. You are a child of God, and I love you whether you perform well or not. Okay?

What followed was the most incredible emotional catharsis I have ever seen. She didn't cry—she bawled for 15 minutes. Eighteen years of performance-based living that could not give her the life, the affirmation, the acceptance, the security, the significance that can only be found in Christ finally came to an end. When the sobbing finally ended, I asked, "May I ask you a personal question? What were you thinking just now?"

"I just hate myself," she said.

I wanted to stand and sing as loud as I could, "No condemnation."

How many people would voluntarily share with another person all the dirt in their lives just for the purpose of sharing it? Not very many, if any. How many people would be willing to share all the dirt in their lives for the purpose of understanding why they feel and act the way they do? Some are willing to do that, but most probably wouldn't unless they were desperate. How many people would be willing to share if in the process of sharing all their dirt, they resolved their problems? Many more would, if confidentiality were assured and the person they were confessing to was filled with the mercy and grace of God.

Steps to Freedom Counseling Method

I have counseled hundreds of people by using both methods, and I can assure you that using the Steps to Freedom will surface more issues in a half-day session than what most counselors are able to drag out of a client in six months. Why? Because I am a good counselor? It has nothing to do with me, but it has everything to do with God, because God is the One who grants repentance. I realize that is an incredible statement, but it is being confirmed around the world. When counselees pray and ask whom they need to forgive, God brings all the names to their minds. When they pray and ask God to reveal every sexual use of their bodies as an instrument of unrighteousness, He does. Why does that even surprise us?

During an advanced conference for Christian leaders, I made the statement about surfacing issues and then followed it with, "I'm not totally sure why this process surfaces so may issues in such a short time." A dear Christian counselor who had been using our material pointed heavenward and said, "I know why. Him!" Exactly. Most of the issues don't surface when people are telling their stories; they surface while they are going through the Steps to Freedom, because they are not telling us, they are telling God.

Dealing with Repressed Memories

Another critically important issue is that of repressed memories. Secular counselors regularly come across clients who cannot recall major events or periods of their lives. They hear as many of the life stories as their clients can remember, but then they come to a wall. Just trying to remember will not usually be enough. Secular therapists, as well as some Christian therapists, try to get past the barrier by using hypnosis, and some psychiatrists are using a prescription drug that is supposed to induce memories. I am opposed to the use of both.

First of all, God never bypasses our minds. All scriptural instruction concerning the mind admonishes us to direct our thoughts externally and actively, never internally and passively. God works through our minds, and I will do everything I can to help people maintain control of their minds. I'm not exactly sure why, but several people I have worked with have had to renounce previous therapy sessions where hypnosis was used to get free from their pasts. Occult practices seek to induce a passive state of the mind. Some eastern religions teach their followers to get their minds out of the way so they can pursue truth directly. That is the most dangerous thing you can do spiritually.

Why don't we follow David's example when he asked the Lord, "Search me, O God, and know my heart; try me and know my anxious thoughts; and see if there be any hurtful way in me, and lead me in the everlasting way" (Ps. 139:23,24). As I mentioned earlier, the Holy Spirit will lead us into all truth, and He "will convict the world concerning sin, and righteousness, and judgment" (John 16:8). The most definitive New Testament passage concerning repressed memories is found in 1 Corinthians 3:20—4:5:

> "The Lord knows the reasonings of the wise, that they are useless." So then let no one boast in men. For all things belong to you, whether Paul or Apollos or Cephas or the world or life or death or things present or things to come; all things belong to you, and you belong to Christ; and Christ belongs to God. Let a man regard us in this manner, as servants of Christ, and stewards of the mysteries of God. In this case, moreover, it is required of stewards that one be found trustworthy. But to me it is a very small thing that I should be examined by you, or by any human court; in fact, I do not even examine myself. I am conscious of nothing against myself, yet I am not by this acquitted; but the one who examines me is the Lord. Therefore do not go on passing judgment before the time, but wait until the Lord comes who will both bring to light the things hidden in the darkness and disclose the motives of men's hearts; and then each man's praise will come to him from God.

According to this passage, we are entitled. So great is that entitlement that Paul prays in Ephesians 1:18, "I pray that the eyes of your heart may be enlightened, so that you may know what is the hope of His calling, what are the riches of the glory of His inheritance in the saints." What we have in Christ is more than we can comprehend, but our riches in Christ are also an entrustment. It is required of us by God to be good stewards of all that we are entitled to, and that we be found trustworthy.

I take that seriously. I belong to God and so does my family, my ministry and everything else that God has entrusted to me. All that I have of lasting value has been freely given to me. I didn't earn it; I can't claim ownership of it. Any part of my message that is true did not originate with me. If it is new, it is not true, and if it is true, it is not new. If you took Christ out of my life, I would be no different than any other lost soul, and neither would you.

Christ Is the Only Way

Before I became a Christian, I didn't know what I know today, and the only reason I do now is because of Christ in me. This book is not my message, and Freedom in Christ Ministries is not my ministry. Both belong to God, and I pray every day that I don't undo what God has done in me, and that we be kept from scandal and the evil one. What I am sharing with you in this book is not *the* way. It is *a* way, and not the only way. Christ is the only way. I hope what I am teaching gives *an* answer for the hope that lies within me, but only Christ is *the* answer.

I fear only the loss of His blessing on my life and ministry. I think I can say with Paul that it is a very small thing to be examined by you or by any human court. I really don't care much what others think of me, and you shouldn't either. I am concerned about what God thinks of me, and I trust that you are concerned as well. To my knowledge, at this moment I have no unresolved issues in my life. I can't think of anybody I need to forgive, and there is nothing I need to confess or renounce. But I am not by this acquitted. In other words, I have not arrived. I am in Christ, but certainly I am not yet perfected.

Paul sums it up well, "Not that I have already obtained it, or have already become perfect, but I press on in order that I may lay hold of that for which also I was laid hold of by Christ Jesus" (Phil. 3:12).

Paul is describing the sanctifying process Dr. Robert Saucy and I are attempting to explain in our forthcoming book. We need to realize as pastors and counselors that clients being examined by us is "a very small thing." God is the One who justifies, and also the One who sanctifies. We are privileged to be used by God, who will work through us to facilitate the process. The Lord is the One who examines us and those we seek to help. He allows us to have some mountaintop experiences when all is well with our souls. Then He gently reveals to us that we are not yet qualified to be a member of the Trinity.

Many proverbs show that rebukes and reproofs are a way of life. Paul says we should:

> Exult in our tribulations, knowing that tribulation brings about perseverance; and perseverance, proven character; and proven character, hope; and hope does not disappoint, because the love of God has been poured out within our hearts through the Holy Spirit who was given to us (Rom. 5:3-5).

We must own up to our mistakes, face our inadequacies, resolve our conflicts and decide to grow up. We can do this because we are already forgiven, and the key is to do it daily. Life is a lot easier if we make small incremental steps toward maturity in Christ than it is if we refuse to grow up. The Lord asks, "What do you desire? Shall I come to you with a rod or with love and a spirit of gentleness?" (1 Cor. 4:21) The choice is ours.

BECOMING FREE AND STAYING FREE

Some of the people we take through the Steps experience complete freedom. For others, gaining freedom is a process. These people may leave their appointments feeling great and alive in Christ. Then, hours, days or months later they are having difficulty again.

Becoming free in Christ is one thing, staying free is another. Paul says, "It was for freedom that Christ set us free; therefore keep standing firm and do not be subject again to a yoke of slavery" (Gal. 5:1). In other words, we can fall back into legalism, and we can fall back into license. "For you were called to freedom, brethren; only do not turn your freedom into an opportunity for the flesh, but through love serve one another" (v. 13). To stay free, people need to know who they are in Christ, the authority and protection of the believer, the nature of the battle that is going on for their minds, and how to walk by faith according to what God said is true by the power of the Holy Spirit.

I can't afford the time to sit down one-on-one and educate these needy people, and you probably can't either. That is what lead me to write the books *Victory over the Darkness* and *The Bondage Breaker*, and produce the video series "Resolving Personal and Spiritual Conflicts." People can read, listen or watch the materials before we meet, and I encourage them to do so. All the material from these resources is covered in my conferences before I take them through the Steps. This greatly increases the chances of people staying free. I cannot guarantee they will choose to be free any more than I can guarantee that every person I have led to Christ will go on to spiritual maturity. That is their choice, but I want to do what I can to increase their chances.

Releasing People from Bondage

One word of caution. Many people cannot read a book or listen to a tape because of the terrible bondage in which they are trapped. In those cases, we have to lead them through the Steps first, but then make sure they have follow-up. After this we encourage them to get into the books and tapes right away. The people must understand certain things to stay free, as the Lord so clearly instructed, "When anyone hears the word of the kingdom, and does not understand it, the evil one comes and snatches away what has been sown in his heart" (Matt. 13:19).

Some people have too much baggage to deal with all at once. If God revealed it all at once, they would probably fall apart. So He graciously reveals one layer at a time. We have to "wait until the Lord comes who will both bring to light the things hidden in the darkness and disclose the motives of men's hearts" (1 Cor. 4:5). So where do we start? We start with what we know. That is why the passage from 1 Corinthians 4 begins with the instruction to be a faithful steward of what God has entrusted to us. Until we are willing to deal with what we know, He won't reveal to us what we don't know. We have to show ourselves faithful in little things before He will put us in charge of greater things.

When people start experiencing difficult days or weeks after their sessions, it may appear they have fallen back into sin or deception, but that may not be the case. God could be revealing another layer of issues to work through. The issues they are dealing with are different from what they were dealing with before.

One lady whose story was featured in *Released from Bondage* went through three major layers in one week. She finally heard an explanation of the "voices" in her head that made sense. She took herself through the Steps and dealt with many surface issues. She felt totally free. Two days later, she started to struggle again and was confronted with the need to forgive her mother. After she worked through all the forgiveness issues, the Lord allowed her to remember all the occultic games she played when she was young. She had totally "forgotten" those times.

Haven't you ever wondered how someone could "forget" such traumatic events in their lives? Was the devil blocking out her memory to keep her from resolving these issues? It may be a possibility in some cases, but it is not the major issue. I think God clouds the past and in severe cases allows the person to dissociate so she can mature in life. Some people don't recall those painful memories until they are 40, 50 or even 60 years old. The Lord waits until they have reached enough maturity and have enough support before He reveals the things hidden in darkness. Even then it will be traumatic, but hopefully they will have the means to resolve it. Eventually, "There is nothing covered that will not be revealed, and hidden that will not be known" (Matt. 10:26).

If we are working with God, we will do all we can to get these people established in Christ. That is their hope and assurance of freedom and victory. The classic model of psychotherapy tries to dig all that information out of the counselees. Potentially, the counselors could get ahead of God's timing and do some incredible damage, but the biggest error is made when they expose all the issues without resolving them. Whenever God reveals something from the past, help the person resolve it. The person will always need to forgive somebody, and will always need to renounce something. Please don't spend the next five years opening up a person without resolving anything. You will do more damage than good. What the person can't remember is probably going to be traumatic when God reveals it.

This is especially true for those who are victims of SRA. Many of these people end up with a multiple-personality disorder (MPD), which is a severe defense mechanism that allows them to dissociate. Those who don't are usually worse off than those who do. I have never met a true MPD who doesn't also have deep spiritual bondages, and I strongly suggest you get the person out of that mode first. If you take the classic approach of counseling with these people 50 minutes a week and spending the next five years breaking down their defense systems, you will end up with basket cases.

I don't believe a truly biblical counseling model has emerged yet for helping MPD victims. It is the ultimate challenge of integration, because it requires an extensive understanding of the spiritual and the psychological. My personal thinking is that the best models of resolution will entail large blocks of concentrated time in an isolated one-on-one session. We have had some tremendous results taking people through the Steps, but we are not suggesting it can be done in one session. Eventually, every personality must be accessed, each must resolve its own issues, and each must agree to come together in Christ. Only Jesus can bind up the brokenhearted.

Prayer for Repressed Memories

Can repressed memories be recovered through prayer? Yes, and we often have counselees pray and ask the Lord to reveal what happened to them at certain times. (I will explain what we do later on in this book.) Let me point out that there is a major difference between the Lord revealing and the person remembering. When God reveals something hidden from the past, it is as though the person is transported back in time. One lady shared that it was as if a window had opened up to her past. Often the pain of the experience is felt again. This is different from accessing another personality that was formed in the past. That personality, too, will experience the past as though it were the present, but the personality that is presently experiencing it is the one that was formed in the past. God isn't revealing anything new to the personality because it already knows too well what has happened.

God reveals the past to people who are new creations in Christ. They are not just products of the past—they are primarily products of the work of Christ on the cross. They have the means to set themselves free from the past by forgiving those who have hurt them and by confessing and renouncing what they have done. That is why God has revealed the past to them. Not because He is using the past against them, but because He wants them to know what has happened so they can finally be free from the past.

What if people pray and nothing happens? Then let it go and get on with your life. Either nothing is there or the timing isn't right. If something in the past is important to know, trust God to reveal it at the right time. Some people become obsessed with what is wrong with them, when the New Testament is wonderfully obsessed with what is right about them. Paul says, "Brethren, I do not regard myself as having laid hold of it yet; but one thing I do: forgetting what lies behind and reaching forward to what lies ahead, I press on toward the goal for the prize of the upward call of God in Christ Jesus" (Phil. 3:13,14).

How do I know those memories are true? What God reveals is true, but memories can be false. For the sake of the people you help, believe what they recall because that is what they have to resolve. But I would never take what I hear from a counselee as gospel fact for the purpose of accusing another person unless I had some hard-core, external and objective evidence to substantiate it.

False memories usually come by way of dreams, suggestive thoughts from irresponsible counselors, counterfeit "words of knowledge" from deceived "Christian" workers and from deceiving spirits. We have been warned "that in later times some will fall away from the faith, paying attention to deceitful spirits" (1 Tim. 4:1). If Satan can put a thought in our minds—and he can—then he can certainly put a thought in the form of a false memory. I have even helped clear the names of Christian leaders who have been falsely accused of being satanists.

We desperately need to depend upon the Lord and exercise godly discernment. "For everyone who partakes only of milk is not accustomed to the word of righteousness, for he is a babe. But solid food is for the mature, who because of practice have their senses trained to discern good and evil" (Heb. 5:13,14). I attempt to explain discernment and distinguish between counterfeit guidance and God's guidance in my book *Walking in the Light*.

The fact is that satanists and abusers are out there, and they will never own up to what they do. Most will never be brought to justice. If legitimate charges are brought against them, they point at the abused and accuse them for trying to tear up the family, and discredit them. They are often believed because they may appear to be doing better than the victim who is deeply troubled because of the abuse. My heart cries for justice, but we will not have perfect justice in this lifetime. God will make it right in the end. The secret sin on earth is open scandal in heaven. "'Vengeance is mine, I will repay,' says the Lord" (Rom. 12:19). Until then, let us do what we can to help people break free from their pasts and from their abusers.

CHAPTER FIVE

COUNSELING THE SPIRITUALLY AFFLICTED

The first power lawn mower I bought many years ago was a basic, no-frills model. It had a pull cord, throttle, grass catcher—and a new owner to push it. Being inexperienced in the ways of power mowers, I pushed it into an irrigation valve and bent the shaft of the engine. It stopped immediately, and I couldn't even turn the engine over by pulling the cord. So I decided to fix it.

First, I had to get the blade off, but it wouldn't budge. I beat on it with a hammer, pried it with a crowbar and tried a dozen other ways before I finally gave up. I threw the pile of parts into a cardboard box and took it to a lawnmower repairman.

He looked at the mess I made, then pointed across the shop. "See that machine over there?" he said. "It straightens the shaft of a power mower engine while it is still in the block. I usually charge 10 bucks for doing it!"

Looking at the damage I had done, I said, "Great, what is it going to cost me now?"

"I'll fix it for 20 bucks," he said with a grin on his face.

"Go ahead," I said. "But tell me, how do you get the blade off the shaft?"

He reached over with a pair of pliers and pulled out a key I hadn't seen, and the shaft dropped right off!

THE KEY OF KNOWLEDGE

My struggle with that lawn mower is similar to the way we Christians sometimes handle spiritual struggles. How many times have we resorted to some power mode out of frustration or ignorance? What we should be doing is looking for the key. Jesus said, "I will give you the keys of the kingdom of heaven" (Matt. 16:19). The keys of the kingdom of heaven open doors that set captives free.

When Jesus was preaching judgment upon the Pharisees and religious lawyers, He said, "Woe to you lawyers! For you have taken away the key of knowledge; you did not enter in yourselves, and those who were entering in you hindered" (Luke 11:52). The "key" is the "key of knowledge." The Lord speaking through the prophet Hosea said, "My people are destroyed for lack of knowledge. Because you have rejected knowledge, I also will reject you from being My priest" (Hos. 4:6). Jesus said, "You shall know the truth, and the truth shall make you free" (John 8:32).

Not much has changed since the time of Christ. Certain pharisaic leaders in the Church today will oppose any personal ministry that encourages people to walk in the light and speak the truth in love. Why do they do this? Jesus said, "Men loved the darkness rather than the light; for their deeds were evil. For everyone who does evil hates the light, and does not come to the light, lest his deeds should be exposed" (John 3:19,20). If people don't repent, they have to run from the light or try to discredit the source of the light. The latter is the option of those who cover up to protect their reputations, or believe they would lose their positions of leadership if people found out the truth about them. Notice how Scripture characterizes them.

First, these leaders have not entered into the key of knowledge themselves. If the Holy Spirit were taken out of their lives and ministry, every activity would continue on as scheduled. They think eternal life is something they get when they die; therefore, being "in Christ" is only positional truth. They are more concerned about controlling others than about developing self-control. They have no idea what freedom is. They go to church to critique the message and the music. We are not supposed to sit in judgment of the message. A biblical message shared in love sits in judgment of us, and we should enter into the worship experience rather than criticize the worship team. Many are caught "in the gall of bitterness and in the bondage of iniquity" (Acts 8:23).

OPPOSITION TO FREEDOM'S MINISTRY

A church board voted to have a video conference. A couple from our ministry provided counseling and counselor training. An older gentleman in the church was against it from the beginning, but he came to the conference anyway. He stood at the back with his arms folded across his chest just waiting to hear something he didn't like. Hoping to reach this dear man, one of our staff members asked him to sit in on a counseling session as a prayer partner. Being retired, this man had the time, so he reluctantly agreed. In one afternoon, he saw a young man come to complete freedom in Christ. That same evening, he asked to be led through the Steps, and the following Sunday afternoon he "entered in" and began to experience the wonderful life that Christ offers. For 60 years he had been living under the bondage of bitterness toward his own father, and for 60 years he was a critical, controlling member of the church. No longer!

Any ministry that turns on the light has to expect opposition. I regularly have people share with me at conferences that they have had thoughts of killing me. One lady said she drove by a gun shop for three weeks in a row before a conference. She fought off the temptation to buy a gun and bring it to the conference for the purpose of shooting me. She glared at me with hatred from the front row on the first evening of the conference. That week I had the privilege of leading her to freedom in Christ. At the end of the week, she gave me a foot washer/massager. The note on the box said, "You washed my feet, now let me wash yours."

A policeman approached me during a break at a conference and said, "Neil, this can't be me! While you were talking, I had overwhelming thoughts to grab a knife and stab you!" Of course, those weren't his thoughts, and by now I hope you know the source of his thoughts.

The members in our ministry have all had people in bondage attack them verbally. Many became our good friends and supporters after they found their freedom in Christ.

OPPOSITION TO THE CHURCH

Nobody opposed the Church with more zeal than Paul did before he encountered Christ on the Damascus road, but when his eyes were opened, nobody promoted it more. We regularly pray for those who curse us, and ask the Lord to open their eyes.

Sadly, some choose to remain in bondage and oppose what God is doing. Paul wrote, "Alexander the coppersmith did me much harm; the Lord will repay him according to his deeds. Be on guard against him yourself, for he vigorously opposed our teaching" (2 Tim. 4:14,15). When Paul wrote his first letter to Timothy, he exhorted him to "fight the good fight, keeping faith and a good conscience, which some have rejected and suffered shipwreck in regard to their faith. Among these are Hymenaeus and Alexander, whom I have delivered over to Satan, so that they may be taught not to blaspheme" (1 Tim. 1:18-20).

Second, pharisaic, controlling leaders hinder those who are trying to enter into knowledge. Jesus said, "Woe to you, scribes and Pharisees, hypocrites, because you shut off the kingdom of heaven from men; for you do not enter in yourselves, nor do you allow those who are entering to go in" (Matt. 23:13). It is hard to be gracious to these "blind guides" (v. 16) when they are attacking you. The damage they do to the kingdom of God cannot be overestimated. I have helped many people find their freedom from these spiritual abusers. Eventually, the abusers' character will reveal who they are, and inevitably they end up in moral failure because the law is powerless to give life (see Gal. 3:21).

THE CURSE OF THE LAW

Legalism is the religion of the self-righteous. It is a subtle and deadly form of bondage because it is almost impossible to confront. The Lord confronted it in Matthew 23, but we are not to judge another person's character. It is hard to discipline these wrongdoers because they are extremely careful not to be caught doing anything morally wrong. They are driven people. Paul says, "For as many as are of the works of the Law are under a curse; for it is written, 'Cursed is everyone who does not abide by all things written in the book of the law, to perform them.' Now that no one is justified by the Law before God is evident; for, 'The righteous man shall live by faith'" (Gal. 3:10,11).

Why is the Church still living under the curse of the law nearly 2,000 years after Christ was on earth? Many do not understand that He redeemed us from the curse of the law, "in order that in Christ Jesus the blessing of Abraham might come to the Gentiles, so that we might receive the promise of the Spirit through faith" (v. 14). Those who enter into the life of Christ can say, "Our adequacy is from God, who also made us adequate as servants of a new covenant, not of the letter, but of the Spirit; for the letter kills, but the Spirit gives life" (2 Cor. 3:5,6).

Third, spiritual abusers actually try to discredit those who are bearing fruit. Jesus didn't fit into the theological system of the Pharisees, so "they were watching Him to see if He would heal him [a man with a withered hand] on the Sabbath, in order that they might accuse Him" (Mark 3:2). Sure enough, the Lord healed the man. What a gracious act of God to heal someone with a withered hand. But what did the Pharisees do? They "went out and immediately began taking counsel with the Herodians against Him, as to how they might destroy Him" (v. 6). If they had really loved the Lord and His people, they would have said, "Thank You for doing that. What a wonderful thing You did."

Why do some people want to discredit those who are doing good works? Some actually believe they are defending the faith, but most are merely hurting people. I learned years ago that people do not cut down other people out of a position of strength, and I also learned not to try to defend myself against them. They will only double their efforts. We need to voluntarily be accountable to wise, godly people for both our message and our ministry, but you can't be accountable to these kinds of people. To do so would only put you under bondage to them. We have to be bond servants of Christ. Every legitimate Christian ministry should establish people free in Christ and enable them to be the people God wants them to be. Another reason for deviant ways is articulated in James 3: 13-18, which also describes the nature of ministry for those who have entered in:

Who among you is wise and understanding? Let him show by his good behavior his deeds in the gentleness of wisdom. But if you have bitter jealousy and selfish ambition in your heart, do not be arrogant and so lie against the truth. This wisdom is not that which comes down from above, but is earthly, natural, demonic. For where jealousy and selfish ambition exist, there is disorder and every evil thing. But the wisdom from above is first pure, then peaceable, gentle, reasonable, full of mercy and good fruits, unwavering, without hypocrisy. And the seed whose fruit is righteousness is sown in peace by those who make peace.

LEADING OTHERS TO KNOWLEDGE

The keys to the Kingdom come through wisdom from above and are sown by gentle, merciful peacemakers who enable others to enter in. Let's go back to our original passage, Matthew 16:19, and finish the sentence: "I will give you the keys of the kingdom of heaven; and whatever you shall bind on earth shall be bound in heaven, and whatever you shall loose on earth shall be loosed in heaven." The Lord makes a similar statement in Matthew 18:18 and then adds, "Again I say to you, that if two of you agree on earth about anything that they may ask, it shall be done for them by My Father who is in heaven. For where two or three have gathered together in My name, there I am in their midst" (vv. 19,20).

Another similar passage, grammatically, is John 20:23: "If you forgive the sins of any, their sins have been forgiven them; if you retain the sins of any, they have been retained." These passages are difficult to interpret and have resulted in church practices that may or may not be biblical. If these passages are translated into the English language in the future tense (i.e., "shall be bound" and "shall be forgiven") then they can be taken to justify extreme sacerdotalism. In other words, the Church has the power to bind, loose and forgive whomever it wishes. The Catholic church has generally taken this position, but only the pope can speak with ultimate authority, and only ordained priests under the authority of the pope can communicate such statements. Some "name-it-and-claim-it" advocates, and those in the "positive confession movement," also operate as though they have the authority to bind and loose whatever they wish.

Other people believe that the tense of the verbs in these passages is best translated as future perfect (i.e., "Whatever you bind on earth shall have been bound in heaven" and "If you forgive anyone his sins, they have already been forgiven"). I personally believe that is the best way to interpret these passages, especially in light of the rest of Scripture. We are called by God to do His will. We are assured of God's presence for the purpose of discerning His will when two or three are gathered together in His name. Heaven—not us—initiates the binding and loosing, which we have the privilege of announcing.

Does this passage teach that we can have infallible communication from God in every question of "binding and loosing"? I think God is capable and willing to communicate with His Church in such a way that it may have the keys to the Kingdom, but I don't think any of us can claim perfect discernment, totally renewed minds or pure hearts. There is always the possibility of two or more people agreeing together on what they want to do, and then claiming this passage to support their activity. In effect, they are putting God to the test by claiming that He has to respond according to His Word. God will respond to His Word, but who initiated what they agreed upon? Was it God or them?

Jesus renounced this kind of thinking when the devil tempted Him to throw Himself down from the pinnacle of the Temple. Satan quoted Scripture, but Jesus responded, "You shall not put the Lord your God to the test" (Matt. 4:7). We don't put God to the test; He tests us. There is no way we can cleverly word a prayer so that God is obligated to do what we ask of Him. God is under no obligation to humankind. He is under obligation only to Himself to keep His Word and His covenant with us. We need to take into account Jesus' words in Matthew 7:21-23:

> "Not everyone who says to Me, 'Lord, Lord,' will enter the kingdom of heaven; but he who does the will of My Father who is in heaven. Many will say to Me on that day, 'Lord, Lord, did we not prophesy in Your name, and in Your name cast out demons, and in Your name perform many miracles?' And then I will declare to them, 'I never knew you; depart from Me, you who practice lawlessness.'"

There must be some application for binding and loosing, and I think there is. The Pharisees had charged Jesus with doing exorcisms by the power of Beelzebul (a high-ranking demon). Jesus responded by saying, "How can anyone enter the strong man's house and carry off his property, unless he first binds the strong man?" (Matt. 12:29). Jesus is the One who ties up the strong man (Satan) and carries off his property. The Lord argues that if His exorcisms cannot be attributed to Satan (see vv. 25,26), then they reflect an authority that is greater than that of Satan.

Satan has gained a right to be in people's lives because of the ground they have given him. To recapture that ground, we have to first bind the strong man by the authority we have in Christ. Notice the order of the commands in James 4:7: "Submit therefore to God. Resist the devil and he will flee from you." We can do this because Jesus said, "All authority has been given to Me in heaven and on earth" (Matt. 28:18). "He had disarmed the rulers and authorities" (Col. 2:15) and "in Him you have been made complete, and He is the head over all rule and authority" (v. 10). We don't minister in our authority, but in His authority, and then only by the power of the Holy Spirit. Paul says, "Be strong in the Lord, and in the strength of His might" (Eph. 6:10).

Based on what has already been accomplished by Christ and established in heaven, we suggest praying before each counseling session as follows:

Dear heavenly Father,
We acknowledge Your presence in this room and in our lives. You are the only omniscient (all knowing), omnipotent (all powerful), and omnipresent (always present) God. We are dependent upon You, for apart from Christ we can do nothing. We stand in the truth that all authority in heaven and on earth has been given to the resurrected Christ, and because we are in

Christ, we share that authority in order to make disciples and set captives free. We ask You to fill us with Your Holy Spirit and lead us into all truth. We pray for Your complete protection and ask for Your guidance. In Jesus' name. Amen.

Then make the following declaration out loud:

In the name and authority of the Lord Jesus Christ, we command Satan and all evil spirits to release (name) in order that (name) can be free to know and choose to do the will of God. As children of God seated with Christ in the heavenlies, we agree that every enemy of the Lord Jesus Christ be bound and gagged to silence. We say to Satan and all his evil workers that you cannot inflict any pain or in any way prevent God's will from being accomplished in (name's) life.

OUR LIMITATIONS IN BINDING AND LOOSING

Is this binding and loosing all-encompassing? In our experience it is not, but it is sufficient to accomplish God's will. Let me explain.

First, if God requires us to do something, the grace of God will enable us to do it. "And this is the confidence which we have before Him, that, if we ask anything according to His will, He hears us. And if we know that He hears us in whatever we ask, we know that we have the requests which we have asked from Him" (1 John 5:14,15). I think we can say with confidence that it is God's will for us to renounce false religious experiences and lies that we have believed, to forgive others and to genuinely repent of our ways that aren't right.

Second, it has been our experience that God grants enough freedom for the person to know, choose and do the will of God. Why aren't people totally free after saying a prayer and making a declaration as given previously? Because that is not the answer to their bondage. If it were the answer, they would call us every night to pray for them. The answer is repentance, and God is the One who grants it (see 2 Tim. 2:25). Freedom comes progressively as people go through the Steps to Freedom.

Third, every passage of Scripture must be understood in light of the immediate and larger context of the Bible. Every ministry and minister of the Church is subject to all governing authorities God has established (see Rom. 13:1-7), and each has the responsibility to be faithful stewards (see 1 Cor. 4:1-3). I have spoken on secular campuses on the topic of "demonic influences in the world today." In each case, I prayed before the meeting with the local leadership of Campus Crusade for Christ, who had invited me. We first committed ourselves to the Lord, then the auditorium and then the sound system. Then we agreed together that every enemy of the Lord Jesus Christ was to be bound in that auditorium, and we prayed against the blinding of the unbelieving.

We prayed this way with confidence because we followed all legal and administrative procedures to reserve that time and place for our use. The Lord had entrusted us with the auditorium, and we were trying to be good stewards by committing it to the Lord. Also, we could agree together to bind the enemy because we were under God's authority and the governing authorities of the university and the land. In every meeting, you could hear a pin drop as I spoke, and many students gave their hearts to Christ.

When I was in India recently, I talked to a young missionary who was under psychiatric care. He and several others had gone into Hindu temples and attempted to bind the enemy, but they were unsuccessful. Why? I think they overstepped their authority. Those temples did not belong to them, and they had not sought permission from the governing authorities to use them for their own purposes.

Can we be in the will of God and at the same time rebel against governing authorities? Romans 13:1,2 gives an answer: "Let every person be in subjection to the governing authorities. For there is no authority except from God, and those which exist are established by God. Therefore he who resists authority has opposed the ordinance of God; and they who have opposed will receive condemnation upon themselves." I appreciate the missionaries' zeal to see others won to Christ, but I seriously question if what they did originated in heaven.

Stewardship is an important part of ministry. We should commit to the Lord everything that God has entrusted to us. It begins with our bodies. "I urge you therefore, brethren, by the mercies of God, to present your bodies a living and holy sacrifice, acceptable to God, which is your spiritual service of worship" (12:1). We should then commit to the Lord our marriages, families, ministries, homes and everything in them. We don't want to leave any room for Satan to have access to ourselves, our families or our ministries.

When I rent a room in a hotel, it is under my stewardship. I have no idea what occurred in that room before I rent it, so I renounce any previous use of the room that would not please my heavenly Father. People hide pornographic material in hotel rooms, use them for adulterous affairs and watch X-rated movies in them. Next, I commit the room and all that is in it to the Lord and command Satan and all his evil workers to leave the room in the name and by the authority of the Lord Jesus Christ. Finally, I ask for the Lord's protection while I sleep.

MAINTAINING CONTROL OF THE COUNSELING SESSION

After we have taken our rightful place in Christ, we need to understand what is happening in the lives of those who want to be free in Christ and how we can maintain control in the counseling process. Several years ago, a pastor's wife made an appointment to see me. A half-hour into our conversation, I said to her, "You really love Jesus, don't you?"

"Oh, yes," she said.

"And you really love the Holy Spirit, don't you?" I asked.

"Oh, yes. He is my comforter," she said.

Then I asked, "But you don't even like God the Father, do you?"

When I said this, she began to cry. Her mother was a legalistic woman who had verbally abused her for as long as she could remember. Her father sat there like a lump and never once came to her defense. This woman loved Jesus because He did something for her; He went to the Cross. The Holy Spirit talks to her. But she thinks her heavenly Father is just like her earthly father. He sits up there in heaven like a lump! Unfortunately, the voice that she thought was the Holy Spirit's, wasn't. A little voice told her not to do certain things or her son would be cursed.

I knew that her understanding of her heavenly Father needed to be corrected, so I gave her a set of tapes on the attributes of God by A. W. Tozer, who wrote *The Knowledge of the Holy* (HarperSanFrancisco, 1978). She listened to the tapes three times. As near as I can tell, it didn't have any effect on her. That shook me to the core. At the time, I was chairman of the practical theology department at Talbot School of Theology. I was responsible for teaching homiletics as well as Christian education. Having a master's and a doctoral degree in education, I was deeply committed to preaching and teaching God's Word, and I still am. But I had just given a person the best possible teaching on the attributes of God, which she listened to three times, and the effect was zero!

I began to wonder how much influence teaching and preaching really has on the average member in our congregations. About that time, Dr. David Seamands, author and professor at Asbury Theological Seminary, spoke at a chapel meeting at Talbot. He showed us a diagram similar to the following one:

Loving and caring ▶	Truth about God is filtered through the grid of:	▶ Hateful and unconcerned
Loving and caring ▶	1. Ignorance	▶ Hateful and unconcerned
Good and merciful ▶	2. False prophets and teachers	▶ Mean and unforgiving
Unconditional grace ▶	3. Blasphemous mental thoughts	▶ Conditional approval
Present and available ▶	4. Unhealthy interpersonal relationships during early developmental years	▶ Absent when needed
Giver of good gifts ▶		▶ Takes away, "killjoy"
Nurturing and affirming ▶		▶ Critical and unpleasable
Accepting ▶	5. Role model of authority figures, especially parents	▶ Rejecting
Just, fair and impartial ▶		▶ Unjust, unfair, partial
Steadfast and reliable ▶		▶ Unpredictable and untrustworthy

Diagram 5-A

I don't recall Dr. Seamands's exact words, but his presentation certainly stimulated my thinking. Apparently, he had students in his seminary, as we did in ours, who would take their theology class exams and answer the questions about the attributes of God correctly, as given on the left side of the diagram. But emotionally, the students would still feel the same about God, as given on the right side of the diagram.

We need to realize that many people have thoughts "raised up against the knowledge of God" (2 Cor. 10:5) long before they take a class on theology or before the people in our churches hear the truth about God from our pulpits. Every legitimate educator and communicator knows that saying something does not ensure reception and integration on the part of the listener.

For the pastor's wife I counseled, hearing the truth about God three times was drowned out by deceiving spirits, unhealthy relationships in her early years and poor parental role models. So how do we help people love the Lord their God with all their hearts and with all their souls and with all their minds? First, we must realize that we can't accomplish this by just preaching and teaching harder and better.

Please don't misunderstand me. I think we ought to have the best possible teaching and preaching. I make my living by doing both, but I also know that some people who sit in my conferences catch only one-tenth of what I say. I have had people tell me months later that they saw my lips move but didn't hear a word I said as I read to them from my Bible.

But we routinely see people go from the right side of the diagram to the left side emotionally in a three-hour counseling session, which helps them find their freedom in Christ. Then, watch the effect of your teaching and preaching. People gobble up the Word of God. They can't get enough of it. And why is this so? Because they have resolved the personal and spiritual conflicts that are critical in their relationships with God, and the Holy Spirit now bears witness with their spirits that they are children of God (see Rom. 8:16). God alone can do this when these people have spiritually connected with Him (entered in). Notice how Paul states this in Ephesians 4:20-24:

> But you did not learn Christ in this way, if indeed you have heard Him and have been taught in Him, just as truth is in Jesus, that, in reference to your former manner of life, you lay aside the old self, which is being corrupted in accordance with the lusts of deceit, and that you be renewed in the spirit of your mind, and put on the new self, which in the likeness of God has been created in righteousness and holiness of the truth.

The truth is *in Jesus*. It is our responsibility to lay aside the old self, put on the new self, and be renewed in the spirit of the mind. "A natural man does not accept the things of the Spirit of God; for they are foolishness to him, and he cannot understand them, because they are spiritually appraised" (1 Cor. 2:14).

The carnal Christians are still operating according to their old nature (flesh). Paul says to them, "I, brethren, could not speak to you as to spiritual men, but as to men of flesh, as to babes in Christ. I gave you milk to drink, not solid food; for *you were not yet able to receive it*. Indeed, even now *you are not yet able*, for you are still fleshly" (3:1-3, emphasis added). Paul explains why they were not able to receive it. They were getting their identities from men and walking like mere men with conflicts of jealousies and strifes. Until we help people resolve these conflicts and establish their identities in Christ, they will not be able to receive solid food no matter how well we preach or teach.

A BATTLE FOR THE MIND

We also need to understand how the spiritual battle going on for the mind is impeding the process. A highly educated professional man asked if he could spend some time with me. He told me he was experiencing great difficulty, and he was willing to drive six hours to meet with me. I sent him a set of my tapes "Resolving Personal Conflicts" prior to our meeting. I wanted him to understand who he was in Christ, how to walk by faith, how to grasp the battle for his mind and how to forgive from his heart. He handed me the tapes and said they were all blank! After I led him through the Steps, he listened to the same set all the way home.

We also need to know that the enemy is more real to the people than God is. Listen to what a victim of satanic ritual abuse wrote in her diary:

Dear God,
    Where are You? How can You watch and not help? I hurt so bad, and You don't even care. If You cared, You'd make it stop or You'd let me die. I love You, but You seem so far away. I can't hear You, or feel You, or see You, but I'm supposed to believe You're here. Lord, I feel them, I see them, and I hear them. They're here. People tell me You're here, but I can't tell. I'm sorry if I'm that bad, God, but I'm trying.
    Please love me and help me. I want to be a part of You. Why won't You help me do that? I know You are real, God, but they are more real to me right now. You know how real they are, Lord, but no one will believe me. Please make someone believe me, Lord. I'm alone in this, and it hurts so bad. Why, Lord? Why? I have no answers, but I have so many questions. Why won't You give me some answers? Why won't You make it stop. Please, Lord! Please! If you love me, You'll let me die.

Ten minutes after recording this entry, this woman tried unsuccessfully to commit suicide. Many people break down and cry when I read this to them in my office. All of them have a distorted concept of God and none of them know who they are in Christ. They fear the possibility of having a mental breakdown. They feel unloved, worthless and rejected. Most think they are different from other people. In our research, we discovered that 74 percent of our church kids believe they are different from others (i.e., Christianity works for others, but it doesn't work for them). Are they different from others? Of course not. But if they believe they're different, would it affect the way they live their lives? Yes, it would.

These kids' spiritual perspective is totally askew. They see themselves as caught between two equal and opposite powers as depicted in the following diagram:

Diagram 5-B

The truth is, God is higher and greater than what can ever be shown on a diagram. He is omnipotent, omnipresent, omniscient, kind and loving in all His ways. Satan is a defeated foe, and we are in Christ, seated with Him in the heavenlies. But the severely oppressed perceive Satan as more powerful, real and present than God in their experiences, as did the lady whose diary entry I cited. Many are not aware that they are spiritually in trouble. Some don't want to give up what they have. The little voice in their heads is the only thing they have. I know it sounds bizarre, but it is not that uncommon.

I deeply believe that what lasts for these people is not what we do, but what *they* do. Yet we have an important role to play as the Lord's bond servants. We must maintain control by working only with the people as we guide them through the process. To do this, I always ask them for cooperation in one major area. They must share with me what is going on inside in opposition to what we are doing or saying. The mind is the control center. If they don't lose control in their minds, we won't lose control of the counseling session. I don't care if the thought is coming from the pit or from an external speaker in the room. The only way it can have any power over them is if they believe the lies. Bringing the lies out into the open breaks the power. All we are up against is deception. No physical monster in the room will beat them up.

EXAMPLES OF FINDING FREEDOM IN CHRIST

One lady said, "They're laughing at you." This can be intimidating unless you understand it is just a scheme of the devil. As soon as it is exposed, the laughing stops. When people reveal what they are hearing, no matter how vile or threatening it is, I always say, "Thank you for sharing that." Then I proceed with the Steps.

But sometimes people are reluctant to share what they are hearing in their minds. This happens for two reasons. First, they won't tell us what is going on inside if they suspect at all that we won't believe them. Second, they may not tell us what they are hearing because they are intimidated. It is common for them to be told they will get thrashed when they go home. This is just an intimidating lie intended to keep them from resolving their conflicts. I told one lady that if she resolved her problems in the counseling session, her problems would be resolved at home as well. She blurted out, "I wish you could prove that to me!" The intimidation may be a threat to their loved ones, such as spouses or children.

An extremely abused lady was threatening suicide in her church before we conducted a conference there. The church leaders set up an appointment with me to meet her during the week. I was able to settle her down, and I convinced her to attend the conference. The night I talked about forgiveness, she came under an attack and had to leave the auditorium! She heard enough to make a list of people she needed to forgive—four pages of names. I asked for her cooperation and then started to pray. Before I could finish, she was headed for the door in panic.

"What are you thinking?" I asked.

"You're going to hurt me," she said.

"No, I'm not," I said. "That is a lie."

The woman had a few more similar episodes, and we dealt with them calmly. We worked through the Steps, and she found her freedom in Christ. When the pastor and I got to his house, the phone was ringing. "Pastor," she said, "they're not here either!"

I let people know that I am not going to bypass or violate their minds, and they are free to leave anytime. I never try to physically restrain anyone, because "the weapons of our warfare are not of the flesh" (2 Cor. 10:4). I have had some people say, "I have to get out of here!"

And I tell them, "You are free to leave anytime." I have never had people leave who didn't come back on their own in about five minutes. I just pray for them while they are gone.

In the vast majority of cases, you will only get spiritual opposition when you start to resolve the problems or when you initially pray. Watch the person's eyes closely. If she starts to look around the room or gets glassy eyed, get her attention immediately. If you are starting to lose her, back off immediately. You have lost control if she cannot respond to you, or if she goes catatonic. In either case, don't panic. If you go out for a cup or coffee, she would probably be alert by the time you came back.

After a conference in Singapore, I got an urgent call from a missionary. A college student had heard me speak the night before and came to the location of the conference to see me, but I had already gone back to my apartment. The student was threatening to kill me, and then he went catatonic. The missionary wanted me to come and help him. I told him the student should be left alone for a while. He would wake up in a few minutes, and when he did, he should make an appointment to see me the next day. I try to never let the devil set the agenda. The student came by my apartment the next day, and I walked him through the Steps. He left being free in Christ.

The key is not to lose control, but if the person should go catatonic, try saying, "Satan, you have no authority here. This person has given her heart to Christ." Then address the person by saying, "You can open your eyes now." In most cases, the person will. The only reason she closed her eyes was because she believed a lie. The effect on the mind is similar to hypnosis.

Occasionally, we have to confront the demonic when the person is too weak in his or her faith. Command Satan in the name of Christ to release the person and go on. I don't recommend trying to cast out demons, because it is premature. The person hasn't cleaned up the garbage yet, and resisting the devil is an individual responsibility. The two most common physical symptoms we observe are headaches and nausea. They usually subside when the person shares what he or she is feeling. In most cases, I ignore the physical symptoms and go on. Both will be gone when the person is free in Christ.

The interference is intended to intimidate us and cause us to respond in fear. We will lose control if we respond in fear of Satan rather than through faith in God. That is exactly what is intended. During one counseling session, a large lady slowly got out of her chair and started walking toward me with a menacing look on her face. What would you do? I calmly said, "I am a child of God, and you cannot touch me." She stopped in her tracks. "Sit down," I said, and she did.

Understand, I was not talking to the lady, but to the deceiving spirits that were controlling her. Incidentally, authority does not increase with volume, so there's no need to shout at the devil. Shouting indicates that you have lost control and are operating in the flesh. It is no different from shouting at your children. You are controlling them by your flesh with fear and intimidation. You are not exercising proper parental authority; you are undermining it.

Once when I was in Europe, I asked a couple of missionaries to help the adult child of another missionary. The two came back looking defeated. One of them had a bruised shoulder and a button missing on his shirt. They had lost control at the very beginning and went into a defensive mode. The next day, I met with the boy. I told him he had to cooperate with me by sharing what was going on inside, because what we were up against was nothing but deception. "No, it's power," he said. I had him renounce that as a lie, and then I asked him to share with me what he was thinking. "They want me to kill you," he said. I thanked him for sharing that, and we had no more interference after that.

In many cases, interference is not experienced at all. So the people wonder if anything was really wrong spiritually, although they sense a newfound freedom. Their problems may not have had demonic origins, but they still resolved huge spiritual issues, which affect their relationships to God. We all need to submit to God even if we have no need to resist the devil. I don't try to figure out the major causes or the origins of people's problems. I don't care if the lies they believed came from the world, the flesh or the devil. The solution is the same. Christ is the answer, and truth will set us free.

In every case, look for the key, put your confidence in Christ and share the truth in love. I received a treasured gift at Christmas recently. It was from a satanic ritual abuse victim who has become a dear friend of mine. The gift is a handmade wreath and has the following poem she wrote attached to the center:

> A friend of mine whose grapevine died, had put it out for trash.
> I said to her, "I'll take that vine and make something of that."
> At home the bag of dead, dry vines looked nothing but a mess,
> But as I gently bent one vine, entwining 'round and 'round,
> A rustic wreath began to form, potential did abound.
> One vine would not go where it should, and anxious as I was,
> I forced it so to change its shape, it broke—and what the cause?
> If I had taken precious time to slowly change its form,
> It would have made a lovely wreath, not a dead vine, broken, torn.
> As I finished bending, adding blooms, applying trim,
> I realized how that rustic wreath is like my life within.
> You see, so many in my life have tried to make me change.
> They've forced my spirit anxiously, I tried to rearrange.
> But when the pain was far too great, they forced my fragile form,
> I plunged far deeper in despair, my spirit broken, torn.
> Then God allowed a gentle one that knew of dying vines,
> To kindly, patiently allow the Lord to take His time.

And though the vine has not yet formed a decorative wreath,
know that with God's servant's help one day when Christ I
   meet,
He'll see a finished circle, a perfect gift to Him.
It will be a final product, a wreath with all the trim.
So as you look upon this gift, the vine 'round and complete,
Remember God is using you to gently shape His wreath.

PART TWO

This section will walk you through each of the

seven Steps involved in helping a person find

freedom in Christ.

CHAPTER SIX

THE FREEDOM APPOINTMENT

Thousands of Christians all over the world are experiencing a new freedom in their relationships with Jesus Christ. They have walked through the Steps to Freedom in Christ and have resolved personal and spiritual conflicts. Many, like yourself, want to go further and lead others to freedom in Christ, which is the birthright of every child of God.

While many Christians need to settle issues of personal identity or spiritual conflict, relatively few have powerful strongholds that require the help of an expert. In this book, I sometimes use the terms "leader" or "encourager," rather than "counselor," because I am not writing primarily to professionals, but to all committed Christians who want to help others find their freedom in Christ.

When walking someone through the Steps to Freedom, you are not "counseling" in the traditional sense. You are helping Christians assume responsibility for their own lives by affirming their identities in Christ, renouncing the lies they have believed, choosing the truth as revealed in God's Word and resolving the personal and spiritual conflicts that are keeping them in bondage.

YOU CAN BEGIN NOW

Though I will provide some depth of information in preparing you to lead someone through the Steps, don't be fooled into believing that knowing this material inside out is necessary in order for you to be a leader-encourager. I knew little of this material when I first began, and I learned most of it through trial and error.

I believe every committed Christian can do what I do to help others find freedom in Christ. It does not require the exercise of a special gift; it requires total dependence upon God, Christlike character and the ability to apply truth. Gifts and unique callings are not transferable, but truth is. We have trained thousands of Christians—students, homemakers, pastors, missionaries—to help others find their freedom in Christ.

If you are free in Christ, have read *Victory over the Darkness* and *The Bondage Breaker*, understand the concepts and have a genuine caring and nonjudgmental attitude toward others, you can begin leading them through the Steps to Freedom today!

Discerning Whom to Counsel

Going through the Steps must be a personal choice, and people should not be coerced into it. Those who have found freedom will often want their spouses or friends to experience the same joy. But taking people through the Steps because others want them to do it is usually not advisable for a number of reasons: (1) they may feel obligated to the person but have no desire to face the truth or get right with God; (2) they may have no sense of need; (3) they may not be totally truthful; and (4) they may have no motivation because they have gone to counseling before without seeing any results. Therefore, we encourage those who have been freed to pray for their loved ones and allow the Holy Spirit to prepare their hearts for an appointment.

In most cases, it is not wise to take second-person appointments. That is, the person seeking help should ask for it personally. You can't help someone who doesn't want to be helped, nor can you help someone who won't assume responsibility for his or her own attitudes and actions.

Addressing Defenses

Be aware of two defenses some people may exhibit. The first comes from those who have tried traditional counseling and haven't seen any results, or from those who don't believe in counseling. In such cases, you can share something like the following: "I want you to know that I care about you, and I believe that you can be free in Christ. I have no desire to psychoanalyze you or offer you advice unless you ask for it. This is more of an encounter with God than the traditional concept of counseling, that of man trying to help man. I believe that your conflicts can be resolved in Christ, and I want to help you understand how your needs can be met in Him."

The second defense comes from those who have been burned by the "Church." They have tried church, and they have tried reading their Bibles and praying, but it didn't work for them. Most of these people are disappointed with God and Christians (usually the authority figures, such as pastors, teachers and parents). They need to understand that institutions and programs, no matter how well intended, cannot set them free. "Who" sets them free is Christ, and "what" sets them free is their personal response to Him.

Christian institutions and programs *should* facilitate that process, but in many cases they do not. In some sad situations, parents and pastors have been the perpetrators. In every case, there are no perfect pastors or parents, and even the best will let others down sometime. The good news is that Jesus loves us perfectly, and He will never let us down, nor forsake us.

In this second category of defenses, you may see demonic deception and interference. One young lady's opening statement to me was, "I don't want to get right with God or anything!" Well-meaning parents had tried to shove religion down her throat. Going to church in the past hadn't helped her at all. She had been date raped in high school and hadn't shared that trauma with anyone because of embarrassment. Sexual promiscuity followed. I have learned to ignore such opening statements and respond with something like this: "I can accept that, but since we have this time together, why don't we see if we can resolve some of the difficulties you are having." In almost every case, the freedom appointment progressed as all others have.

EVERYONE IS A CANDIDATE

Everyone who desires a one-on-one appointment to walk through the Steps is a candidate. Often, a person without a deeply troubled history needs the objectivity of a fellow believer to uncover bondages and choose the truth. As stated earlier, the one common denominator with everyone who was caught in one form of bondage or another was the ignorance of their identities and positions in Christ. Trying to help them gain the assurance of salvation in Christ before their freedom in Christ has proven to be counterproductive. The assurance comes after they have resolved the issues that are critical between themselves and God.

At one conference, the wife of a professional person made a guarded inquiry about some needs in her life. One of our staff members simply suggested what going through the Steps to Freedom could mean to her. But he left the decision to her.

Later, she asked for an appointment and walked through the Steps. The issues were not extreme, but she felt abused because of legalism in her childhood. It was deeply moving to observe how earnestly she chose to be free of her bitterness and to see the joy she expressed after dealing with forgiveness in Step Three. After the conference, she sent me a testimony regarding the many effects of her freedom in the lives of her husband and family.

There are others with backgrounds of more serious trauma, such as the teenager who had seen her father strangling her mother. A few months after she went through the Steps, a friend of this teenager wrote: "Kim is doing great. The voices are gone. The blank stare in her eyes is gone, and she is back to the quiet, calm Kim that I used to know."

Another woman wrote: "I feel like a different person. I don't have this big dirty black hole inside me that needs to be filled up by my husband's abuse or my abuse of food. I found out who I am. I'm a precious child of God. If Jesus can change that much pain in me, He can help others, too, and I want to be utilized by Him...I now have three girls I am discipling."

PREPARATION OF THE PERSON SEEKING HELP

The best scenario is for people who want to go through the Steps to have attended a Personal and Spiritual Conflicts Conference, listened to or seen the tape series or read *Victory over the Darkness* and *The Bondage Breaker*. Being exposed to this teaching in advance of the appointment will result in far greater resolution. They will have some understanding of what the issues are, the truth about their identities in Christ, the authority and protection of the believer and how to take decisive steps to resolve their conflicts. When people have been struggling for years and now realize that legitimate help is available, they are more willing to invest the time to read books and gather helpful information. If they are unwilling to take some initiative to help themselves by reading a book or listening to tapes, I would question how serious they are about getting well.

Many people, however, can't read the books or even listen to the tapes. I have had people tell me months after an appointment that they saw my lips move but didn't hear a word I was saying.

PLANNING YOUR TIME

We strongly recommend that you complete the Steps in one appointment. This will usually take anywhere from three to five hours. That's a sacrificial commitment to make for the sake of another person, but you will find that the hours invested will accomplish far more than meeting only one hour at a time, week after week. Greater resolution results when you hear people tell their stories and then deal with all of their sin and pain while the memories and emotions are surfaced and fresh. If you deal with only one Step at a session and the people leave with their issues only partly resolved, they will be much more vulnerable to the enemy.

If a surgeon opens a wound but fails to provide proper closure, germs will be afforded an opportunity to cause infection, and the healing process won't be given a reasonable chance. Most counseling techniques focus only on the opening-up process, but lacking a theology of resolution, they leave the wound open. (I could see why you would do that if you didn't believe in germs.)

PRAYER PARTNERS

We recommend prayer partners for support, but our primary reason is to train others. We multiply our efforts by modeling. At conferences, we often include two, and sometimes more, prayer partners for the purpose of training. This has seldom been a problem when those you are helping have been advised in advance. In fact, they often express gratitude for the time commitment and intercessory prayer that has been given for them.

Usually, it is desirable for men to help men and women to help women, but there are times when it may be necessary for the opposite to occur. Since women are often quicker to recognize their needs and to ask for help, there are more women seeking appointments. Therefore, mature men sometimes help women, but a woman prayer partner is recommended for those sessions.

It is not wise to use the spouse of the one you are helping as a prayer partner because the person needs to assume personal and total responsibility, and not rely upon a spouse. Also, issues may arise that the individual would hesitate to share in front of the spouse. The same would apply to parents and older children. With young children, on the other hand, it is often better for the parent to take them through the Steps (using the children's version), or at least for the parent to sit in as a prayer partner. The trust between a parent and younger child is important and sometimes necessary for the child to feel safe. However, if an adversarial relationship exists between the parent and child, then it will be virtually impossible for the parent to help the child.

If a person says that he or she would like to bring a close friend to be a prayer partner, we explain that his or her freedom depends upon their being totally open and honest about everything, past and present. So, if having a friend present would inhibit him or her, it would be better for the friend not to be there. On the other hand, we must respect the need for safety. This process may seem simple and straightforward to us, but to the person it may be extremely intimidating. The person often struggles with threatening thoughts and fears of losing control in some horrible demonic encounter. The person needs to know that he or she will be respected, believed and helped in a safe and controlled way. Having a trusted friend present may give the person a sense of safety and provide emotional support.

In more severe cases, such as victims of satanic ritual abuse (or other extreme traumas), it is best for the person seeking help to ask his or her professional counselor, discipler or a trusted friend to be in the session. Or, if the person has a primary caregiver, the option should be given to bring that person to the appointment. Knowing what issues were dealt with as he or she went through the Steps, a counselor will be better able to follow up and continue the process of recovery/discipling.

LOCATION

The setting is important. Try to have comfortable chairs, proper room temperature, quiet, freedom from interruptions, access to a rest room, tissues, a wastebasket for tissues and water to drink.

The most desirable location would be an appropriate room in your church. It is not advisable to go to the homes of the people you will help since that may not be neutral ground, and you may experience disturbances, either spiritually or from family, pets, phone calls and so on.

SETTING THE APPOINTMENT

When someone asks for an appointment, it is a good idea to do a brief interview in order to learn:

1. Name and phone number;
2. Reason for the appointment;
3. Further clarification to determine possible involvement in abuse or the occult, if needed;
4. Whether he or she has attended a Freedom in Christ

Conference or read *Victory over the Darkness* or *The Bondage Breaker*.

If the person has not had any exposure to a conference, tapes or books, explain the importance of reading at least *Victory over the Darkness*, and if possible, *The Bondage Breaker*, prior to the appointment.

If a person knows the teaching and is ready for an appointment, the following explanation should be given:

1. During the session, a leader will hear her story and then take her through the Steps to Freedom.
2. The appointment will last anywhere from three to five hours.
3. There is nothing to be afraid of, although condemning, doubting and fearful thoughts may try to prevent her from keeping the appointment. The appointment itself is a quiet and controlled process that will help resolve personal and spiritual conflicts.
4. Nothing will be done to violate her will. She is free to come and free to leave at any time.
5. There will be a prayer partner or two present.
6. Everything will done be in confidence.

Some leaders prefer to use the Confidential Personal Inventory before taking someone through the Steps (see appendix C). The inventory is most helpful when the person can fill it out and return it in advance of the appointment, so the leader will have adequate time to review it and perhaps highlight areas where further information would be helpful.

When the person requesting help and you, the leader, are in agreement that all of the necessary preparations are in order (the exposure to the conferences or the books, the interview, the inventory, the prayer partners), the time and place for the appointment can be scheduled.

Before the Appointment

Arriving 15 minutes prior to the appointment gives the leader and prayer partners an opportunity to have prayer in the room they will be using. We have the privilege to be good stewards of all that the Lord has entrusted to us. Start by committing yourselves and the space you are in to the Lord. Some have found it helpful to ask the Lord to surround it with His angels as a hedge of protection from influences of the enemy and to offer themselves to God as His servants, standing in His power and authority. I verbally announce that all authority has been given to the Lord Jesus Christ in heaven and on earth (see Matt. 28:18), and therefore Satan has no authority in this time, place or in our lives.

There should be a copy of the Steps to Freedom for each person, paper and pencil for the leader, and drinking water and tissues.

You can help create a calm environment by being as prepared as possible. Prearrange the seating. Choose a comfortable chair for the person you are helping, and seat yourself directly across from him or her at a distance that will ensure good eye contact. Seat the prayer partners off to the side, out of the direct line of vision, between you (the leader) and the person you are helping.

STARTING THE APPOINTMENT

After introductions, ask the person who has come for help to fill out a Statement of Understanding (see appendix B), explaining that you are not a professional counselor or therapist (if this is the case) but a brother or sister in Christ desiring to be an encourager with the truth of Scripture.

A gracious and relaxed leader and prayer team will make a person feel welcome when he or she arrives for the appointment. Having never done this before, most people are apprehensive. They may think you are going to cast a demon out of them, because that is all they've ever heard about. They may be having thoughts or hearing voices telling them such things as: *This isn't going to work, Sit close to the door so you can escape if you need to, This leader can't be trusted,* or *If you tell them how dirty you are inside, they won't like you.* You can help relieve those fears by the way you relate to the individual.

So after introductions, there are assurances the person seeking help will need to hear. You may want say:

> There is nothing you could share that would shock or embarrass me. There is nothing you could share that would cause me to think less of you. We know who the enemy is, and it is not you. After hearing a person's story, we care more deeply for him or her, because now we understand the trauma that has been experienced. Also, everything you say will be in confidence. The prayer partners are here to pray for us and to gain experience in order to lead others to their freedom.

INTRODUCING THE STEPS AND
ACKNOWLEDGING CHRIST'S LORDSHIP

The people you help need to be reminded of their identities in Christ, that they are not just products of their past and don't have to be victims anymore. They need to know that Satan has no power over them unless they allow it. You can remind them of that by reading the preface page of the Steps to Freedom in appendix F. Or, as you gain experience, you may prefer to paraphrase that content as follows:

I'd like to remind you of God's attributes. God is omnipotent (all powerful), His power is greater than we can comprehend. He defeated Satan at Calvary in fulfillment of Genesis 3:15, "He shall bruise you [Satan] on the head." "He had disarmed the rulers and authorities, He made a public display of them, having triumphed over them through Him" (Col. 2:15). Though you may feel you are being pulled by two equal but opposite powers, that is not the case. That is deception. You must choose to "be strong in the Lord and in the strength of His might" (Eph. 6:10).

God is omnipresent (everywhere at once). He is here right now. As Psalm 125:2 says, "As the mountains surround Jerusalem, so the Lord surrounds His people." Satan cannot be everywhere at once. There is a hierarchy of his emissaries, but they are like little gnats. They get in your face and distract you.

God is omniscient (all knowing). He knows the thoughts and intentions of your heart (see Heb. 4:12), and He loves you unconditionally (see Rom. 5:8). He knows the trauma you have experienced, and He stands ready to set you free from your past, if you will submit to Him. Satan cannot perfectly read your mind, although he can give you thoughts to deceive and condemn you.

My role is to help you understand and assume your position in Christ by resolving the personal and spiritual conflicts that are critical between yourself and God. What counts is not what I can do for you, but what Christ has already done for you. He came to "destroy the works of the devil" (1 John 3:8) and to give you life (see John 10:10). He is the only One who can set you free as you submit to Him. Jesus said, "All authority has been given to Me in heaven and on earth" (Matt. 28:18). Would you personally choose to believe that and profess it as true? (Wait for a positive response.) Then would you also choose to believe and profess as true that Satan has no authority here? (Wait for a positive response.)

I need cooperation from you in a major area: If you get thoughts or feelings that are negative and contrary to what we are doing, please share them with me. Your mind is the control center of your life. As long as you don't lose control, then we won't lose control during our time together. Once the lie is exposed to the truth, the power of the lie is broken. It doesn't make any difference if the thoughts you are hearing are coming from a loudspeaker on the wall or lies from Satan. The only way they can have any power over you is if you listen to them and believe them. Demons are like cockroaches. They scurry around in the dark, but when the light of God's truth shines, they run for cover. Don't be afraid to say whatever it is you are thinking or hearing, regardless of what it is. I have heard it all before, and I don't think you could surprise or shock me. I know those threatening and condemning thoughts aren't coming from you, because you "joyfully concur with the law of God in the inner man" (Rom. 7:22). As we address each issue, I will try to help you understand this battle for your mind by helping you to renounce the lies and choose the truth.

THE LEADER SHOULD BE IN CONTROL

It is of utmost importance that the leader—rather than the person seeking help—be in control of the session. This is not difficult and instructions will be given throughout this book. Actually, the one who is in control is the Lord, if the leader is truly the Lord's bond servant. I always start every session with a verbal prayer acknowledging my total dependence upon Him, for apart from Christ I can do nothing (see John 15:5).

A loss of control would mean that the person you are helping is no longer in control of his own mind, and some form of interference is interrupting the process designed to bring freedom. Some of the interference you could encounter might include:

- Deception (lies the person is believing): Your most important weapon is to know the truth of God's Word and to pray for wisdom.

- Fear and flight: If the person does get up to leave, never attempt to restrain him or hold him back. If a person leaves, simply pray and wait patiently. Usually, he will return in a few minutes. This happens very rarely and only in extreme cases.

- Mental interference (confusion, noise, voices in the person's head): The best way to deal with mental interference is to become aware of it and address it briefly, but otherwise to ignore it. Watch the person carefully, especially his eyes. If he starts to cloud over, drift away or lose focus, get his attention immediately. If you don't get his attention and have him assume responsibility for his thoughts, you will lose him. I ask what he is thinking, or to share with me what is going on in his mind. When he tells me, I always thank him for sharing it with me, no matter how vile or threatening it is.

- Physical interference: Internal interference may manifest itself with physical symptoms. The most common are banging headaches and nausea. Simply address the problem directly in prayer, affirming that the enemy is a defeated foe and has no authority to inflict bodily pain. Usually, the physical symptoms stop or subside when the person acknowledges them, and you can continue on with the Steps.

THE PRAYER AND DECLARATION

The prayer and declaration at the beginning of the Steps acknowledge our dependence upon Christ and our authority in Him. As you read the declaration, insert in the blanks the first name of the person you are helping.

Prayer:

Dear heavenly Father, we acknowledge Your presence in this room and in our lives. You are the only omniscient (all knowing), omnipotent (all powerful), and omnipresent (always present) God. We are dependent upon You, for apart from Christ we can do nothing. We stand in the truth that all authority in heaven and on earth has been given to the resurrected Christ, and because we are in Christ, we share that authority in order to make disciples and set captives free. We ask You to fill us with Your Holy Spirit and lead us into all truth. We pray for Your complete protection and ask for Your guidance. In Jesus' name. Amen.

Declaration:

> In the name and authority of the Lord Jesus Christ, we command Satan and all evil spirits to release (name) in order that (name) can be free to know and choose to do the will of God. As children of God seated with Christ in the heavenlies, we agree that every enemy of the Lord Jesus Christ be bound and gagged to silence. We say to Satan and all his evil workers that you cannot inflict any pain or in any way prevent God's will from being accomplished in (name's) life.

HEARING THE STORY

The Steps to Freedom in appendix F contain a brief list of questions about family and personal history intended to draw out the essential information you need. In order to help the person stay focused and brief, you may want to preface your time by saying, "I'm going to ask you some questions to learn what I need to know before we go through the Steps together—just a brief outline of your life. Other pertinent details will surface as we go through the Steps. When I'm finished, I'll give you an opportunity to add anything you might want me to know if you feel it's important."

The primary reason for delving into the history is to glean important information about the person. I always start with the parents and grandparents. Were they Christians? Did they ever participate in any cults or occultic experiences? I want to know if there are any generational issues that are contributing to the person's problems. Then you need to hear a brief chronological history of the individual's life, which should include at least the following:

Marital history of parents and grandparents
Brothers and Sisters? How are they presently doing?
What was the spiritual, emotional and physical climate of the home?
What kind of friends did they have?

Was school a good or bad experience? Why and why not?
What traumatic events were experienced?
What were their church experiences?
Do they have nightmares or spiritual visitations?
What have their thought lives been like?
What emotional problems do they struggle with?
Are they taking medication? What for?

Please see the Confidential Personal Inventory in appendix E for other issues that may need to be addressed. You do not need to hear every detail of the person's life history. The details will come out as you walk him or her through the Steps.

Hearing people's stories also demonstrates that you care for them. They need to know that you believe them and will not judge them regardless of what you hear. Ironically, I still hear people say, "I know you won't believe me, but...!"

Remind them that there is no condemnation for those who are in Christ and that this is a time for them to be totally open and honest because their freedom depends upon it. While listening, take brief notes and mark the issues you might want to address. It is best not to deal with problems while listening to their stories. Wait until the appropriate Step, and do it in that context.

A word of caution: If you use the Confidential Personal Inventory, don't rely upon it totally. Often a person will be reluctant to write down some of the most critical issues you will need to address. On the other hand, using the inventory may give you an indication of where to gently ask some probing questions. What are you looking for?

- A dysfunctional family background: mental illness, chronic depression, chronic illness, addictive problems, involvement in the occult or false religions, extreme legalism or control, extreme permissiveness or neglect, an adoption, living overseas under pagan influences and so on;
- Personal problems: depression, fear, anxiety, unresolved anger, a failure to forgive, lust, pride, rebellion, addictions, the occult, mental or physical illness, rape, abortion, compulsive behavior, an evil or frightening presence, difficulty with relationships or sexually deviant behavior;
- Spiritual problems: lack of assurance of salvation, false beliefs, not knowing their identities in Christ, not knowing that Satan

is a defeated foe, not knowing the limitations of Satan's power, unaware of the nature of the battle for the mind.

The above lists are only suggestive of the various kinds of problems for which we should listen. People don't always know or cannot specifically say what their bondages are. But as they tell their stories, there will be indicators—surface issues that point to root problems. The more you meet with people, the more you will become sensitive to what might be an indicator and how to pursue it. Remember, you are not alone in the counseling session; the Holy Spirit knows every detail of the person's life and is committed to be your guide.

A common pitfall is to get bogged down and spend too much time hearing the story. The life history may seem important to the person you are helping, but the resolution comes from going through the Steps, which surfaces the critical issues that need to be addressed. You need to gently guide them through the process of telling their stories and assure them that the details and the abuses of the past will be acknowledged and dealt with as you go through each Step.

Hearing the story should take less than an hour. Normally, a good time to take a break is after Step Two. The time needed for Step Three will vary greatly, because forgiveness is a primary issue and the number one ticket to freedom from their pasts. After Step Three, you will generally be able to finish within an hour.

AN UNCLEAR SALVATION EXPERIENCE

The Steps to Freedom are designed for someone who has a personal relationship with Jesus Christ as Savior and Lord. But many people who don't have assurance of their salvation come for help. That's not surprising, considering they are being harassed by the enemy and are believing lies. The very fact that they are troubled about their relationships with God and have turned to the Church for help suggests that they are Christians. The accuser wants us to question our salvation, because without it we have no hope. Thoughts such as *How can you be a Christian and do that?* or *God doesn't love you* are so common that you can almost expect them from anyone with unresolved conflicts.

Also, many people do not remember the specific time of their salvation decisions. The questions in the Confidential Personal Inventory dealing with their spiritual histories will help clarify the issue. If they are uncertain, you may simply ask, "Would you like to follow me in a prayer right now affirming your relationship with Christ?" Then lead them to pray, "Lord Jesus, I thank you for dying on the cross for my sins. I now confess with my mouth that you are my Lord, and I choose to believe in my heart that Jesus was raised from the dead. I now receive Him into my life to be my Lord and Savior."

Sometimes non-Christians who have been searching come to an appointment with their hearts so warm and hungry that they gladly choose to believe the truth and invite Christ into their lives.

It is not necessary to belabor this portion of the session or require that they word their testimonies exactly the way you would. These are wounded people who want to be made whole in Christ. As they go through the Steps, they will affirm their relationships with Christ in many more ways. Assurance of salvation comes as they work through the Steps.

IDENTIFYING STRONGHOLDS AND REMOVING GROUND

Taking a person through the Steps to Freedom in Christ is not just a matter of mechanically confessing sins and repeating prayers. The goal in counseling people with the Steps is to connect them with God. Those in bondage often lack the objectivity to do this on their own. As a leader, you can help them discern what needs to be addressed.

There may be a battle going on for the minds of the people you help. Though you can pray for them and encourage them, you can't fight the battle for them. The battle can be won only as they personally choose truth. Their freedom will be the result of what *they* choose to believe, confess, forgive, renounce and forsake.

While the battle is going on and they are experiencing painful memories, there is a natural tendency to reach out and hold their hands or pat their shoulders. Most of the time, it is best to avoid touching them until the session has been completed. In severe cases, and until people are free, the conflict within them may cause resistance to the Holy Spirit in you, and touching could impede progress. Also, those who have experienced sexual abuse could perceive touching as the opposite of what you intended. Your compassion can be conveyed by your facial expression or words during the session, and perhaps an appropriate hug afterward will be in order.

Be prepared to confront false concepts. Almost all of the people you help will have some false concept about God or themselves that may potentially keep them in bondage. That is why it is highly recommended that they read

Victory over the Darkness and *The Bondage Breaker,* or hear the *Resolving Personal and Spiritual Conflicts* tapes before the session. This will save a lot of time, because they will already have a basic familiarity with the key concepts, and only a brief review will be necessary.

The difference between an experienced lay leader and one who is beginning to use the Steps is the ability to identify strongholds (or lies) and focus on areas where the person has given ground to the enemy by willful or involuntary involvement in sin. The only way for you to sharpen that ability is *through* experience. It will never be learned fully from a textbook.

STRONGHOLDS CAN SURFACE AT ANY TIME

The evidence of a stronghold or belief in a lie can surface at any time during the session. It may be revealed in the Confidential Personal Inventory, hinted at or stated by the person while you are hearing his or her story, or uncovered while going through the Steps.

For example, when Sue went through the Steps, she first told of a supportive family and love for her father and mother. Later, she revealed that when she was a little girl someone had robbed her of her innocence by taking advantage of her sexually. When she told her father, he did nothing about it, and she questioned whether he even believed her. Suddenly, she blurted out, "I hate my father." She had not wanted to face and acknowledge that hatred before. The way her father related to her throughout her life, along with the abuses from other men, developed a stronghold in her life that kept her from trusting men and God her Father.

Strongholds will be clearly identified and destroyed by going through the Steps because the person has believed lies and is now embracing the truth. When Sue recognized and renounced the lies that she was worthless and couldn't trust anyone, she won the battle. By the end of the conference she gave me a hug, which was significant because of her previous mistrust. She said, "I believe I can trust now."

FURTHER COUNSELING FOR LIFESTYLE ISSUES

Some strongholds, particularly addictions, will be exposed and renounced, but even after the bondage has been broken, the individual will require further discipling and support. Lifestyle issues will continue to surface, and additional counseling will be beneficial if it is Christ-centered.

Tim was caught in the web of homosexual behavior. After going through the Steps in a personal appointment, he was elated with the sense of freedom and joy he felt. A letter received a few weeks later proclaimed his belief that he was now free from the weight of his past. But a second letter, sent a few months after the first, gave a different appraisal.

Tim had taken a backward step, but he had not forgotten what he had learned in going through the Steps. He learned that he had not won a once-and-for-all victory, and that it is one thing to gain freedom and another thing to maintain it. After confession, he began practicing resisting the enemy and choosing truth on a daily basis. When we saw him nearly a year after first taking him through the Steps, Tim was *maintaining* his freedom daily.

I would encourage you to read through the stories in *Released from Bondage* as a companion to this book. One chapter deals with the "onion effect." That is, some people are like onions and others are like bananas. The "bananas" have total recall of all their pasts and every issue that needs to be dealt with. They can find total freedom in one session, and never look back as they continue to grow in Christ. The "onions," however, have their issues revealed one layer at a time. God will reveal at the right time the things hidden in darkness (see 1 Cor. 4:1-5). For these people, it would be too overwhelming to face all the issues at one time. So God graciously reveals them one at a time.

These people will work through the Steps and resolve all that they know, and experience great freedom. Then a week or month later, they experience difficulty again. It would be easy to conclude that the process didn't work. It did work, but now they are dealing with *another* layer of the onion. God doesn't reveal those past events until enough maturity and support structure is in place to face and resolve the issues. If we want to work with God, we should help these people be established in Christ and provide them with the means to resolve the issues as they surface. I strongly recommend that you don't keep trying to surface issues without resolving them. Like any other issue in life, God will not allow us to move on unless we are good stewards of what He has already entrusted to us. Why should He show us more if we aren't willing to face and resolve what we already know?

What if people don't know what has happened to them in their pasts? What if they pray and nothing surfaces? Then help them find out what is right about them in Christ, because that is where their hopes lie anyway. Paul said, "Brethren, I do not regard myself as having laid hold of it yet; but one thing I do: forgetting what lies behind and reaching forward to what lies ahead, I press on toward the goal for the prize of the upward call of God in Christ Jesus" (Phil. 3:13,14).

CHAPTER SEVEN

EXPOSING THE LIES

STEP ONE: COUNTERFEIT VERSUS REAL

The first Step to freedom in Christ is to renounce previous or current involvement with any activity or group that denies Jesus Christ, offers guidance through sources contrary to the Word of God or requires secret ceremonies or covenants. To renounce is the first step toward repentance. The Greek word for repentance is *metanoeo*. The word has two components. The first, *meta*, means "after," which implies change. The second, *noeo*, means to perceive. This comes from the root word *nous*, which is usually translated as mind. It literally means a change of mind, but it is much more sweeping in its application.

When the Pharisees and the Sadducees came to be baptized by John, "He said to them, "You brood of vipers, who warned you to flee from the wrath to come? Therefore bring forth fruit in keeping with repentance'" (Matt. 3:7,8). He discerned that their repentance was incomplete. They wanted the blessing of God but didn't want to give up their traditions, practices and religious positions. Neither did Simon when Philip preached the gospel in Samaria, even though he had professed to believe and was baptized. Peter said to him, "You have no part or portion in this matter, for your heart is not right before God. Therefore repent of this wickedness of yours, and pray the Lord that if possible, the intention of your heart may be forgiven you. For I see that you are in the gall of bitterness and in the bondage of iniquity" (Acts 8:21-23).

THE NEED TO RENOUNCE

The public declaration "I renounce you, Satan, and all your works and all your ways" has historically been a part of the Church's profession of faith since its earliest days. To this day, Catholics and members of most liturgical churches are required to publicly profess that at confirmation. In the Early Church, believers would literally face west and make that declaration. Then they would face east and declare their belief in God. Understand that the statement is generic. Every work of Satan and every way of Satan had to be renounced in order for repentance to be complete.

To be completely free from the past, we have found it necessary for each person to specifically renounce every false religion, false teacher, false practice and every means of false guidance that he or she has participated in. Many people come to our churches and make professions of faith in Christ but continue in their old ways of seeking guidance and hang on to their old practices. That is not complete repentance. If we declare something as true, then it is just as important to declare the counterfeit as false. You cannot believe the truth and the lie at the same time and be free in Christ.

The skeptic would argue that all this business of renouncing Satan and his ways has been taken care of at the Cross because our sins are all forgiven. It's true that the Cross washed away our sins, the Resurrection gave us life and the ascension of Christ to the right hand of the Father assured us of the authority and power to live a victorious life in Christ. But the moment we are born again, our *minds* are not totally transformed. That is why Paul said, "Do not be conformed to this world, but be transformed by the renewing of your mind, that you may prove what the will of God is, that which is good and acceptable and perfect" (Rom. 12:2). The Cross, the Resurrection and the Ascension make all that possible. Now we can repent and renew our minds. We can renounce the lies, the false guidance and the false teachers. We can choose the truth because "we have the mind of Christ" (1 Cor. 2:16).

DEMONIC FORCES AT WORK

The Bible clearly teaches that demonic forces are directly involved in false religions and the occult: "But the Spirit explicitly says that in later times some will fall away from the faith, paying attention to deceitful spirits and doctrines of demons" (1 Tim. 4:1). These deceptive belief systems and false teachings are counterfeits. They mimic the truth but are in fact satanically inspired lies. They are taught by false teachers often representing themselves as followers of Christ (see 2 Cor. 11:13-15).

When assessing counterfeits of Christianity, no criterion is more important than the person of Jesus Christ. If there is any foundational belief adhered to other than expressing Jesus Christ as the Son of God, the King of kings, and the great I AM, then it becomes suspect as a false religious experience (see Matt. 26:63; John 8:58; 1 Cor. 3:11; Rev. 19:16).

Another identifying trait of false religions and the occult is an offer of salvation or enlightenment through something other than faith in the finished work of Christ. Satan blinds people to the gospel of Jesus Christ, because he knows there is no other name given among men by which salvation will occur (see Acts 4:12; 2 Cor. 4:4; 11:3,4,14). New Age proponents insist that we are not separated from God by our sin and therefore have no need to repent. They say we *are* God and only need to be enlightened. What a lie!

Another mark of counterfeits is that they are aimed at satisfying our need to be significant and our "right" to be happy. They offer a special quality of life, esoteric knowledge or special power that is available by tapping into cosmic energy sources, or from secret rituals, ceremonies or covenants. Every late-night television channel advertises psychics who offer success and guidance to a happy life.

The very nature of the occult is revealed by the meaning of the words *hidden, concealed* or *secret*. What is really hidden from view, however, is the true nature of Satan. His goal is to keep humanity in bondage by drawing us away from the truth that would free us (see John 8:32). Repentance sets us free as we renounce the lie and choose the truth.

TAKING A VERBAL STAND

Some have suggested that 2 Peter 2:10,11 and Jude 8 teach that believers should not stand verbally against Satan or his spiritual forces. But a close look at the context of these passages reveals their true intent. The writers were referring to unbelievers trying to exert an independent authority over the demonic realm. They were like the seven sons of Sceva, who were also unbelievers trying to cast out demons in Jesus' name without His authority (see Acts 19:11-16). This is the essence of occult practice—humans manipulating demons to do their will.

Jude 1:9 says that even "Michael the archangel, when he disputed with the devil and argued about the body of Moses, did not dare pronounce against him a railing judgment, but said, 'The Lord rebuke you.'" Two important points about this passage: First, we are not pronouncing a "railing judgment" against anybody. Only God can judge, and we are commanded *not* to judge. Resisting the devil and renouncing our involvements with him is not pronouncing a railing judgment. Every believer has the right and the responsibility to exercise his or her authority in Christ by resisting the devil. Second, look at the context of Jude 1:9. The passage refers back to the time of Moses when Satan was not yet a defeated foe and the Church was not seated with Christ in the heavenlies.

Believers are not being self-willed and despising authority when they obey the command to submit to God and choose to resist the devil, even in a verbal way (see Jas. 4:7). On the contrary, they are recognizing God's authority over their lives and His authority over the demonic realm (see Eph. 1:20,21; Col. 2:15; 1 Pet. 3:22). They are standing in their position at Christ's right hand (see Eph. 2:6) and standing against the devil, using the sword of the Spirit (see 6:10-17). They are exercising "dependent authority" in Christ.

The biblical precedent for open renunciation is found in Acts 19:18-20. Many of the new Christians in Ephesus had been deeply involved in false religions and the occult through worship at the Temple of Artemis. Luke writes in verse 18: "Many also of those who had believed kept coming, confessing and disclosing their practices." The open disclosure of occult practices was followed by the positive action of ridding themselves of anything associated with that darkness. "And many of those who practiced magic brought their books together and began burning them in the sight of all" (v. 19).

BRINGING EVERYTHING INTO THE LIGHT

When we walk people through the Steps to Freedom, we are not always aware of what still needs to be brought into the light. Even they may not realize that certain religious or occult experiences have given a foothold to the enemy.

In this first Step, they will pray and ask God to bring to mind all previous involvement with cult or occult practices, false religions and false teachers, whether done knowingly or unknowingly. Often, people remember something they had not thought about for many years, and they begin to see how a long accumulation of false input has strongly influenced their minds.

Two important objectives will be accomplished during Step One. First, strongholds from false belief systems will be exposed and broken by agreeing with God through verbal renunciation. Second, people will learn how to handle lies and strongholds that surface later.

Beginning Step One

As you begin this Step, you are helping people take back any ground gained by the enemy in their lives, issue by issue, step-by-step. To help them understand the spiritual significance of what they are doing, you may want to use an illustration like the following:

> Suppose there is a 40-year-old man who has never done much right in his life. At a meeting, for the first time in his life, he hears about Jesus. His heart responds, and he prays, "Lord, I confess that I have sinned, and I ask You to forgive me and to come into my life and be my Savior and Lord."
>
> If you and I were in the room when that man prayed, we may not have seen anything happen visibly. But in the spiritual realm, his sins were forgiven, he passed from death to life and from eternity in hell to eternity in heaven. All of this because he wanted to be right with God. God hears and answers prayer, and neither Satan nor his demons, nor any other person could block what God wanted to do in that man's life.
>
> We're going to go through a series of prayers now. Many of them are short, simple prayers like the one that man prayed. As you are honest and sincere before God, every prayer you pray is going to be like the prayer of that man. Bonds the enemy has on your life will be broken because of your authority as God's child.

Explain that everything done in the session is done aloud, because there is no indication in the Bible that Satan can read our minds. God knows our innermost thoughts, but Satan is not God, and we should never ascribe the divine attributes of God unto him.

Confessing with the mouth that Jesus is Lord is taught in Romans 10:9,10 and throughout Scripture. Even Jesus stood up against Satan by verbally quoting Scripture. So the person you are helping will be declaring vocally that he or she is under the protection and authority of Jesus' name, choosing allegiance to Him and renouncing ties to the evil one.

The person begins by praying the first prayer in Step One aloud:

> Dear heavenly Father,
> I ask You to guard my heart and my mind and reveal to me any and all involvement I have had either knowingly or

unknowingly with cultic or occult practices, false religions and false teachers. In Jesus' name I pray. Amen.

CHECKING THE LISTS

Those you help should silently read the lists that follow, placing a check by any activity where there may have been involvement, no matter how innocently. They have asked the Lord to show them the occult activities, so trust the Lord to do it. It is God who grants repentance, leading to the knowledge of the truth, so that we may escape from the snare of the devil (see 2 Tim. 2:25,26). They should take seriously any impression they receive and check it, because there is nothing harmful in renouncing a counterfeit, and it is essential not to overlook anything God wants to surface.

Sometimes people ask for a definition of the terms. These are usually honest questions, but be cautious not to be led off target on a mental excursion. Answer with just a sentence or two. (Some leaders prefer to read the list to the people they are helping, giving a brief explanation of each item and having them check the ones that apply.)

It is not necessary to know or understand every cult, false religion or occult practice in order to help people, though becoming familiar with the terms is recommended. (See the appendix in the companion study guide for this book for definition of terms.) They must be honest about their participation, because they can't just renounce a cult. They need to renounce what they did and believed in, as well as all the vows, covenants and pledges they made. For instance, one lady who had come out of the Mormon Church needed to renounce her secret initiation, and the ceremonies in baptisms and marriages for the dead in which she participated.

If you are unfamiliar with something they have participated in, have them write it down in a blank space and explain what their participation was. If they checked something but are not sure they participated in it, explain that they are simply renouncing any trust in the occult and breaking any possible connection. In that case, they may want to change the wording of the prayer to: "Lord, I confess that I *may* have participated in...."

One area that sometimes needs explanation is *incubi* and *succubi* (sexual spirits). These may manifest themselves in vivid sexual dreams or fantasies, or by a presence in their rooms that aroused them sexually. If they identify with any of those experiences, suggest that they check "sexual spirits." Many will not volunteer such information because of its vile nature and their embarrassment. If they stood against it at the time, there is nothing to renounce. It is no sin to be under attack. If they participated with the sexual spirits, then they need to renounce any involvement and every sexual use of their bodies as an instrument of unrighteousness.

The lists are not exhaustive, so when they have finished checking off the items, ask them if they are aware of anything else they have participated in that they should renounce. One lady tripled the size of the list given in the Steps! Let the Holy Spirit bring those thoughts to their minds, and as He does, let them note the thoughts on the page. Any number of things might surface: books, photos, movies, music or other materials, religious customs or traditions, praying to idols or angels by name, beliefs such as atheism, agnosticism, hedonism, involvement in legalism or any type of works to earn God's approval.

They may or may not add items, and it is not the leader's responsibility to exhaust the possibilities. Use discernment and allow God to do His work.

FIVE ESSENTIAL QUESTIONS

When those lists are complete, proceed to the five questions included after the list. Have the person underline any area of involvement, or write a brief explanation.

Question one addresses seeking guidance from sources other than God. In hypnosis, a person looses control of the mind and becomes vulnerable to the will of another person. God never bypasses our minds. He works through them. We should never surrender our responsibility to think and choose the truth. We invite the Lord to search our hearts and our minds. New Age thinking uses the premise that human beings possess tremendous power and potential for enlightenment, setting the stage for man to be elevated above the need for God. Looking for wisdom independent from God is the oldest deception in the Bible (see Gen. 3:1-5). To seek guidance from ghosts or spirits through an intermediary, such as a medium (or present-day channeler) or spiritist, is strictly forbidden by God (see Lev. 19:31).

Question two explores ways in which demons may have been invited into people's lives under the guise of "spirit guides" or "imaginary friends." If they answer the question in the affirmative, ask for any name or names associated with those experiences, and have them write those names in the blank space. Those guides should be renounced specifically. Continued relating to an imagined friend could open the door to a demonic entity who purports to be a friend and companion and offers guidance. If that imaginary friend is talking back to them, it isn't imaginary. People who knowingly dabble in the occult often seek a guide or guides who come to them from the spirit world. It is not unusual for some people to experience sorrow as they choose to break and renounce those relationships.

Parents need to exercise discernment in evaluating the imaginary friends of their children. I don't want to stifle the creativity of young children because we all played games, assumed fanciful roles or created fantasies. But when the imaginary friends talk back, visit a child at night or in dreams, tell them to do things that are wrong or offer guidance, there is reason to be concerned.

Question three focuses directly on the battle for the mind. Those who hear audible voices or noises recognize their harassment, but many others have believed that they themselves were the *source* of their negative thoughts. The enemy is the accuser of the brethren. Almost everyone has dealt with condemning thoughts that come directly from the enemy or indirectly from the harmful programming of their minds. In either case, these thoughts must be taken captive and not be allowed the power to control our lives (see 2 Cor. 10:5).

The issue is, who will decide what we think about? To apply this, you may want to use the following illustration:

> If I were to come to your house tonight and knock on your door, you would first come to the door to see who is there, and then you would have a choice to make. You could open the door to allow me to come in, or you could close the door to deny me access. In the same way, when the enemy tries to invade your mind with lies and accusations, you have a choice to make. You can choose to allow those thoughts to come in, or you can deny them access. To "open the door" to enemy lies, you simply remain passive. You let him set the agenda for your thoughts. To "close the door," you take your thoughts captive; you decide what you choose to believe.

You may want to suggest to people you are helping that they can drive a proverbial stake in the ground here by assuming responsibility for their own minds. Before now, they may not have realized how passive they have been about entertaining negative thoughts. It may be new to them to realize that they no longer need to allow the "recorder" to replay every conversation, that they can choose to not "run around in their heads" or listen to condemning thoughts. Many people in alcoholic-recovery groups advise others not to pay attention to the committees in their heads.

Hopefully, people will learn to take captive every thought as a way of life after going through the Steps to Freedom and learning to cooperate with the Lord in the renewing of their minds. The Lord has promised a peace and quietness of mind (see Phil. 4:4-9). One leader says, "Your mind can be a quiet sanctuary for you and God. Jesus died for your peace of heart and mind." So this is a point of decision, a time to take responsibility under the Lordship of Christ. Therefore, when they pray to renounce the other items they have checked on the page, encourage them to insert the words of question three in each blank, personalizing the prayer like this:

> Lord, I confess that I have paid attention to the voices or thoughts in my mind and believed those repeating, nagging and condemning messages as though a dialogue was going on in my head. They were foreign to what I now choose to believe. I ask your forgiveness, and I renounce paying attention to those voices or thoughts in my mind, and I renounce giving in to the dialogue in my mind.

Question four relates to any religious or spiritual experience that was not of God. This would include such experiences as: being visited at night by an evil presence or apparition, particular superstitions they believed as children, having visited a questionable church or participated in some religious experience. They should mention any demonically oriented dreams and nightmares, counterfeit experiences or gifts. A missionary in China participated in a Buddhist temple funeral in which he had to take off his shoes before he entered. He felt uncomfortable about doing it at the time, and that night he came under intense attack. It didn't stop until he renounced that act of worship to pagan gods.

There are authentic spiritual gifts, and there are counterfeit spiritual gifts. One person was paranoid with fear because her New Age masseuse and mentor had whispered and prayed over her many times to receive gifts before she became a Christian. Many cults practice tongues, and occult healing is common. Some have been exposed to these and other practices, and have been deceived into believing that they were in a Christian context. If the people you are helping raise the issue, doubting the authenticity of a gift they have received, they can simply pray, "Lord, if this gift of _____ is not from you, I renounce it." Include anything that has unusual spiritual connotations, but let the *Lord* bring it to *their* minds.

A note of caution here. Do not spend an inordinate amount of time exploring every minute detail of any one item that needs to be renounced. It is usually sufficient to cover the basic issue and move on through the Steps to Freedom.

I have learned that testing the spirits is a responsibility that is best put back on those I'm helping. I encourage them to pray, asking the Lord to show them the true nature of their gifts, experiences and thoughts. A young man told me that the voice in his head pleaded, "Don't send me away. I want to go to heaven with you." With my prompting, he prayed, "Lord, please show me the true nature of this voice." Before he could finish the prayer, he cried out in disgust. What he saw or heard I don't know, but he knew it wasn't from God.

Question five mentions satanic rituals, which could have been practiced in a group or independently, passively or actively. If there is any history of satanic ritual or secretive rituals indicated—or if you suspect it by the volume of the items checked on the cult and occult lists, by family involvement or by obvious blocked memories—you will want to have them read the Special Renunciations for Satanic Ritual Involvement at the end of Step One. This is done separately at the conclusion of this Step and after they renounce the counterfeits they checked, those they added and those they wrote in response to the five questions.

CONFESSING AND RENOUNCING

The person you are helping should confess his or her involvement and renounce the group or activity individually, repeating this prayer aloud for each counterfeit checked or written on the page:

> Lord, I confess that I have participated in _____.
> I ask your forgiveness, and I renounce _____.

You could demonstrate this by reading the first prayer yourself: "Lord, I confess that I have participated in the Ouija board (or whatever his or her first item is). I ask your forgiveness, and I renounce the Ouija board."

KEEP CONTROL

For you to have control while leading someone through the Steps means that you are aware of what is happening with the person you are helping.

So stay alert. Watch for any omissions from his or her list as he or she prays. Have the person tell you if he or she has interference of any kind: negative thoughts, voices or a feeling of sickness or pain. These may indicate a stronghold where the person may be caught unaware, and you may need to use gentle control and encouragement.

But since most people are not accustomed to saying everything they think and feel, you can help by watching their eyes and facial expressions, and listening to their tones of voice. You can often detect interference before there is a loss of control and ask, "What's going on? What are you hearing?"

Those issues need to be addressed promptly to maintain control. Usually, for the person to say aloud what is happening is enough to break the harassment. If necessary, you can pray in the authority of Christ against the interference. In rare cases, a person will continue to be bombarded with voices. If this happens, you can give the following illustration:

> Suppose we're trying to carry on a conversation in a room where there are speakers playing loud music or a talk show. If we wanted to continue our conversation, we would simply ignore the speakers. In the same way, you can choose to ignore those voices or thoughts. You can say, "I'm a child of God, and I will continue to work through the issues and find my freedom in Christ."

When a person takes authority in that way, the problem eventually subsides.

Satanic Renunciations

The majority of people you lead through the Steps will not require the renunciations for satanic ritual abuse (SRA). But you will need to use them if there has been: an actual memory of an event or events; ritual involvement by family members or a family history of the occult or cults; an extremely large number of cult or occult items checked; severe nightmares; sexual dysfunction; or blocked memories. (One encourager who is herself a survivor of child molestation takes people with that background through some of the renunciations. She feels that a child's innocence and virtue was sacrificed to Satan through the molestation.)

If people have been involved in satanic rituals, covenants and assignments, they need to renounce each one as the Lord reveals them. Some are already aware of the issues; for others, the memories may surface as they work through the renunciations.

At first I had trouble believing the stories of those who were professing to be victims of SRA. But after a while, I started to see a remarkable pattern. Notice that every satanic renunciation is an antithesis of true Christianity. What we are up against is the Antichrist. Our names are written in the Lamb's Book of Life, while satanists will sign their names or force others to sign their names in a goat's book of life. We are the brides of Christ, so satanists will have a mock ceremony where they are wed to Satan. They literally drink blood and eat flesh during a satanic ritual. Jesus said, "Truly, truly, I say to you, unless you eat the flesh of the Son of Man and drink His blood, you have no life in yourselves" (John 6:53). We celebrate this truth symbolically in communion. You can see what they are counterfeiting in each one of their rituals.

MULTIPLE PERSONALITY DISORDER

Many SRA victims end up with a multiple personality disorder (MPD). This is a severe defense mechanism that allows them to develop somewhat normally apart from the rituals. Those who develop multiple personalities in order to cope with abuse are better off than those who don't. I personally have never come across a true MPD who doesn't have severe demonic problems as well. We meet with three or four MPD sufferers in every conference we conduct all across the country. And during our advanced conferences, when I ask how many counselors and pastors are dealing with this, the majority raise their hands. This is not some isolated phenomenon that a few extremists are waving the flag about. Professional Christian counselors and churches are dealing with it in every community in our country.

Such dissociative disorders go beyond the scope of this book. However, let me make some general comments. Try as best you can to help the host personality and any other primary personalities to resolve their spiritual issues first. We take people through the Steps and all the general satanic renunciations and have them renounce any other specific assignments, rituals or covenants that they made or were forced to make. SRA victims cannot always discern whether the voices in their heads are demonic or other personalities. Eventually, every personality will need to be accessed and all will have to resolve their own issues and agree to come together in Christ. It may sound simple, but it isn't.

You can make three serious mistakes with victims of SRA. The first is trying to cast out a personality or asking the victim to tell it to go away. It can't leave. It is a part of them. Such rejection will only further alienate the already damaged personality.

The second error is trying to integrate a stupid demon into their personalities. I have seen or heard about well-meaning pastors and counselors making both of these two mistakes. It is hard to say which holds greater potential for harm.

The third error is treating everything you hear as gospel fact. If the devil can deceive you with his lies, he is certainly capable of putting in a few false memories. I would never accuse a suspected abuser based only on what I heard in a counseling session unless I had some other external, objective and "hard" evidence to support it. That is especially true when the accusations are against a leader in your church. Paul says, "Do not receive an accusation against an elder except on the basis of two or three witnesses" (1 Tim. 5:19). I believe that our major obligation is to set the captive free, and we don't have to make any accusations of others to do that. Let God deal with them. "Never take your own revenge, beloved, but leave room for the wrath of God, for it is written, 'Vengeance is mine, I will repay,' says the Lord" (Rom. 12:19).

Accepting What Victims Recall

On the other hand, I am going to believe everything victims tell me for their sakes, because that is what they recall, and therefore, that is what they have to resolve. If I discern that what they are "recalling" is nothing but deceptive lies, then I have them pray, asking the Lord to reveal the source of their memories. I never trust what they seem to recover in dreams or what others say about the person claiming that God told them. When God reveals the things hidden in darkness (see 1 Cor. 4:4,5), He will reveal it to the person, not through some medium. "For there is one God, and one mediator also between God and men, the man Christ Jesus" (1 Tim. 2:5).

If there has not been any known involvement in satanic rituals but you suspect it, you may want to preface their declarations by saying:

> I'd like to ask you to work through the satanic renunciations, even though we don't know for sure whether you were involved or whether any of these things actually happened. What we do know is that renouncing a lie that has never been believed or an experience that has never happened will not do any harm. We are not suggesting that it has happened to you; we are just

checking to see if anything bad has happened to you. Plus, you are not only renouncing the counterfeit, you are announcing the truth about your relationship with Christ.

The renunciations and announcements are read across the page—first renouncing the act in the kingdom of darkness, and then announcing the truth in the Kingdom of light. (See chapter 10 in *Released from Bondage* for further help on dealing with SRA.)

TRUST GOD IN THE PROCESS

Trust the Holy Spirit to guide you, just as you are trusting Him to guide the person you are helping. When George went through the Steps, he was heavily in bondage to sexual addictions. He had no memory of being involved in satanic rituals. But when he told about the things he practiced, they sounded so ritualistic that the helper asked him to go through the satanic renunciations. When he came to the statement "I renounce any and all covenants that I made with Satan," George pushed his chair back, covered his face with his hands and began to sob, saying, "I think I did that."

At that moment, George remembered a time when he was alone in the bathroom, and Satan appeared to him in the mirror, promising all the beautiful women he could ever want if only he would tell Satan that he loved him. George resisted at first, but then began to see visions of beautiful women until he finally responded to Satan's invitation. That was an opening for the enemy in George's life, and he was exploited by other abusive experiences that put him in deep sexual bondage. That day, those bondages were addressed and broken, and with continuing help George is now a free man.

Before we leave this Step, we sometimes advise people to discard any books, photos, materials, artifacts, music or any other items or gifts they own that may be tied to anything on their list. These may be symbols of allegiance to other gods, and if so, they are counterproductive to walking in the Kingdom of light. Follow the example found in Acts 19:19, where believers got rid of anything associated with darkness. Recognizing that Satan could continue to use the tools of their former religious practices, they publicly destroyed about 50,000 days' wages worth of books, a mind-boggling sum. These New Testament believers would make any sacrifice to be rid of Satan's influence in their lives and prevent his further influence in their families.

Helping Them Choose Truth

Here, and at any time while going through the Steps to Freedom, you may discern specific events that have had a dramatic effect on the life of the person you are helping, or specific lies he or she has believed that have become like a curse. It will be helpful if you lead the person through specific renunciations that would address those areas.

For example, in one session, a woman had nagging fears and anxieties about her experiences with her aunt who was heavily involved in witchcraft. She was helped to pray, "I renounce any way in which Satan is using my relationship with my aunt against me. I renounce anything she said or did to me, and anything she may have done on my behalf. And I thank You, Lord, that I am not a victim of those experiences. I am a child of God and free to be the person You want me to be."

Another woman had been led into a life of prostitution by her mother. She remembered that at a very young age a fortune-teller said to her, "Honey, you have a beautiful face and body. That will help you make it through life." She was encouraged to renounce that curse and the lie that she should use her appearance and body to meet her needs, and she was encouraged to announce aloud the truth that her body is a temple of the Holy Spirit and that God would supply all her needs (see 1 Cor. 6:19; Phil. 4:19). Whenever you renounce a lie or any counterfeit experience, you should also affirm the truth and the Christian practices that enable us to live free in Christ.

CHAPTER EIGHT

CHOOSING THE TRUTH

STEP TWO: DECEPTION VERSUS TRUTH

When Julie came to one of our conferences, there was no question about her deep desire to find freedom. She didn't just ask for an appointment to go through the Steps to Freedom, she pursued it! As the session began, it didn't take long to find out why. With deep emotion, she told the story of her troubled life: a violent alcoholic father...sexual molestation....pornography...demonic experiences in her room...exploitation by legalists at church.

She earnestly dealt with Step One on the occult, and she had composure as she went through Step Two (Deception vs. Truth). But it was at the end of this Step that a beautiful thing happened. After reading through the Doctrinal Affirmation, she put her book down, looked at her leader, and tears welled up in her eyes. Overwhelmed with the truth of who God is and who she is as His child, she said, "Wow! That is soooo great!" It was apparent that she was experiencing the life-giving freedom found only in Christ.

TRUTH FREES

Our Lord had just partaken of His last supper with His disciples. He knew the path toward the cross was set before Him, and He knew that He would soon be leaving earth. Left behind would be 11 of the chosen 12 apostles, who would face the god of this world and continue the work Christ had begun. Satan had already deceived one of the disciples into betraying Christ.

Jesus turned to the Father and prayed, "I do not ask Thee to take them out of the world, but to keep them from the evil one" (John 17:15). He revealed how this can be accomplished in His "High Priestly Prayer": "Sanctify them in the truth; Thy word is truth" (v. 17).

Believing the truth about who Christ is, why He came and who we are in Him is the essence of the liberating gospel. Knowing the truth set forth in God's Word is the mark of a true disciple. "If you abide in My word, then you are truly disciples of Mine; and you shall know the truth, and the truth shall make you free" (8:31,32).

Girding our loins with truth is our first line of defense against the father of lies (see Eph. 6:14). We acknowledge this truth in the inner self (see Ps. 51:6), because a genuine faith is more than just intellectual assent or the accumulation of knowledge (see 1 Cor. 8:1). God's truth is meant to penetrate the heart, the very core of our beings (see Heb. 4:12). Only then will His truth bring about freedom and lasting change in the "inner man" (2 Cor. 4:16).

THE NEED FOR TRANSPARENCY

But truth also implies truthfulness, which means that our lives should be transparent before God and others, so that we are not living a lie. When David lived a lie, believing he could cover up his sin with Bathsheba, he suffered greatly. When he finally found freedom by acknowledging the truth, he wrote, "How blessed is the man...in whose spirit there is no deceit!" (Ps. 32:2). He learned from experience what Paul later taught: "Therefore, laying aside falsehood, speak truth, each one of you, with his neighbor, for we are members of one another" (Eph. 4:25).

One major characteristic of those who are caught in the bondage of sin is this: they lie. Bulimics lie about their binging and purging. Alcoholics hide their addictions and secretly stash bottles around the house. Sex addicts can keep their sin hidden for years. The first step in recovery is to get out of denial and face the truth. The only thing a Christian must admit is the truth. "If we say that we have fellowship with Him and yet walk in the darkness, we lie and do not practice the truth; but if we walk in the light as He Himself is in the light, we have fellowship with one another, and the blood of Jesus His Son cleanses us from all sin" (1 John 1:6,7).

One of the primary reasons Julie, the girl mentioned earlier, found so much resolution is that she held back nothing. She was ready to walk in the light and speak the truth to someone who knew how that truth could set her free. She found forgiveness, cleansing and freedom. Truth is never the enemy; it is a liberating friend. Jesus is the perfect embodiment of truth, the liberating light, the best friend a man or woman could ever have. "In Him there is no darkness at all" (v. 5). Jesus is the truth, and He is setting people free.

SATAN IS THE DECEIVER

Jesus described Satan as the father of lies. "Whenever he speaks a lie, he speaks from his own nature; for he is a liar, and the father of lies" (John 8:44). He cannot speak from truth because there is no truth in him, though he can distort the truth, even using Scripture, as when he tried to tempt Jesus (see Matt. 4:6).

Satan keeps people in bondage by deceiving them and by blinding the minds of the unbelieving (see 2 Cor. 4:4; Rev. 12:9). It follows that the power of Satan is in the lie and that the battle is for the mind. If he is able to deceive Christians into believing things that are not true about God or about who they are in Christ, they will live in spiritual impotency. When the lies are exposed, Satan's power over the believer is broken.

Asking the Lord to reveal the deception and declaring the truth in the Doctrinal Affirmation in this Step is a powerful experience for many who have been deceived for years. Some, like Julie, will become increasingly confident as they verbalize God's truth. Some will struggle just trying to read through the Doctrinal Affirmation. I have seen some take as long as 30 minutes.

Most Christians honestly desire to live righteous lives but have distorted concepts of God and are ignorant of their positions and identities in Christ. As they make this public declaration of faith before witnesses (prayer partners), they are choosing God's truth about His nature, character and redemptive plan for life.

DOING BATTLE

The battle *is* for the mind, and Satan will twist Scripture or tell half-truths to subtly deceive. So we must trust God to expose the deceit, remembering that the weapons we fight with are not the weapons of the world. On the contrary, they have divine power to demolish strongholds. In this Step, we use truth to "demolish arguments and every pretension that sets itself up against the knowledge of God, and we take captive every thought to make it obedient to Christ" (2 Cor. 10:4,5, *NIV*).

As the person you are helping processes this Step, be dependent on the Lord for discernment. Steps One and Two are by the far the most spiritually contested. So pay close attention to the people you are trying to help. Watch their eyes and look for any indication of interference. If they start to drift away, get their attention immediately by asking, "What's going on in your mind? Share with me." You might hear any number of answers, but regardless, the help they need is the same. Ask them, "Where is that coming from?" and "Is that the truth, or is it a lie?" You are helping to expose the nature of the battle for their minds.

For some the light bulb suddenly comes on. One lady blurted out, "Do you know what I'm hearing now? It's just a thought! That's all it is! I don't have to believe that trash anymore." She got it. Another lady approached me at a conference with a bunch of cards she had printed up and was handing out to anyone who wanted one. Each card contained the following questions, "Where did that thought come from? A loving God?"

Sometimes the voices, noises or laughter in the background of the person's mind is too overwhelming for him or her. You may have to stop and pray as you did at the beginning of the counseling session, or have the person exercise authority by calling upon the name of the Lord and telling the voices to stop in Jesus' name. One person couldn't get through the doctrinal statement without my prayer support. It was as though her tongue was swelling up in her mouth. Her speaking became garbled. Four times I had to command Satan to release her by the authority of the Lord Jesus Christ.

The primary approach is to maintain control by exposing the lies and revealing the battle for the mind, and then ignore it. Help people to understand the concept of not paying attention to deceiving spirits. Remember, freedom doesn't come from swatting flies, it comes from taking out the garbage. The way we overcome the father of lies is by choosing the truth. We are not called to dispel the darkness; we are called to turn on the light. The freedom progressively comes by resolving the conflicts. The noise in their heads is just an attempt by the enemy to get them off the track that leads to freedom.

OTHER SYMPTOMS OF ATTACK

During the Steps, the person you are helping may feel physical symptoms such as nausea, light-headedness or headaches. Though these sensations are very real, you should recognize them as nothing more than harassment. The strategy of Satan is to get people to respond in fear, which elevates him as the ultimate fear object. God is the only legitimate fear object, because He alone is omnipresent and omnipotent (see chap. 5). Fear of anything other than God is mutually exclusive of faith in God, and Satan knows that.

In most cases, the physical pain will subside when they share it, but like the voices, the best approach is to ignore it. The symptoms will disappear as the conflicts are resolved. If they seemingly can't go on, then pray for them as you did for the voices or have them declare: "I renounce this attack and announce that my body is a temple of the Holy Spirit, and I choose to continue to seek my freedom."

While reading the Doctrinal Affirmation, a person may say, "I feel like I'm just reading words." You can help the person by asking, "Isn't it your desire to be sincere?" The person will answer, "Yes." Then suggest, "Renounce the lie that you are just reading words, and declare the truth that this Scripture is what you choose to believe." It will be evident to you when someone has difficulty reading the doctrinal statement. Critical points of truth are being contested. Like buzzards hovering over a dying person, it indicates where the problem is. Having the person renounce the lies he or she has believed, or is presently hearing, and choosing the truth will thwart the plans of the buzzards and bring life to the dying body.

Marcy's difficulty in getting through the Steps was not that she had been involved in gross sins or satanism. She was a sincere and attractive Christian who was being mentally "beaten up" with lies and accusations. She had been deceived into thinking that God was not a good God, that she couldn't trust Him, that she would never be free from her past. This vulnerable, hurt and fragile lady had to be slowly and gently guided through the Steps, renouncing all the lies as they surfaced. A few days later, she wrote this:

> God is different from what my concept of Him has been, and I *choose* to trust that new concept. I am His child, and I choose to believe that He will relate to me as a good father would. I am a new person. This day is new, and I await eagerly to experience it as a new creature, free from my past.

GOING THROUGH STEP TWO

We have not found it necessary to explain every detail of the Steps. Most people will have previously read or heard the teaching. I usually give a brief explanation of what we are trying to resolve and then ask the person to pray the prayer at the beginning of each Step. God is the one who reveals and grants repentance. The Holy Spirit is the Spirit of truth, and He will lead them into all truth—the truth that liberates.

We encourage people to read through the Steps at home after we are done. Most will read through them more thoroughly, and many will work through issues that surface later or issues they chose not to deal with in your presence. Your desire is to move them along with understanding and deal with lies they have believed, overcome resistance or reinforce a truth they need to hear.

The Steps are written in such a way that they can be a self-guided tour, and many have worked through the issues on their own. We are receiving letters from people all over the world who have done just that. Some people have started taking others through the Steps by reading all of the light print and asking the person they are helping to pray the prayers. You may choose to do that as well, or you may want to underline and read the main points. In any case, it is God who sets people free, and He will use you regardless of your experience if you are yielded to Him and compassionate toward others.

An easy way to bridge from Step One to Step Two would be to simply say: "In Step One we dealt with counterfeit Christian experiences. In Step Two we want to determine if you have been deceived in any way. Scripture does say that we can fall away from the faith by paying attention to deceiving spirits (see 1 Tim. 4:1). We can also deceive ourselves. We need God's help to do this."

Then ask the person to pray aloud the following prayer:

> Dear heavenly Father,
>
> I know that You desire truth in the inner self and that facing this truth is the way of liberation (John 8:32). I acknowledge that I have been deceived by "the father of lies" (v. 44) and that I have deceived myself (1 John 1:8). I pray in the name of the Lord Jesus Christ that You, heavenly Father, will rebuke all deceiving spirits by virtue of the shed blood and resurrection of the Lord Jesus Christ. By faith I have received You into my life, and I am now seated with Christ in the heavenlies (Eph. 2:6). I acknowledge that I have the responsibility and authority to resist the devil, and when I do, he will flee from me. I now ask the Holy Spirit to guide me into all truth (John 16:13). I ask You to "Search me, O God, and know my heart; try me and know my anxious thoughts; and see if there be any hurtful way in me, and lead me in the everlasting way" (Ps. 139:23-24). In Jesus' name I pray. Amen.

After they have prayed the prayer, proceed by saying:

Satan's purpose is to cause us to think and live contrary to God's plan for us. Some of the ways he tries to do that are included in the two lists: Self-deception and Self-defense. Scripture reveals several ways that we can deceive ourselves, and before we came to Christ, we learned how to defend ourselves in order to survive and hopefully succeed. Now that we have come to Christ we no longer have to do that. Christ is our defense. We are forgiven and accepted just as we are. This is what allows us to be honest and real people who walk in the light and speak the truth in love. We don't have to hide, cover up or pretend anymore. We may have done all of those things at one time or another in our lives. But what I'd like you to do is to take your pen and quietly go through those lists, and place a check mark in front of the items that you can identify as patterns of behavior in your life.

Then just sit quietly, and let the person go through the lists. Occasionally, there will be a question about the meaning of one or two of the statements that will require a brief explanation. (As an alternative, you may choose to read the statements under self-deception and self-defense aloud, and have the person you are helping check the items that apply to him or her personally.)

Self-deception

___ Being hearers and not doers of the Word (see Jas. 1:22; 4:17)
___ Saying we have no sin (see 1 John 1:8)
___ Thinking we are something when we aren't (see Gal. 6:3)
___ Thinking we are wise in this age (see 1 Cor. 3:18,19)
___ Thinking we will not reap what we sow (see Gal. 6:7)
___ Thinking the unrighteous will inherit the Kingdom of God (see 1 Cor. 6:9)
___ Thinking we can associate with bad company and not be corrupted (see 1 Cor. 15:33)

Self-defense (defending ourselves instead of trusting in Christ)

___ Denial (conscious or subconscious)
___ Fantasy (escape from the real world)
___ Emotional insulation (withdraw to avoid rejection)
___ Regression (reverting back to a less threatening time)
___ Displacement (taking out frustrations on others)
___ Projection (blaming others)
___ Rationalization (defending self through verbal excursion)

Identifying areas of self-deception and self-defense is another way for people to discover wrong beliefs so they can continue to deal with them. Some people will read quickly through the lists, make their check marks and be finished in just a minute or two. Some will labor over the lists, being very subjective and slow in making a decision. Resist the temptation to help them check their lists, but encourage them to take responsibility the best they can. The way you can help most is to keep encouraging them to trust the Holy Spirit and to go ahead and make a decision.

As they go through these lists, people with backgrounds of severe trauma may check many or all of the items under self-defense and may express concern about that. You can encourage them by explaining that as they realize their true identities in Christ, they will know they are forgiven and totally accepted by Him, that He is the only defense they need, and they will begin to cope in new healthy ways.

When they have completed the lists, ask them to commit those areas of deception to the Lord using the following prayer:

> Lord, I agree that I have been deceived in the area(s) of
> _____. Thank You for forgiving me. I commit myself
> to know and follow Your truth. Amen.

Whereas in Step One they repeat the prayer separately for each item they checked or wrote in, in Step Two they can read the prayer only once, and when they come to the blank, they can read their entire list of the things they checked in both categories, then complete the prayer.

FOR THOSE WHO STRUGGLE WITH FAITH

The paragraphs between the previous prayer and the Doctrinal Affirmation are important and in many cases should be covered. This is the section that explains: "Choosing the truth may be difficult if you have been living a lie (been deceived) for many years" and "believing the truth is a choice....Of course you can believe God. Faith is something you decide to do, not something you feel like doing." You may want to read those paragraphs aloud.

Many people struggle with faith. Satan's first tactic with Eve was to make her doubt God and believe Him to be a liar (see Gen. 3:1-5). People need to see that they can stop believing Satan, their failed experiences and their damaged emotions, and start believing God and His Word.

OBJECTIVITY IS ESSENTIAL

One of the values of being led through the Steps by another believer is having someone more objective about the person's life than he or she is able to be. The most difficult people to work with are those who are highly subjective and passive. They believe any little thought that comes to their minds. They have never understood the need to assume responsibility for their own thoughts. One person told me, "The idea of taking every thought captive to the obedience to Christ never crossed my mind."

Their feelings (thoughts) tell them that they are hopeless, and they need someone to do something *for* them. They are prime candidates for cults or sick legalistic pastors who maintain control over their people by doing their thinking for them. These people believe that God won't hear their prayers, that they don't have enough faith, or that it will work for others but not for them. Those lies have been played over in their minds for so many years that they have become a stronghold. They need to know that they are not helpless victims and that there is hope for them, but they will need to personally assume responsibility for choosing the truth, regardless of how they feel.

Most of these people think they are helpless victims with no wills of their own. You could gently point out any lie that surfaces and help them exercise their choice to verbally renounce the lie and choose the truth. That will begin to expose and break the spiritual strongholds, but habitual patterns of denial and deception will need to be changed over time. It may be helpful to share the following illustration:

> Suppose there is a dirt road leading to your house in the country. If you continually drive over that road through rain and mud, ruts will be formed. Over time the sun will dry those ruts and make them hard as concrete. The easiest thing, as you drive that road, would be to allow the car to drift along in those ruts. It will be a rough ride compared to the smooth ride that you could have on the surface right beside the ruts. You can immediately feel the resistance on the wheel to return to the ruts in the road when you only make a half-hearted effort to steer out of them.
>
> If you want to get out of the rut, you will have to be totally committed and willing to make deliberate choices. In the same way, if you no longer want to be controlled by the strongholds or "rut thinking" that the world, the flesh and the devil has cemented in your mind over years, you need to be committed to

breaking those strongholds and make deliberate choices based on the truth of God's Word. You choose; you don't passively let the liar and your old patterns of thinking decide. You take every thought captive in obedience to Christ and choose His truth. This is how we renew our minds—by knowing and choosing the truth, and by letting the Word of Christ richly dwell within us (see Rom. 12:2; Phil. 4:8; Col. 3:16).

THE DOCTRINAL AFFIRMATION

Unless they experience extreme difficulties as mentioned earlier, let the read through the Doctrinal Affirmation. No matter how difficult it may I to read through it, have them persevere. This is an opportunity for them I take a stand and witness to who they are in Christ. If there is a word or state ment they do not understand, then take the time to explain it. The immed ate impact for most will be negligible.

I have often used the doctrinal statement as a litmus test to show then their newly found freedom after they have completed the Steps. I have sai to many, "Remember how difficult it was to read through that Doctrina Affirmation earlier? Why don't you read it again and see if you can tell any difference." Some can hardly believe the difference. Suddenly it is under-standable, as is the Bible. Most have a hunger and thirst for the Word of God in a way that they have never experienced before.

EXPOSING LIES AND AFFIRMING TRUTH

A woman wrote to one of our staff members, "Going through the Steps to Freedom has been the most exciting part of my Christian walk." She had struggled with voices and screaming in her head, nightmares and apparitions in her room, and strong deception through lies and condemnation. After viewing the *Resolving Personal and Spiritual Conflicts* videos, she said, "I have been unwilling to take responsibility for my own thoughts. I have wanted some kind of help from the outside without being willing to do the work necessary for myself." But now she has. In a letter she wrote to Jesus, she said, "I confess my unbelief, my selfishness, my obsessive thoughts. I renounce the lies that would destroy and incapacitate me. I ask Your for-giveness and forsake all thinking that would destroy the truth that is in me." Attached to her letter were six typewritten pages of lies she had believed, accompanied by Scripture verses she found that exposed those lies and affirmed the truth.

The same woman wrote this letter to the person who took her through the Steps to Freedom:

> As I've thought about and weighed what happened in God's presence and your office, I am awestruck at the reality that not only has Christ completely severed the spiritual bond between myself and Harold and all the others I was involved with, but that He also touched the deeper issue—a place where I have held the belief that I actually became the slut, whore, adulterer, the "evil one," the "witch" that mom and dad had always said I was.
>
> Facing the reality of that truth—or rather the lies that I have believed about myself—has been more than I ever believed God could make clean or redeem. I could not escape the embarrassment, nor could I forgive my willing participation. The violations were easier to renounce because I was not choosing them for myself.
>
> Is it possible that as I've continued to renounce both the sexual acts themselves and the beliefs that I became the embodiment of the evil I participated in, that the Lord would expunge the record...and change my life...that I am no longer identified by the names my father gave me, but I am truly a new person in Christ...that I am as you said, "clean as a hound's tooth"? I have always thought of myself as a slut and an adulteress who was just taking up space in the Church, but who could never take a position of responsibility or ministry because my past is so evil.
>
> It's like God has taken a giant sponge to the battered and bloody portion of my life that has been a major stronghold, absorbed all the blood, all the pain, all the lies. And as He took all this away, He left me new and free and clean in Him. I don't have to contend with the weight of that sin because it's forgiven, nailed to the cross through the blood of Jesus.
>
> I have known all the lies in my head and have wanted to believe that God's Word was true; today I know it in my heart and spirit. As I renounced these things, I thought, *How can these words set me free?* How could they not? They are the power of God.
>
> Today, I don't just believe God is cleansing me; I *know* I'm

clean! I don't just believe God will free me from my past; I *know* I'm free! I am no longer Avery's daughter, his sex toy. I am no longer Harold's mistress. I am no longer the embodiment of the evil I participated in. I am a child of the King, called and chosen by Him. Cleansed, forgiven, made new to live in His family forever. Free to love and give and enter into relationship with Him and the Church, to be the person He has called me to be. Praise His name!

Truth set her free! It can free those you help also!

CHAPTER NINE

OVERCOMING THE PAST

STEP THREE: BITTERNESS VERSUS FORGIVENESS

As I talked about forgiveness one evening during a conference, a woman sat shivering with fear on the front steps of the church. Threatening and condemning thoughts raced through her mind.

During the same session of another conference, someone darted out of the auditorium and into the lobby, exclaiming, "I can't stay in there any longer!"

At the seminary where I taught, a young student abruptly got up and walked out of my lecture on forgiveness.

Most people don't outwardly respond so dramatically, of course, but why do some have such strong reactions? Because this is the number one ticket to freedom for most people. Of the hundreds of people I have had the privilege to help find their freedom in Christ, forgiveness has been the primary issue, and in some cases, the *only* issue that needed to be resolved.

Ask any of our staff members what affords Satan the greatest access to the Church, and based on years of experience, they would say *unforgiveness*. One severely victimized lady had an "asthma attack" as I spoke and had to leave the auditorium. She heard enough to know that she needed to prayerfully make a list of people she needed to forgive. She came the next day for a personal appointment with four pages of names. The atrocities associated with any one of those names would send an average person into a tailspin.

WHY SOME PEOPLE RESIST FORGIVENESS

Some people react negatively to the idea of forgiving others, because they see it as another form of victimization. It rips at their sense of justice. So they reason, "Oh, sure, just forgive and keep getting slapped around!" To them it is another sign of weakness, a continuation of the sickening saga of codependency.

On the contrary, forgiveness is a courageous act that requires the grace of God. Forgiveness is not tolerating sin. Scriptural boundaries must be set up to stop further abuse.

Many don't want to forgive because they want revenge. Seeking revenge is letting the devil set the agenda. It puts you on the same level as the abuser and usurps God's role of exacting justice. Paul writes, "Never take your own revenge, beloved, but leave room for the wrath of God, for it is written, 'Vengeance is Mine, I will repay,' says the Lord" (Rom. 12:19). Some people just want the soul satisfaction of hating the wretch. But hanging on to our bitterness only sickens the soul. Trying to cover it up doesn't fool anyone, least of all ourselves, because "the heart knows its own bitterness" (Prov. 14:10).

We have discovered that in almost every case people don't know how to forgive, nor do they understand what constitutes forgiveness. Those we work with have been hurt, and many have been hurt badly. After helping hundreds work through the painful memories of unspeakable atrocities, my heart goes out to them in ways I can hardly explain. Most of our staff members are close to tears all the time. After hearing hundreds of stories, I still can hardly believe what people are capable of doing to one another.

I went through a soul-searching period a few years ago. I didn't want to hear any more horrible stories. In fact, I don't think I could hear them today if I didn't see resolution. What keeps me going is the freedom that comes when people work through the Steps and forgive from their hearts. I thank God that there is an answer for these wounded people.

I have said to hundreds of people in counseling sessions, "I'm so sorry that happened to you." Instead of having fathers who would protect and provide for them, they had fathers who took advantage of them sexually. Instead of having mothers who would comfort and encourage them, they had mothers who verbally abused them. Instead of having pastors who would shepherd them, they had legalistic men who tried to control them under a cloud of condemnation. What some thought would be safe dates, turned out to be date rape. *Ad infinitum nausea!*

The vast majority of the victimizers will never come back and ask for forgiveness. They won't even acknowledge they did anything wrong. Many times I have stood before a group of ladies and said, "I want to acknowledge and apologize for the way men in general have looked at you as sex objects, and for the way we have touched you and violated you. As a father, husband and a man, I'm asking for your forgiveness. Would you forgive me? Would you forgive us?" Unless you were there, you could hardly believe the impact this has. I have vicariously asked forgiveness a number of times in personal counseling to help people work through their anger and bitterness toward others. Why? Because I wanted to acknowledge their pain and the injustice of their abuses at the hands of others. I wanted to give them the best possible opportunity to finally be free from their abusive pasts.

INTRODUCING STEP THREE

In the entire process of helping people find their freedom in Christ, no other Step requires greater patience, sensitivity or skill than this one. I prefer to establish who it is people need to forgive before I explain what forgiveness is and how they can do it. I originally started this way because I was concerned that they may not share all the names if they knew beforehand what I was going to encourage them to do. Other members of my staff prefer to explain forgiveness first. Regardless, the individuals need to pray and ask the Lord to reveal to them who it is they need to forgive. I usually explain to them, "In this prayer, all you are asking for are the names of the people you need to forgive." Then I will have them pray as follows:

> Dear heavenly Father,
>   I thank You for the riches of Your kindness, forbearance and patience, knowing that Your kindness has led me to repentance (Rom. 2:4). I confess that I have not extended that same patience and kindness toward others who have offended me, but instead I have harbored bitterness and resentment. I pray that during this time of self-examination You would bring to my mind those people I have not forgiven, in order that I may do so (Matt. 18:35). I ask this in the precious name of Jesus. Amen.

MAKING THE LIST

When they have finished praying, ask them to list the names that come to their minds. I usually record the names for them, but some of our staff members prefer to have the people write down the names on blank pieces of paper. If they begin to discuss the people they're thinking of, encourage them to just write the names and deal with the "why" later. First names only are sufficient, or they can refer to the individuals as Dad, Mom, first-grade teacher and so on. In some cases they have forgotten their names or never knew them. Ninety-five percent of the time, Mom and Dad are mentioned first. The first few names given are usually the people who contributed to their greatest source of pain. You might encourage them to start with the early years and work up to the present.

The leader and prayer team should sit quietly and prayerfully while the names are written. Be careful to notice if they have left out the names of obvious persons. Having heard their stories at the beginning of the sessions, you can offer suggestions of people they overlooked. They may have only a few names, or they may fill several sheets of paper. (Perfectionists usually have short lists, because they blame themselves for problems.) Allow enough time to ensure that the list is complete.

WORKING THROUGH BLOCKAGES

I have had some people pray the prayer and then say, "Well, I don't think there is anybody I need to forgive."

"That may be the case," I respond, "but would you share the names that are coming to your mind right now?" A list of 25 names might suddenly appear, and I will spend the next hour or two helping him or her work through it.

Some people's way of dealing with the pain is to cover up the abuse and live in denial. Many say, "I don't know why I'm thinking of this person." Chances are, they will know when they get to that person in the process of forgiving. The Lord wants us free in Him, so He will bring to mind both the people and the events that we are chained to in unforgiveness. When we forgive, we set the captive free, only to realize that we were the captives.

You do not want to play the role of the Holy Spirit, of course, but if someone has difficulty thinking of *any* names, or if only one or two names are mentioned, you might suggest that the person repeat the portion of the prayer requesting God to bring names to mind. Or you could gently probe a bit: "Are there any relatives you need to forgive? How about teachers? Employers? Friends at school, work or church?"

Occasionally, people will have short lists because they have truly dealt in depth with most of the forgiveness issues in their lives. You can usually discern whether that is the case by how they respond to the Steps and how they deal with the names they do have. Regardless, people cannot be forced beyond their understanding of the issues or their willingness to forgive. Forgiveness is a crisis of the will, a hard-core choice to forgive from the heart.

DEALING WITH SELF AND GOD

The two most overlooked names on the lists are: "myself" and "God." In many cases, anger toward self or God is greater than anger toward any other person. Why is that? Let me offer an explanation, which I also take the time to explain in almost every counseling session.

There is a real line that is drawn in life that separates responsibilities. On one side of the line exists all the issues that God and only God can deal with. He is the Creator, Sustainer and the Redeemer of life. We can't create anything. We can be creative and shove the rocks around and spread the paint on the canvas, but we cannot bring something out of nothing into existence. We can't play God, nor can we do anything to save ourselves. We should not try to be another person's conscience, nor convictor of his or her sins. We have to trust God for what He alone can do. For all those issues, we rest in the sovereignty of God and trust Him to be and do all the things He said He would.

Everything on the other side of the line is *our* responsibility, which is revealed to us in the Word of God. We cannot pray and ask the Lord to do for us what He has required us to do. He won't do it, and I'm not sure that He even can! God has to stay true to Himself and true to His Word. He cannot change and neither does His Word. He has communicated to us His ways, and He will always work that way. The only biblical basis by which we can boast is that we understand Him and know His ways (see Jer. 9:23,24; 1 Cor. 1:31).

ASSUMING OUR RESPONSIBILITY

Suppose there is a difficult member of your congregation who is causing disunity. A number of you meet regularly to pray and ask the Lord to remove the person. Nothing happens! Why won't God do something about it? After all, it is His church. Doesn't He care about it? Actually, He has done all He has needed to do for the problem to be resolved. He has defeated the devil, given life, power and authority to the Church, and communicated to us the means by which we are to relate to one another. Church discipline is *our* responsibility. God has said we must first go in private for the purpose of winning a brother. If he or she won't hear us and be reconciled, then we are to confront the person with two or more other witnesses, and so on.

It becomes more complex in our Western world when dealing with spiritual problems because we haven't received much instruction regarding this.

For example, imagine that a person comes under some type of spiritual attack in his bedroom at night. He pulls the covers over his head and silently cries out to God for help. Nothing happens! Why not? Hearing no response from heaven, he begins to struggle with the following thoughts: *Come on, God, You can do something about this. You're all-powerful. Why won't You help me? Maybe I'm not a Christian. Maybe God doesn't love me. Maybe I'm different from others.* Whose responsibility is it to resist the devil?

The devil capitalizes on our ignorance and irresponsibility by pummeling us with thoughts such as, *God isn't going to help you. He doesn't love you. How can you be a Christian and do the things you do? Look how weak and helpless you are.*

People who have encountered such thoughts frequently come to my conferences seeking help. They are ticked off at themselves and/or God, and disillusioned by the Christian life. Some cry out, "Come on, God, accommodate me one time. Won't You please make one exception just for me?" Would you really want Him to? If He did, He would no longer be God. Our hopes lie in the fact that He will remain true to Himself. The conflicts will be resolved when we assume our own responsibilities, decide to do it His way and trust in the finished work of Christ.

RECEIVING FORGIVENESS

The concept of "letting go" of anger, guilt and condemnation toward self is something many have never considered. Those feelings may be rooted in our failures to accept God's cleansing and receive His forgiveness. Only God can forgive our sins, which separate us from Him, and He has. But we need to forgive ourselves for our failures, for letting God down and for hurting others. Otherwise we are believing the subtle deception that we must atone for our own sins.

Believers paralyzed by condemnation are being victimized by the accuser of the brethren, or by their own faulty consciences, rather than the truth of God's grace. The latter is psychological guilt based on years of performance-based living and legalistic Christianity. These kinds of people live as though Christ's death was not sufficient to cover their sins. Sometimes I feel like saying, "Go ahead, hang on the cross if you want to, but it won't do you any good." Colossians 2:18 says, "Let no one keep defrauding you of your prize by delighting in self-abasement."

These kinds of people will not be presumptuous in forgiving themselves, because they are not *accomplishing* forgiveness. We know that only God can forgive sin through His Son. The forgiveness we're speaking about here is *receiving* forgiveness from God. Forgiving ourselves is saying in effect, "Lord, I do believe that You have forgiven me and cleansed me of those sins which I have confessed to You. Because of Your great love and grace—not because I deserve it—I choose to no longer condemn myself when You have forgiven me. I receive Your forgiveness."

RELEASING BITTERNESS TOWARD GOD

Bitterness toward God is far more common than most people would feel free to admit. But when they become honest about their anger toward God, another stronghold begins to crumble. They believe God has been unfair and let them down...by failing to answer an important prayer...allowing them to suffer by not rescuing them...not endowing them with certain blessings, looks, gifts, abilities, success or financial security.

Obviously, God doesn't need to be forgiven, because He cannot commit any sin of commission or omission. But we need to destroy "speculations and every lofty thing raised up against the knowledge of God" and take "every thought captive to the obedience of Christ" (2 Cor. 10:5). Satan's scheme is to turn us against God by raising up thoughts against Him. These deceptive thoughts often come in first-person singular form: *God doesn't love me. He isn't going to do anything to help me.* They cause us to rebel against His Lordship. Satan is defeated when we release God from our own false expectations and stop blaming Him for our own failures and the failure of the Church to adequately equip the saints so they can stand.

Understand that people don't forgive others because of what they did to them; they forgive others for what they *think* others have done to them. Bitterness isn't always rooted in reality. It is rooted in their *perceptions* of reality. I have had people put my name on their lists for silly things like not answering the phone when they called. But I wasn't home or I would've answered the phone! I didn't do anything wrong, but they thought I did, so they needed to forgive me. Roots of bitterness can spring up whereby many are defiled (see Heb. 12:15), all because of a misunderstanding.

THOUGHTS RAISED UP AGAINST GOD

That is why it is not blasphemous to "forgive" God, because the bitterness is not based in reality but in thoughts raised up against the knowledge of Him. God understands that concept much better than we do, because He alone knows the thoughts and intentions of our hearts (see 4:12). The only way to overcome bitterness is to forgive.

I have never had anyone work through their bitterness toward God without immediately acknowledging the fact that God hasn't done anything wrong. I have never been successful at helping people overcome their bitterness toward God by defending Him. First of all, God doesn't need me to defend Him. Second, we have to start where people are at. It is futile to tell people they shouldn't feel the way they do toward God or anyone else. They can't change the way they feel. It is a subtle form of rejection when we won't accept or acknowledge their frustration and pain. If you find it uncomfortable having people "forgive" God, or if you think it is absolutely wrong, then you might try having them pray, "Lord, I know You haven't done anything wrong, but I want to repent of the anger I have against you for...." Either way, the feelings must be dealt with or it won't do much good to go on, because God is their only hope.

Most people won't submit to God if they are bitter toward Him or think they can't trust Him. I can only tell you from experience that working through the bitterness toward God brings tremendous healing and restoration. Job is a good example of a believer who repented of anger toward God: "Therefore I retract, and I repent in dust and ashes" (Job 42:6). Forgiving others is not a self-righteous activity, nor a blaming exercise. It is a humbling and healing experience that faces the hurt and the hate, and then chooses the way of the Cross.

FACING THE NEED TO FORGIVE

Once the list is complete, it's time to address the meaning of forgiveness. We can't assume that people know how to forgive from the heart, so take time to cover the explanation in the Steps to Freedom. You can do this by reading it in its entirety, or by emphasizing key points and adding brief explanations as necessary, or enumerating the main points by memory if you know them well. These points are:

1. Forgiving is not forgetting.
2. Forgiveness is letting go of resentment. You don't heal in order to forgive; you forgive in order to heal.
3. Forgiveness is not seeking revenge.
4. Forgiveness is letting other people off your hook, knowing that they are still on God's hook.

5. Forgiveness is something you do for your sake; it is between yourself and God.
6. Forgiveness is God's way of stopping the cycle of abuse. (Some say, "But they hurt me!" And I respond: "They're still hurting you! Forgiving is how you stop the pain!")
7. Forgiveness is agreeing to live with the consequences of another's sin. You pay the price of the evil you forgive.
8. Forgiveness allows God to touch your emotional core. You acknowledge the hurt and the hate in order to forgive from the heart.
9. Forgiveness is a crisis of the will. It is a choice that is only possible by the grace of God.
10. Forgiveness sets the captive free. What is to be gained by forgiving is freedom from the abuse and abusers.

GIVING UP OUR RIGHT TO BLAME

Some people deal with their emotional pain by pointing fingers. "That person violated me" or "I'm suffering because of that person." While that may be true, it doesn't resolve the problem. In many cases, blaming someone else can be a cover for their own guilt. For others, it reveals a heart that is more prone to seek revenge than to forgive.

To place the blame on somebody else can be nothing more than an excuse to stay in bondage. The reason that many still feel the emotional pain from the past is because they haven't forgiven. I can empathize with these people because they have been hurt. But I also care enough to help them realize that bad things happen to good people all the time, and it may happen to them again. I can't guarantee that a lady will not be sexually assaulted, but I can say that God has a means by which that event doesn't have to control her for the rest of her life. These people can't fix their pasts, but by the grace of God they can be free from them.

Forgiveness is an act of the will whereby we give up our claim to seek revenge for an offense against us. God could have justifiably exercised His wrath against us and all mankind. Instead, "He made Him who knew no sin to be sin on our behalf, that we might become the righteousness of God in Him" (2 Cor. 5:21). Was it difficult for Jesus to accept His assignment? He said to Peter, James and John, "My soul is deeply grieved, to the point of death" (Matt. 26:38), and He cried out, "My Father, if it is possible, let this cup pass from Me; yet not as I will, but as Thou wilt" (v. 39). The will of our heavenly Father was that Jesus go to the cross, but the grace of God was incredibly evident even in His hour of agony. As Jesus looked down upon those who would crucify Him, He said, "Father, forgive them; for they do not know what they are doing" (Luke 23:34).

The Cross reveals the cost of forgiveness and the pain of bearing the penalty of someone else's sin. At the Cross, Jesus died once for all the sins of the world (see Rom. 6:10). He paid the penalty for my sins, your sins and all the sins committed by others against all the people you and I have the privilege to help find their freedom in Christ. The victim cries out, "Where is the justice?" It's in the Cross. Forgiving others would be a moral outrage without the Cross.

In the same manner that God has forgiven us, God wants us to forgive others. "Let all bitterness and wrath and anger and clamor and slander be put away from you, along with all malice. And be kind to one another, tender-hearted, forgiving each other, just as God in Christ also has forgiven you" (Eph. 4:31,32). Remember, the grace of God will always enable us to do the will of God. Why then do so many Christians try to forgive over and over again, but still feel tormented and confused? Many haven't understood how to forgive from the heart, and others haven't taken the next step of resisting the devil. "Submit therefore to God. Resist the devil and he will flee from you" (Jas. 4:7). Therefore they remain in bondage to the injustices of their pasts.

GIVE SATAN NO ADVANTAGE

One of the most definitive teachings on forgiveness is in Matthew 18:21-35. Several issues stand out in this passage. First, we are to continue forgiving no matter how many times we have been sinned against. Second, the degree that we have been forgiven by God is far greater than the degree we will ever have to forgive others. Third, repayment is impossible. Fourth, we are to forgive from our hearts or be tormented by the accuser of the brethren. If we will not forgive as we have been forgiven, our heavenly Father will hand us over to the torturers (see Matt. 18:34,35). That's not because He doesn't love us; that's because He wants us to live free and productive lives in Christ. In the same way, God disciplines because He loves us.

In 2 Corinthians 2:10,11, Paul warns us of Satan's entrapment when there is unforgiveness: "Whom you forgive anything, I forgive also; for indeed what I have forgiven, if I have forgiven anything, I did it for your sakes in the presence of Christ, in order that no advantage be taken of us by Satan;

for we are not ignorant of his schemes." We are not to sin through anger, because that gives the devil an opportunity (see Eph. 4:26,27,31,32).

JUSTICE, MERCY AND GRACE

Consider these simple definitions of justice, mercy and grace when applied to relationships: Justice is giving people what they deserve. If God were perfectly just in dealing with us, we would all go to hell. God is a just God, and "The wages of sin is death" (Rom. 6:23).

Mercy is not giving people what they deserve. "But when the kindness of God our Savior and His love for mankind appeared, He saved us, not on the basis of deeds which we have done in righteousness, but according to His mercy" (Titus 3:4,5). Justice had to be served, so Jesus took upon Himself the wrath of God.

Grace is giving us what we don't deserve. "For by grace you have been saved through faith" (Eph. 2:8). Forgiveness and eternal life are free gifts from God.

So the Lord instructs us to, "Be merciful, just as your Father is merciful" (Luke 6:36). The point is, we are not to give people what they deserve (be merciful); we are to give them what they don't deserve (be gracious). We are called to love people, not because they are lovable or deserve to be loved, but because we have become "partakers of the divine nature" (2 Pet. 1:4). God loves us because it is His nature to love us. "God is love" (1 John 4:8). "By this all men will know that you are My disciples, if you have love for one another" (John 13:35). This ability to love one another is possible only by the grace of God, as is the ability to forgive as we have been forgiven.

The most common Greek word in the New Testament translated "to forgive" basically means "to send away" or "to let go." In forgiving, we *send away* the devil so he can't torment us, and we *let go* of the past so it can no longer have a hold on us. The pain and anger is released as we forgive from our hearts.

ERRORS TO AVOID

Two major errors are to be avoided when addressing the issue of forgiveness. The first is more common among counselors. Influenced by secular resources, some counselors teach that forgiveness is a process and tell many that they are not ready to forgive. They tell people they have to go through all the painful memories first and then they will be able to forgive. The problem is they will never get there. Rehearsing the painful memories week after week only deepens the wounds and reinforces the abuse. The implication is that one has to heal in order to forgive, but in actuality, it is the other way around. We forgive in order to heal.

The other error is more common in the Church. The extreme version would sound like this: "You shouldn't feel that way; you just need to forgive." The problem is, they just bypassed forgiveness. We have to forgive from the heart. Forgiveness is a hard choice, which includes: (1) allowing God to surface every offending person and painful memory; (2) agreeing to live with the consequences of the other person's sin without seeking revenge; and (3) letting God deal with the offending person in His way and in His timing.

All forgiveness is efficacious or substitutionary. Christ paid the price for our sins, and we pay the price for those who sinned against us. In a practical sense, forgiveness is agreeing to live with the consequences of another person's sins. "But that isn't fair," some protest. Of course it isn't, but we will have to do so anyway. Everybody is living with the consequences of somebody else's sin. We are all living with the consequences of Adam's sin. We have the choice to live in the bondage of bitterness or in the freedom of forgiveness.

GETTING TO THE EMOTIONAL CORE

Just before you lead a person to pray through his or her list of names, you may want to read this sentence: "Stay with each individual until you are sure you have dealt with all the remembered pain—what he or she did, how he or she hurt you, how he or she made you feel (rejected, unloved, unworthy, dirty, etc.)." This is important because facing those specific issues is what enables people to get down to the emotional core, where the damage was done and the healing can take place. Forgiving generically results in generic freedom and healing.

Many people have sincerely tried to forgive but weren't able to because they didn't understand the real source of their bitterness and the subsequent lies they have believed about themselves. Forgiving someone for hurting you may only be dealing with the symptom. You may need to ask the person, "What specifically happened to you?" "How did you respond at the time?" and "How has it affected you today?" Anger, sadness and depression are only the emotional consequences of what happened.

Physical, emotional, spiritual and sexual abuse can also severely damage their self-concepts. Their identities become wrapped around the abuse. A rape victim may feel like a whore, and the emotionally battered person may feel worthless. Forgiving the person for making her feel like a whore or feeling worthless will not get it done. She would need to say something like this: "I forgive that man who raped me, for forcing me to have sex with him against my will, and for violating my body, which is a temple of God, when I wanted to glorify God in my body. And I renounce the lie that I am a whore or that my body is dirty." (More will be said about this kind of renunciation in Step Six.) Or they may need to pray, "I forgive my mother for saying I will never amount to anything and for constantly putting me down by saying _____ (be specific). I renounce the lies that I have believed about myself. I am not the terrible person my mother said I was; I am a child of God, and I choose to believe what God says about me."

Hurtful experiences in early childhood shape our self-perceptions. Over and over again, we hear people tearfully pray: "Lord, I forgive my father (or mother) for beating me, for never caring about what was happening in my life, for not believing me when I told him about the sexual abuse. I forgive him for what he said and did that caused me to feel dirty, unloved and worthless." Such negative programming contributes to a distorted sense of self. Forgiving others connects them to a loving Father who sees them as His children, cleansed by the blood of the Lamb.

Mental strongholds are torn down as people forgive those who have offended them. They have lived under the condemnation of those labels for years. "Therefore, there is now no condemnation for those who are in Christ Jesus" (Rom. 8:1, *NIV*). Now the lies can be exposed so they can live according to the truth of who they really are in Christ.

PREPARING THEIR HEARTS

We often share with these hurting people that bitterness is to the soul as cancer is to the body. If you knew that you had a form of cancer that could be removed by surgery, wouldn't you say to the doctor, "Go for it! Get it all!"? Bitterness, like cancer, affects every part of our bodies, souls and spirits. Forgiving from your heart those who have hurt you is God's way of removing the cancer.

Tragically, this cancer of the soul is a communicable disease that can be spread to others. That is why the Word of God says, "See to it that no one misses the grace of God and that no bitter root grows up to cause trouble and defile many" (Heb. 12:15, *NIV*). Entire families and churches can be defiled by roots of bitterness.

Having covered the main points of forgiveness, you may want to read the paragraphs preceding the forgiveness prayer before you continue:

> As you pray, God may bring to mind offending people and experiences you have totally forgotten. Let Him do it even if it is painful. Remember, you are doing this for your sake. God wants you to be free. Don't rationalize or explain the offender's behavior. Forgiveness is dealing with your pain and leaving the other person to God. Positive feelings will follow in time; freeing yourself from the past is the critical issue right now.
>
> Don't say "Lord, please help me to forgive" because He is already helping you. Don't say "Lord, I want to forgive" because you are bypassing the hard-core choice to forgive, which is your responsibility. Stay with each individual until you are sure you have dealt with all the remembered pain—what they did, how they hurt you, how they made you feel (rejected, unloved, unworthy, dirty, etc.).
>
> You are now ready to forgive the people on your list so that you can be free in Christ with those people no longer having any control over you. For each person on your list, pray aloud:
>
> Lord, I forgive (name) for (specifically identify all offenses and painful memories or feelings).

AS THEY PRAY

Most people realize they need to forgive and that failing to do so will rob them of the freedom they desire. So they pray through their lists and immediately begin to experience a sense of release or freedom. Others may express opposition during forgiveness, especially regarding those who have hurt them deeply. One young lady said, "I can't forgive my mother. I hate her!" I responded, "Now you can. The Lord isn't asking you to like your mother. You can't deny or play with your emotions that way. The Lord wants you to forgive so you can put a stop to the pain you have experienced."

Some are reluctant to forgive others for the wrongs they have done, because they think they are judging people by forgiving them. When a young anorexic girl came to her father on the list, she said, "I feel like I need to ask him to forgive me." I told her, "Maybe you do, but that is not what we are dealing with here. We are dealing with your pain." Sometimes people are torn between feelings of love and loyalty for their parents and the need to face the pain they caused and forgive them for it. Help these individuals understand that forgiving their parents for being something less than perfect is not condemning them. We do not blame our parents for their imperfections; they had parents who were imperfect, too. But facing the truth and forgiving their parents is what stops the cycle of abuse that continues on from one generation to another.

As they work through their lists, make sure they stay with each person until they deal with every painful memory that God brings to their minds. Many people have tried to shove these painful memories down into their subconscious. Such suppression is considered a conscious denial. Others cannot honestly recall what happened to them. I believe the Lord is involved when that happens. The pain was too great to deal with at the time, so the Lord causes the repression only to reveal it at a later time when there is enough maturity, adequate support and the means to resolve it. The Lord frequently brings back repressed memories during this process. Some attempt to deal with their pain by denying that anything bad ever happened or by pretending that it didn't really bother them. Since you have heard their stories and know some of the offenses, you will need to help them face reality for their sakes. Denial and cover-up are never God's way.

EMOTIONS VARY

Forgiving from the heart will be an emotional catharsis for many, while others will remain emotionally blocked and unable to feel anything. A missionary lady looked at her list and slowly pushed it away. Then she pulled it back, and then pushed it away again. She said, "My counselor has been trying to get me to cry for three months." I had said nothing about crying. Finally, she took the list and started with the first name. "Lord, I forgive..." and collapsed in tears. Years of emotional pain surfaced as she forgave one person after another.

Some may work through their lists rather stoically. We have to allow for different temperaments. Shedding tears is not the only way of expressing grief and pain. I have seen some consciously and deliberately come to terms with their abuses and painfully choose to forgive from their hearts without shedding a tear. However, they may have never identified the true sources of their pain. In such cases, you could ask, "How did that make you feel at the time?" or "When you think about it now, how does it make you feel?" You may see a flood of emotions unleashed. Some may forgive without showing any emotion until they come to a particular name, and then the release comes. We all need to rely upon the Lord to discern whether the forgiveness is genuine or contrived. There is no substitute for experience and spiritual maturity on this issue, but we can't wait until we are perfect before we attempt to help others.

FACING THE PAIN AND MOVING ON

The primary objective to keep in mind as they go through forgiveness is not the question of who was right or even God's justice; it is helping them face the truth, acknowledge the pain, forgive the offenders and move on. For many, this may be the first time they have ever acknowledged, understood or faced the root of their pain. Allow them to experience the pain and express their emotions. They have chosen to stuff their feelings and live in denial for the fear of that happening, but that is exactly what must happen. They can't be right with God and not be real.

We often hear people say, "I've never told this to anyone before." We must believe and accept without judgment the feelings and perceptions of the people we are trying to help, because that is what they have to deal with, whether their perceptions were right or not.

Nobody is more emotionally inhibited than the victims of satanic ritual abuse. They have been programmed that way. They were told, and it was probably demonstrated, that if they cried someone would be hurt. I have seen tears form in their eyes and roll freely down their cheeks when they renounce the lie that their crying would cause the death or injury of anyone. Until they break that stronghold, they can't forgive from their hearts. Don't think for a moment that Satan doesn't know that.

Even some people with "ordinary" childhoods have learned not to express their emotions, especially negative ones. "Real men don't cry" they have been told. Or "Being emotionally expressive is wrong and a sign of weakness." If the person you are trying to help is emotionally inhibited, ask, "Were you ever told that it was wrong or weak to express your emotions? What happened to you when you were emotionally honest in your home? Do you believe it is wrong to be emotionally honest?" To be free in Christ, the individual must forgive those who trained him or her and renounce the lies he or she has been taught concerning his or her emotional nature. The one who is free in Christ will be emotionally free as well.

One woman had never been able to feel emotional sadness for herself but could weep for others. Her father had molested her when she was a child, and to guard his secret, he threatened her with more harm if she ever cried or told anyone. When this surfaced while going through forgiveness, she was encouraged to renounce the lie that she should not feel her own emotions and announce the truth that God created her with the emotional ability to experience joy, sorrow, laughter and tears. As she did that, a tear began to form in the corner of her eye. "Now you can cry," she was told. Immediately she began to weep, and she continued to sob for some time, moving the leader to tears of his own.

As I said before, some people are like bananas. The peel is removed and all their problems are resolved the first time they go through the Steps. Not everyone, however, will cover their entire past in one session. Many are like onions. The first time through, they will take off the first outer layer. They may feel a great sense of joy as though a weight has been lifted. They dealt with all they knew, but they may recall other things in the coming days. Now they will know what to do when painful memories surface, or new offenses take place. We need to help them resolve what they do know. If there is more, the Lord will surface it at the right time (see 1 Cor. 4:1-5). Sometimes the atrocities are too much to be revealed all at once.

KEEP THE FOCUS

Try to keep the focus on the people and specific offenses that need to be forgiven. Offering lengthy explanations for what happened can be nothing more than a verbal excursion or subtle form of rationalization. The person you're helping needs to specifically forgive the offenses that have been committed in the presence of a loving heavenly Father.

Discourage people from offering excuses for the offender. Whenever I hear something like "Lord, I forgive my father because I know he didn't mean it," I'll stop them. They are trying to justify the abuse, or excusing the abuser, instead of acknowledging their own pain, facing the truth and forgiving from the heart. They wrongly believe that they have to lie and cover up in order to protect the family name, or that they deserved the abuse.

It is extremely important to remain nonjudgmental, regardless of what is revealed. Many women fear condemnation when they admit they have had abortions. Men are often afraid of admitting failure or need. Many people are ashamed to confess that they have harbored anger toward God because of unfortunate circumstances or losses. A positive, affirming, nonjudgmental attitude is paramount to enable them to be open and honest about specific issues.

Although you want to stay focused, allow this process to be unhurried. This is not a timed exercise. After making his list, a pastor said, "You don't have enough time."

I said, "I'll stay all night if I have to," and I meant it.

This 43-year-old man began to cry. "You are the first person who has ever said that to me," he said.

It's critical that we never start this Step without finishing it.

EXPRESSING COMPASSION

You may be surprised at your own feelings as an encourager. Listening to the person you are helping may surface strong emotions in yourself. It is normal and acceptable to feel empathy toward experiences of loss or personal violation. The individual's stories may arouse feelings of anger in you. Be sure that you don't pick up his offense. You are there to help the person get rid of his anger and bitterness. We have often consoled ourselves by remembering that there will be a day when Christ will bring justice to all.

If someone's story brings tears to your eyes, use the tissues yourself! Romans 12:15 tells us to "weep with those who weep." I'm not ashamed of that. I'm ashamed of myself when I don't care and empathize with the person's pain. But use discernment. Don't get bogged down in pity, because you know the resolution and healing you foresee.

As I mentioned earlier, I often say, "I'm so sorry that happened to you." But I don't say, "I know how you feel." After all, I cannot know exactly how the person feels, and to indicate that I do might bring a rebuttal. I try to sit silently and pray while the individual works through the list, because I want the process of forgiving to be only between God and that person. I openly share my own painful experiences when it is appropriate, but not during this time.

DEVELOP AN IDENTITY LIST

As the person you're helping works through his or her list, it is helpful to quietly make a "before and after" identity chart. Take a clean piece of paper and draw a line down the center of the page. At the top of the left column, write the words "Birth and Before Freedom Identity." At the top of the right column, write "In Christ Identity." (For a sample identity chart, see appendix C.)

While the person is working through the forgiveness list, listen for words that describe the beliefs he or she formed about him- or herself as a result of abuse. In the left-hand column, under the caption "Birth and Before Freedom Identity," record such words as: "dirty," "unloved," "abandoned," "not worth anything" and "can't do anything right." Especially record those words associated with the people of influence in their early years (mother, father, siblings, etc.). Those were the years when belief systems and behavior patterns were formed.

You may need to help them identify those feelings with the first few people on their lists. Some will do that quickly; others are just beginning to be in touch with their emotions. If they forgive an offense but seem to be at a loss for words, you could ask, "How did that offense make you feel about your value or character? How do you think that person felt about you then? How about now?"

Sometimes you will have a list of six or more descriptive emotions related to only one name on the forgiveness list. For emotions that you sense the person has deep pain, you may want to lead the person to pray: "Lord, I forgive (name) for causing me to feel (list feelings)." It's important to realize that the feelings were how the person *interpreted* the offense. They are not blaming the other person, but dealing with their own pain. However, since it's usually true that the perceptions they had of themselves as a result of childhood pain are repeated in their adult conflicts, they will probably forgive the same feelings over and over again.

When they have finished praying, you may choose to put that chart aside until the end of your session when you can explain it more carefully in the context of their identities in Christ. Or you may choose to now read the list of feelings that describe how they viewed themselves. The impact of hearing those words will help them see how they have allowed themselves to be victimized by lies. The following is an illustration you might want to use before reading the list:

> When you go to a store and buy a can or package of food off the shelf, it has a manufacturer's label describing the contents. As you and I go through life—the bad experiences, the things done to us, the things said to us, the wrong things we were involved in—Satan, the god of this world, is there with paper and pencil writing a label for our lives. But now that you are in Christ, you are no longer a product of your past; you are a product of the work of Christ on the cross. All the old labels of the world don't describe the contents of who you are anymore.

SPECIAL RENUNCIATIONS

If you are a beginner at leading people through the Steps, don't be intimidated by the following information. It is not imperative that you use it. As you become experienced, you will more readily discern where there are bondages, and this might be a time when you would lead them in one or several renunciations addressing the most significant lies they have believed about themselves and God. Some examples follow:

- For those who have been betrayed by a parent and transferred that mistrust to their heavenly Father: "Lord, I renounce the lies I've believed about You because of the way my earthly father treated me. I announce the truth that You are not like my earthly father. You are totally loving and faithful."
- For those who think they are responsible for holding their dysfunctional families together and for being a parent's emotional support: "Lord, I renounce the lie that I am responsible for being a savior to the people around me or that I must always be responsible for others by being the strong one. Thank you, Lord, that it's all right for me to be honest about my own need. Thank you that when I am weak, You are strong within me" (see 2 Cor. 12:9, *TLB*).
- For those who have been constantly put down by the authority figures in their lives: "Lord, I renounce the lie that I am unworthy and insignificant. I announce the truth that I am (name), your special child. Lord, and I am precious to You." Or "Lord, I renounce the lie that I am a helpless victim as I felt when I was a child. I announce the truth that I can do all things through Christ who strengthens me" (see Phil. 4:13).

Don't be concerned about exact wording. The Holy Spirit is the wonderful Counselor, and He will lead both you and the person you are helping to understand and know the truth.

SEEKING FORGIVENESS FROM OTHERS

Some are reluctant to forgive others because they believe they have to go to those people to discuss the issues. The prospect of facing their abusers is too traumatic to even consider. To forgive others, they only need to go to God.

They have confused the issue of forgiving others with the need to ask for forgiveness, which is spelled out in Matthew 5:23-26. The Lord requires us to go to others before we go to Him and seek reconciliation if we know that someone has something against us. In appendix A, I have given some specific instruction on how to do this.

The important thing to remember is that *if we have hurt someone else,* we need to go to that person first before we go to God. But *if we have been hurt* by others, we need to forgive them by going first, and in some cases only, to God. Forgiveness must precede reconciliation.

I believe God has forgiven all mankind, but not all have received that forgiveness, and therefore all are not reconciled to Him. "If possible, so far as it depends upon you, be at peace with all men" (Rom. 12:18), but it doesn't always depend upon you. You cannot be reconciled with someone who doesn't want to be reconciled. We want to see these people free from their abuses and their abusers. Reconciliation may come, and I would pray for it, but only if the abusers will own up to their abusive ways and honestly seek forgiveness. Always remember that the freedom of the abused is never contingent upon whether the abuser will own up to it. They must be willing to forgive from their hearts regardless of what the abuser does, or they will be controlled by their abusers all their lives.

A young missionary had worked through all our material and was helping others find their freedom in Christ. Then during a period of engagement to his future bride, he began to experience major spiritual difficulty. He went through the Steps on his own several times. Nothing he did seemed to help. I encouraged him to ask the Lord what was keeping him in bondage. When I asked him if there were some people he needed to go to and ask forgiveness, there was immediate confirmation.

READY TO MOVE ON

Forgiveness is often a draining experience, even for you and the prayer team. Spiritual strongholds have been identified and renounced. A major conflict has been resolved between the person you are working with and God, so Satan has no right to torment them anymore. They usually feel exhausted. You all may be a little weary, but a word of encouragement: A brief break, a stretch, a glass of water, and you are ready to go on to the next Step.

CHAPTER TEN

SURRENDERING TO GOD'S AUTHORITY

STEP FOUR: REBELLION VERSUS SUBMISSION

Jane came to her appointment thinking her greatest need was to resolve a relational issue in her family, but what surfaced during the Steps was an extremely abusive marriage that ended in divorce and then a remarriage into the same cycle of abuse. Her past training and the pressure of family and friends had taught and reinforced the belief that submission is being passive to physical and emotional abuse. Her strategy for survival was based on her own ability to cope.

Many of the people you help will come from abusive backgrounds, and most victims are women. Some make a conscious choice to never be pushed around again and become rebellious. Others spend the rest of their lives accommodating their abusers, hoping someday they will finally live up to their expectations and receive the acceptance and affirmation they believe they must have in order to be worthwhile people. I have asked hundreds of such people, "What if your mother or father never accepted you or gave you the affirmation you believe you need?" Both the rebel and the codependent must find their acceptance and identities in Christ, not the people around them.

WHO IS IN CONTROL?

While sharing the plan of salvation, one of our staff members asked a man, "Who would you say is in control of your life right now?"

"I am," the man replied, "and I like it that way."

God never designed our souls to function as masters. At any one time, we are either serving "mammon" or Jehovah God (see Matt. 6:24). But says the poet, "I am the master of my fate and the captain of my soul." Oh, no, you aren't! Self-seeking, self-serving, self-justifying, self-glorifying and self-centered living are in actuality serving the world, the flesh and the devil. And all the while we are being deceived into thinking we are serving self.

Denying ourselves is the way of the Cross. Saying no to ourselves and yes to God is the ultimate struggle in life. Believing we *are* God is to buy the biggest lie of all. It originated in the garden when Satan said, "You will be like God" (Gen. 3:5). Playing God is the biggest mistake we can make. It seems so sacrificial to surrender all to God, but what are you really sacrificing? You are sacrificing the lower life to gain the higher life. It seems to be the great ambition of man to be happy as animals instead of being blessed as children of God. You are sacrificing the pleasure of things to gain the pleasure of life.

What would you exchange for love, joy, peace, patience, kindness, goodness, faithfulness, gentleness and self-control? A new car? A better home? A higher position? The belief that those things will give you love, joy and peace is the lie of the world. You are sacrificing the temporal to gain the eternal. Some sacrifice! In reality, it is the magnificent defeat. Only when we come to the end of our resources do we discover His resources. Lordship is not a negative doctrine. If we make Him the Lord of our lives, He also becomes the Lord of our problems.

LEARN TO TRUST GOD

Beth was raised in a legalistic church-going family. When she met and married Todd, who was a Christian, she fully expected that her life would be satisfying and that he would be able to meet all of her needs. Her fantasy faded as her marriage failed. Disillusioned and angry with her parents and husband, Beth developed a deep distrust of God. This led to open rebellion and despair, dabbling in false religions and a worldly lifestyle.

She was given some of the Freedom in Christ books and tapes, but for months she was afraid to read them and listen to them. Through loving persuasion, she eventually ventured out to call one of our staff couples who befriended and encouraged her. Later, she was taken through the Steps to Freedom.

The changes in her life are beautiful to see. The rebellion is gone, and she says, "I feel like I'm in love." And she is in love...with the lover of her soul, Jesus. Before, she used to "make things happen" by controlling people or situations in the hope that her needs would be met. But she gave up her struggle for self-fulfillment, and now the Lord is filling her with a growing sense of peace and security. She says, "I no longer *want* the things I craved before; I just want to know Jesus better." She was encouraged to read *Living Free in Christ*, and she began to understand how Jesus meets the needs of our lives.

When we "take things into our own hands," we have the feeling of being in control. But what do we really control? When we were born? Who we were born to? When we will die? The circumstances of life? No, the only real control we have is deciding whom we will choose to follow and serve. Paradoxically, only when we surrender completely to God do we have self-control (see Gal. 5:23).

LIVING UNDER AUTHORITY

According to 1 Samuel 15:23, "Rebellion is as the sin of divination [witchcraft], and insubordination is as iniquity and idolatry." Defiance against authority places us in the camp of the enemy and subject to his influences. The god of this world, the prince of power of the air, is roaring around like a hungry lion seeking someone to devour. God says, "Get in ranks and follow Me. You are under My protection if you are under My authority." Satan was the originator of rebellion, so when we rebel, we are following his lead. If people truly understood the reality of the spiritual world and the choice they are making, they would immediately renounce any rebellion and submit to God.

We live in a rebellious age. Everyone sits in judgment of those who are in positions of authority over them. We go to church and critique the choir or the music instead of entering into the experience of worshiping God. We sit in judgment of the sermon instead of letting the sermon sit in judgment of us. How many times have you heard people coming out of church criticizing the music or the message? We bad-mouth our president, our governors, our pastors, our teachers, our spouses and our parents. I had an elder in my church years ago who was critical of everyone he knew and couldn't figure out why his children were all rebellious.

We are commanded by God to submit to and pray for those who are in authority over us. Romans 13:1,2 says, "Let every person be in subjection to the governing authorities. For there is no authority except from God, and those which exist are established by God. Therefore he who resists authority has opposed the ordinance of God; and they who have opposed will receive condemnation upon themselves." God's desire is that we yield ourselves to Him and demonstrate this allegiance by being submissive to those He placed in authority over us. We surrender our "right to rule" and trust God to work through His established lines of authority for our good. It is a great act of faith to trust God to work through less than perfect people.

Scripture does teach that there are times when we must obey God rather than man. When governing authorities require us to do something that God commands us not to do, or try to prevent us from doing something that God requires us to do, then we must obey God rather than man, as did the members of the Early Church (see Acts 5:29). We also have no obligation to obey people who try to exercise authority outside their jurisdictions. Your employer or school teacher has no right to tell you what to do in your own home. A policeman cannot tell you what to believe or where to go to church, but he can tell you to pull your car over.

RELATING TO AUTHORITY

Daniel is the epitome of submission, and by example he showed us how to respond to the king when he had overstepped his authority. First, don't be disrespectful of the king or of those who are carrying out the king's commands. Nebuchadnezzar wanted those who were in his service to eat the food he chose. Daniel made up his mind not to defile himself with the king's food so he sought permission from his immediate superior to eat as he thought God required. Because he was not defiant, nor disrespectful, "God granted Daniel favor and compassion in the sight of the commander of the officials" (Dan. 1:9). Daniel offered a creative alternative that allowed the commander to save face in the sight of the king and to also fulfill the wishes of the king to have wise and healthy servants.

The Lord's Prayer (Matt. 6:9-13) is a model for how we are to appeal to those who are in authority over us. First, we must have a right standing. "Our Father who art in heaven, hallowed be Thy name." In our judicial system, we must approach the judge in a court of law with respect. It would be considered contempt of court if we didn't. We humbly address the judge as "Your honor."

If there are any unresolved personal issues between yourself and the one you wish to make an appeal to, you better get them resolved first. That is true for our God as well as judges in our courts of law. We couldn't approach God until He found a way to forgive us, and any judge who is personally biased toward the accused must remove himself from the case. If a teenager has been disrespectful and disobedient to his father, he better get that straightened out before he asks for the keys to the car.

Second, we must be committed to authorities' success and do their will. "Thy kingdom come. Thy will be done, on earth as it is in heaven" (v. 10). We need to be committed to the success of those in authority over us and to do nothing that would hinder them from carrying out their God-given responsibilities. No person in leadership can accomplish much without the loyal support of those who are under him. And those who are in a support role will not prosper in their rebellion. Scripture says, "Obey your leaders, and submit to them; for they keep watch over your souls, as those who will give an account. Let them do this with joy and not with grief, for this would be unprofitable for you" (Heb. 13:17).

One of Satan's more potent strategies is to discredit spiritual leaders. I will guarantee you that your loyalty to those who are in authority over you will be tested. Nowhere is this more true than in Christian ministries and in the home. Everybody will be tempted with subtle seed thoughts such as: *I don't like the way he did that; I could do it better than that; This is what I would do if I were in that position,* or *I'm the one who should be running the show around here.* Whether those thoughts come from the pit, from other disloyal members or from your own flesh, consider the following words from James 3:13-18:

> Who among you is wise and understanding? Let him show by his good behavior his deeds in the gentleness of wisdom. But if you have bitter jealousy and selfish ambition in your heart, do not be arrogant and so lie against the truth. This wisdom is not that which comes down from above, but is earthly, natural, demonic. For where jealousy and selfish ambition exist, there is disorder and every evil thing. But the wisdom from above is first pure, then peaceable, gentle, reasonable, full of mercy and good fruits, unwavering, without hypocrisy. And the seed whose fruit is righteousness is sown in peace by those who make peace.

Most leaders will listen to our appeals if they know we are concerned for their responsibilities and their reputations. The Lord withheld judgment upon the Israelites when Moses petitioned Him. He based his appeal on the reputation of God (see Num. 14:11-19). God can only bless us if we are submissive (see 1 Tim. 2:1,2), and in doing so, we find favor with God (see 1 Pet. 2:18-20). Life will always be more difficult if the one we are serving is failing in his responsibility. Every passage that commands us to be submissive ends in a promise for the ones who are—and condemnation for those who aren't.

Third, our appeals must be based on legitimate needs. "Give us this day our daily bread" (Matt. 6:11). Every leader is subject to the needs of those he serves, and the Lord will bring conviction upon those who do not hear the legitimate cries of their people. However, requests for selfish desires may justifiably go unanswered. Few things can turn off a parent more than an ungrateful child who demands more than what is needed.

Fourth, our appeals must come from hearts that are free from bitterness. "And forgive us our debts, as we also have forgiven our debtors" (v. 12). Anyone who has allowed a root of bitterness to spring up and defile others should not expect favor from those who are in authority. When Simon requested authority from the apostles, Peter refused saying, "You are in the gall of bitterness and in the bondage of iniquity" (Acts 8:23).

Fifth, our appeals should be for proper direction in life. "And do not lead us into temptation, but deliver us from evil" (Matt. 6:13). Every human institution has been given its authority by God "for the punishment of evildoers and the praise of those who do right" (1 Pet. 2:14).

TRUST GOD'S PROTECTION

The second principle that we should learn from Daniel is to trust God to protect us and provide for us when we cannot in good conscience do what the king commands. King Darius was persuaded to "establish a statute and enforce an injunction that anyone who makes a petition to any god or man besides you, O king, for thirty days, shall be cast into the lions' den" (Dan. 6:7). Daniel could not honor that decree and continued to pray and give thanks to almighty God (see v. 10). He ended up in the lions' den, and you know the rest of the story.

If your boss wants you to lie, don't be disrespectful. Appeal to him or her as outlined above and offer an alternative. What if the boss won't take your suggestion and says, "If you won't do what I tell you to do, then I will get someone in here who will"? Then let him or her get someone who will, and trust God to provide you with another way out of the situation or another place to make a living.

DEAL WITH ABUSE

What if the authority figure is abusive? Is it being rebellious to turn him in? Absolutely not! It sickens me when I hear of Christian leaders who tell battered wives and abused children to go home and be submissive. "But that is what Scripture requires," says the abuser. That is not all Scripture says on the issue. God has established governing institutions to protect battered wives and abused children. The heart of God goes out to the weak and the defenseless. The Church should be the first to respond. "This is pure and undefiled religion in the sight of our God and Father, to visit orphans and widows in their distress" (Jas. 1:27).

Turn the abusers in to the authorities whom God has established. I say this for two reasons: First, abusive leaders have obviously abdicated their responsibility to provide for and protect those whom they were charged by God to watch over. Being abused by the one in authority over you is double jeopardy. Not only are you being abused, but you have also lost your God-intended protection.

Second, it never does abusers any good to be allowed to continue in their abuses. They are hurting people who need help. If they aren't stopped, the cycle of abuse will just continue on. I'm not taking this stand because I want revenge. I strongly take this position because I also care for the abusers. They have a right to find their forgiveness and freedom in Christ like anybody else, but they won't if they are allowed to continue on. If you were abused by your father, and your mother knew about it but wouldn't do anything to help you, who would be harder to forgive? I think it would be the mother.

When a person has forgiven an abusive authority figure, help him or her set up scriptural boundaries that will stop the cycle of abuse. A word of caution: I am not saying that we don't have to be submissive to any human authority simply because they are not perfect. If that were the case, nobody would be submissive to anyone but God. What I am saying is that there is a biblical means by which we can appeal to those less-than-perfect people who are in authority, and there are times when we must obey God rather than man. Determining when to reject man's authority requires discernment and a deep inner conviction based on truth that cannot be compromised regardless of the consequences. You are acting rebelliously if you refuse to submit simply because you would prefer to do it your way.

THE MEANING OF SUBMISSION

Because of abusive authority and legalistic teaching, the term "submission" has a negative connotation for many people. To them, a submissive person is a doormat who never questions those in authority. Some accept the doormat role and identity, while others deeply resent all authority figures, including God. But God is not like the authority figures who were abusive. He has our best interests at heart. Submitting to His will and His way is the only means by which we can have any sense of social order. Little would be accomplished in our marriages, families, churches, businesses and governments without some authoritative structure. When none exists, there can only be anarchy. The authority of God provides for the peaceful coexistence of His people, who are called to live and work together.

In Ephesians 5:21, before Paul instructs wives to be submissive to their husbands, he says that we are all (both men and women) to "be subject to one another in the fear of Christ." This means that all Christians are to be "willing to cooperate" in their relationships under God-given authority structures. Everybody is under the authority of somebody or something, and we are all subject to the needs of one another, because we are all called to love one another.

SUBMISSION, REBELLION AND THE SEARCH FOR SIGNIFICANCE

What do Paul and Peter mean when they call for wives to be submissive to their husbands (see Eph. 5:21-24; 1 Pet. 3:1-6)? Why do some women rebel against the idea of submission? Why do some men abuse the authority God has given them in the home? Why do Peter and Paul remind men of their responsibility to lovingly meet the needs of their wives (see Eph. 5:25-33; 1 Pet. 3:7)? These are difficult and critical questions encountered when treading into the minefield of role relationships in marriage. Much of the confusion and virtually all of the emotional energy that fuels the debate comes from buying into a wrong view of the source of our identities and significance. People tend to get their identities from the things they do and their significance from their positions and titles. They wrongly conclude that having an authoritative position and the control of others equals significance.

Our identities are not determined by what we do; they are determined by who we are in Christ. It is not what we do that determines who we are; it is who we are that determines what we do. Before coming to Christ, we did get our identities from our professions and positions in the natural order of things. But now that we are in Christ, "There is neither Jew nor Greek, there is neither slave nor free man, there is neither male nor female; for you are all one in Christ Jesus" (Gal. 3:28). This passage does not eradicate social roles or eliminate authoritative structure. It clearly teaches that our essential identities are in Christ, and we are to live out our roles in life as children of God. Our significance is not determined by our positions in this life but by our positions in Christ. When the mother of the sons of Zebedee was trying to get her sons seated next to Christ, our Lord used the occasion to instruct us concerning positions of ministry. "You know that the rulers of the Gentiles lord it over them, and their great men exercise authority over them. It is not so among you, but whoever wishes to become great among you shall be your servant, and whoever wishes to be first among you shall be your slave" (Matt. 20:25-27). Every leader is subject to the needs of those who serve under him. Headship is not a right to be demanded; it is an awesome responsibility.

IDENTITY DETERMINES SIGNIFICANCE

The world says you are nothing, therefore you better scheme, achieve and get ahead by employing devious methods such as malice, guile, hypocrisy, envy and slander (see 1 Pet. 2:1). The Bible tells us that we are something, therefore we should be submissive (see vv. 2-17). The scriptural commands concerning roles in relationships are given in a context where the significance question has already been settled by our identities and positions in Christ.

> But you are a chosen race, a royal priesthood, a holy nation, a people for God's own possession, that you may proclaim the excellencies of Him who has called you out of darkness into His marvelous light; for you once were not a people, but now you are the people of God; you had not received mercy, but now you have received mercy (vv. 9,10).

For both Paul and Peter, our significance flows from our true identities, which are not dependent on some role in a human relationship (see Eph. 1:3—2:10).

So the correct formula is: our position in Christ and identities as children of God equals significance. If a wife's sense of significance flows from her relationship with God, she can respond to her husband's leadership because in fact she is equally significant in God's plan for her personally, her marriage and her family. As a man I don't need to demand respect or "lord it over" others to have any sense of worth. I am already significant as a child of God and secure in Christ. I am free to be the true servant-leader God calls me to be. The fruit of the Spirit is not spouse control, nor child control; it is self-control. Both the husband and wife can respond with grace to a less-than-perfect spouse, because they don't need the other person to meet their need for significance (see 1 Pet. 3:8-12).

Submission, authority and control concern not only man/wife issues, or parent/child issues, or employer/employee issues. Submission is primarily a relational matter between the creature and the Creator. When we know who we are as children of God, we don't have to rebel, we don't have to dominate and control. We yield to the Lordship of Christ, secure in our position in Him, and relate to others with love and forgiveness.

DEALING WITH REBELLION

God's order is: "Submit therefore to God. Resist the devil and he will flee from you" (Jas. 4:7). Submitting to God enables us to resist the devil. The prayer that begins this Step is a commitment to forsake rebellion and choose a submissive spirit, as follows:

> Dear heavenly Father,
>   You have said that rebellion is as the sin of witchcraft and "insubordination is as iniquity and idolatry" (1 Sam. 15:23). I know that in action and attitude I have sinned against You with a rebellious heart. I ask Your forgiveness for my rebellion and pray that by the shed blood of the Lord Jesus Christ all ground gained by evil spirits because of my rebelliousness will be canceled. I pray that You will shed light on all my ways that I may know the full extent of my rebelliousness. I now choose to adopt a submissive spirit and a servant's heart. In the name of Christ Jesus, my Lord. Amen.

AREAS OF REBELLION

When the person you are helping has finished praying, you can call to his or her attention the list of possible areas of rebellion and ask her to place a check by any that apply:

- Civil government (see Rom. 13:1-7; 1 Tim. 2:1-4; 1 Pet. 2:13-17);
- Parents (see Eph. 6:1-3);
- Husband (see 1 Pet. 3:1-4);

- Employer (see 1 Pet. 2:18-23);
- Church leaders (see Heb. 13:17);
- God (see Dan. 9:5,9).

It won't be necessary for the individual to explain the acts of rebellion to you. You have heard his or her story and know most of his or her issues already. He or she does need to know that rebellion is not just an act, it is an attitude. Some may be standing up on the outside but sitting down on the inside.

If you are counseling a man, you may want to suggest that he consider whether he may have been defiant or rebellious toward his wife. We are to "submit to one another," and a husband should be listening to what God might want to say to him through his wife and his children. In some instances, a wife may have a more discerning spirit toward God than he does. The common phrase in our ministry uses is, "Men, listen to your wives." In a similar fashion, children often pick up things that parents overlook.

CHOOSING TO BE SUBMISSIVE

The next prayer is an opportunity for the person to submit these areas of rebellion to God:

Lord, I agree I have been rebellious toward _____.
Please forgive me for this rebellion. I choose to be submissive
and obedient to your Word. In Jesus' name. Amen.

As in Step Two, the person doesn't have to repeat the prayer for each item. When the person comes to the blank, he or she should read the things that were checked and then complete the prayer.

Be careful that the individual doesn't brush over any deep roots of rebellion. This Step may require more counseling to help the person live under authority, especially if there is a long history of rebellion or authoritative abuse. Learning to be assertive will be difficult for a person who has been passive for years, as learning to be submissive will be for those with a rebellious nature.

UNCOVERING ABUSE

A distinction needs to be made between spiritually setting oneself free by asking forgiveness for a rebellious spirit and taking responsible action against abuse or harassment. Offering forgiveness does not mean that the person should remain in an abusive situation or that he or she should refrain from seeking professional counsel or legal protection if necessary.

If you discover that the person you are helping is presently experiencing abuse or harassment, assure her or him that you will talk further on this issue after you complete the Steps. Issues of Abuse are discussed in appendix D.

CHAPTER ELEVEN

RELYING ON THE LORD

STEP FIVE: PRIDE VERSUS HUMILITY

In the northern reaches of Canada, an old story is told of two geese and a turtle who developed a deep friendship. As the nights became shorter and cooler, the geese started talking about flying south for the winter. One evening as the three animals huddled together, the geese wondered openly about their friend the turtle.

"We're sure going to miss you," said one goose. "Since you can't walk south for the winter, what are you going to do?"

"I have an idea," said the turtle. "Why don't we find a sturdy stick that the two of you can hold in your mouths. I will hold on to the stick in the middle with my powerful teeth. Then when you fly south for the winter, I will fly with you."

"Do you think you are strong enough to hold on for that long?" asked the other goose.

"Sure, I'm very strong," said the turtle.

Several weeks later, somewhere in Montana, a farmer looked up and saw the most incredible thing he had ever seen. He rushed into the house to tell his wife. When she ran outside and saw these two geese flying overhead with a stick in their mouths and a turtle hanging between them, she cried out, "What an incredible idea! Who thought of that?"

The turtle made the unfortunate mistake of saying, "I did! It was my idea!" And down...down...down...went the turtle.

THE UGLY FIVE-LETTER WORD

Pride is a killer. It comes before a fall. Pride is an ugly five-lettered word with

I in the middle. Pride says, "It was my idea, and I can do it in my own power." Pride is the origin of evil.

Scripture says of Satan, "But you said in your heart, *'I will* ascend to heaven; *I will* raise my throne above the stars of God, and *I will* sit on the mount of assembly in the recesses of the north. *I will* ascend above the heights of the clouds; *I will* make myself like the Most High.' Nevertheless you will be thrust down to Sheol, to the recesses of the pit" (Isa. 14:13-15, emphasis added). Hell is where we say, "My will be done." Heaven is where we say, "Thy will be done."

Notice the connection between pride and spiritual warfare in the following two passages:

> But He gives a greater grace. Therefore it says, "God is opposed to the proud, but gives grace to the humble." Submit therefore to God. Resist the devil and he will flee from you (Jas. 4:6,7).
>
> All of you, clothe yourselves with humility toward one another, for God is opposed to the proud, but gives grace to the humble. Humble yourselves, therefore, under the mighty hand of God, that He may exalt you at the proper time, casting all your anxiety upon Him, because He cares for you. Be of sober spirit, be on the alert. Your adversary, the devil, prowls about like a roaring lion, seeking someone to devour. But resist him (1 Pet. 5:5-9).

SELF-SUFFICIENCY HAS A PRICE

After Jesus fed the 5,000, He sent the disciples across the Sea of Galilee while He went up to the mountain to pray. In the middle of the sea, the disciples encountered a storm: "And seeing them straining at the oars...He came to them, walking on the sea; and He intended to pass by them" (Mark 6:48). I believe the Lord intends to pass by the self-sufficient. Go ahead and row, He will let you.

The only answer the world has for those who are caught in the midst of the storms of life is "Row harder!" The devil says, "You can do it by yourself, but if you need a little extra power, I can arrange that for a small price." Pride says, "I think I can get out of this by myself. All it requires is a lot of hard work, human ingenuity, and maybe a little luck." God says, "I won't interfere with your plans. If you want to try to save yourself, solve your own problems or meet your own needs, you have My permission. But you won't be able to, because in the final analysis, you absolutely need Me, and you necessarily need each other." All humanity is on a sinking ship that is going nowhere without God.

Pride can sneak up on the best of us. King Uzziah was a godly man who reigned for 52 years (see 2 Chron. 26:3), and "he did right in the sight of the Lord" (v. 4). His accomplishments were exceptional. He built a strong army and fortified the city. "Hence his fame spread afar, for he was marvelously helped until he was strong. But when he became strong, his heart was so proud that he acted corruptly, and he was unfaithful to the Lord his God" (vv. 15,16).

The more we are able to accomplish by the grace of God, the more susceptible we are to pride. More than one Christian leader has fallen when he started receiving glowing accolades. "Therefore let him who thinks he stands take heed lest he fall" (1 Cor. 10:12).

FALSE AND TRUE HUMILITY

What is humility? Is it groveling around in poverty, proclaiming our worthless state? No, that is counterfeit humility that leads only to defeat. Paul says, "Let no one keep defrauding you of your prize by delighting in self-abasement" (Col. 2:18).

Is humility proclaiming that God is everything and we are nothing? No, that is another form of false humility. Christ didn't go to the cross for nothing. He was crucified to establish and build up a fallen humanity. Throughout the New Testament, we are admonished to build up one another, and we are strongly warned against any attempt to tear down one another.

Paul tells us, "For through the grace given to me I say to every man among you not to think more highly of himself than he ought to think; but to think so as to have sound judgment, as God has allotted to each a measure of faith" (Rom. 12:3). That is not a call for self-abasement; it is a call for sound judgment. Paul says of himself, "By the grace of God I am what I am, and His grace toward me did not prove vain; but I labored even more than all of them, yet not I, but the grace of God with me" (1 Cor. 15:10).

All of us are what we are by the grace of God! To deny that would be to discredit the work that Christ accomplished on the cross. To believe that we are more than we are, or to believe that we are products of our own doing, is to join the ranks of the deceived millions who have fallen victim to pride. Humility is confidence properly placed. So Paul says, "Put no confidence in the flesh" (Phil. 3:3). But we ought to have all the confidence that our faith can muster in God and in what He can do through us. I personally want myself and every child of God to reach the highest potential in Christ. "By this is my Father glorified, that you bear much fruit, and so prove to be my disciples" (John 15:8). Pride says, "I did it." True humility says, "I did it by the grace of God."

Cowering in some corner in unbelief or groveling around in mock humility in utter defeat brings no glory to God. Instead, you should, "Let your light shine before men in such a way that they may see your good works, and glorify your Father who is in heaven" (Matt. 5:16).

The glory of God is a manifestation of His presence. When we glorify God in our bodies, we manifest His presence in the world. The only way we can do that is to live victorious lives and bear much fruit. And the only way we can do that is to abide in Christ (see John 15:5). That is why we are trying to help people come to terms with their prides—so they can be established in Christ, "in whom we have boldness and confident access through faith in Him" (Eph. 3:12).

AVENUES OF PRIDE

We come from diverse backgrounds, but pride, rebellion and self-will are consequences of the Fall and common to all humanity. The whole aim of Satan is to get self-interest recognized as the chief end of man. Satan is called the "prince of this world" because self-interest rules this world. The iniquity that is passed on from one generation to another is a distortion of, and preoccupation with, self-will. This is the chief characteristic of the false prophet and teacher. Peter says they "indulge the flesh in its corrupt desires and despise authority. Daring, self-willed, they do not tremble when they revile angelic majesties" (2 Pet. 2:10). They operate from independent spirits and won't answer to anyone. An even more sober scenario is given in Matthew 7:20-23:

> So then, you will know them by their fruits. Not everyone who says to Me, "Lord, Lord," will enter the kingdom of heaven; but he who does the will of My Father who is in heaven. Many will say to Me on that day, "Lord, Lord, did we not prophesy in Your name, and in Your name cast out demons, and in Your name perform

many miracles?" And then I will declare to them, "I never knew you; depart from Me, you who practice lawlessness [iniquity]."

Strongholds of pride are not only passed on from one generation to the next, but each new generation will develop its own basis for pride by seeking fame and fortune in the worldly system in which it is raised. Self-glorification can come by accumulating wealth, garnering social status, acquiring academic degrees and even obtaining biblical knowledge. There is nothing wrong with having wealth, social status, academic degrees or biblical knowledge—if they are obtained by the grace of God for the purpose of doing His will.

Pride is the chief characteristic of the world: "For everything in the world—the cravings of sinful man, the lust of his eyes and the boasting of what he has and does—comes not from the Father but from the world" (1 John 2:16, NIV). All temptation is an attempt to get us to live our lives independent of God. Under such temptation, people unwittingly serve the world, the flesh or the devil. They have been deceived into thinking they are benefiting themselves, but such temporal gratification quickly fades away. Jesus counters by sharing the way of the Cross, the foundational principle for our lives in Christ, which is the repudiation of the old natural life and embracing the new joyful union with the resurrected life of Christ.

Though the immediate evidence of pride is self-centeredness, the root of pride is self-exaltation. It is at this point that we are most like the god of this world. Though no legitimate Christian would identify with such blatant blasphemy, self-exaltation expressed by subtle attitudes of pride and self-righteousness will keep a person from humbly admitting the need for Christ's righteousness. Such pride is an open invitation to the god of this world, which may render impossible the ability to carry out even the best of our intentions. Notice how this proved to be true in the life of Peter.

Jesus said to Peter, "Simon, Simon, behold, Satan has demanded permission to sift you like wheat; but I have prayed for you, that your faith may not fail; and you, when once you have turned again, strengthen your brothers" (Luke 22:31,32). Notice that Jesus didn't say He would not permit Satan to sift Peter like wheat. He just said He would pray for him, and afterward Peter was to help others.

What right did Satan have to ask permission of God? The previous context reveals that a dispute had arisen among the apostles regarding who was the greatest (see v. 24). Such pride can coexist with the best of intentions. Peter said, "Lord, with You I am ready to go both to prison and to death!" (v. 33). Sadly, he had already forfeited his right. Before the cock crowed, Peter denied his Lord three times.

A BIBLICAL VIEW OF OUR WORTH

A proper sense of self-worth comes from recognizing and appropriating the biblical fact that we are loved and valued by our heavenly Father. Our value is not based on our own merit but on the fact that we are His precious children for whom Christ was willing to die. We are blessed with every spiritual blessing...chosen in God...holy and blameless before Him...predestined to adoption as sons...have redemption and forgiveness...the riches of His grace are lavished on us (see Eph. 1:3-14).

The problem is not that we don't have tremendous riches in Christ; the problem is we don't see them. So Paul says, "I pray that the eyes of your heart may be enlightened, so that you may know what is the hope of His calling, what are the riches of the glory of His inheritance in the saints" (v. 18).

GOING THROUGH STEP FIVE

The flow from Step Four to Step Five is generally smooth, since you will have already dealt with pride from the standpoint of control and rebellion in Step Four. The two Steps are closely linked because the source of a rebellious attitude is often in pride. To introduce this Step, it is sufficient to simply paraphrase or read the paragraph preceding the prayer in appendix F.

If necessary, you may choose to briefly explain the need to face the issue of pride by saying something like:

"God is opposed to the proud, but gives grace to the humble" (Jas. 4:6). By acknowledging pride, we are declaring what Satan refused to declare—that we are totally dependent upon God. By exposing and confessing pride, we are acknowledging our desire to be free from the self-life. Then we will be free to begin living by grace and deriving our spiritual strengths and identities from God, through Christ.

The person you are helping then prays as follows:

Dear heavenly Father,
     You have said that pride goes before destruction and an arrogant spirit before stumbling (Prov. 16:18). I confess that I have lived independently and have not denied myself, picked up my

cross daily, and followed You (Matt. 16:24). In so doing, I have given ground to the enemy in my life. I have believed that I could be successful and live victoriously by my own strength and resources.

I now confess that I have sinned against You by placing my will before Yours and by centering my life around self instead of You. I now renounce the self-life and by so doing cancel all the ground that has been gained in my members by the enemies of the Lord Jesus Christ. I pray that You will guide me so that I will do nothing from selfishness or empty conceit, but with humility of mind I will regard others as more important than myself (Phil. 2:3). Enable me through love to serve others and in honor prefer others (Rom. 12:10). I ask this in the name of Christ Jesus my Lord. Amen.

ACKNOWLEDGING SPECIFIC AREAS OF PERSONAL PRIDE

After praying this prayer, the person then has the opportunity to check areas of pride that may be present in his or her life. You may want to prepare him or her by saying something like this:

> The Lord may bring several things to your mind that rob you of the blessings of God because of pride. In addition, here is a list of some of the more common ways that people choose to live their lives independent of God by trusting in their own wisdom and resources. Most of us have done each of these things at certain times in our lives, but just identify the ones that may be a tendency in your life, a stronghold that would keep you in bondage to self and pride instead of humbly drawing on God's resources.

Then wait quietly while the individual checks those areas that apply. (Some leaders choose to read the statements aloud.)

__ Stronger desire to do my will than God's will
__ More dependent upon my strengths and resources than God's
__ Sometimes believe that my ideas and opinions are better than others'

__ More concerned about controlling others than developing
self-control
__ Sometimes consider myself more important than others
__ Tendency to think that I have no needs
__ Find it difficult to admit that I was wrong
__ Tendency to be more of a people pleaser than a God pleaser
__ Overly concerned about getting the credit I deserve
__ Driven to obtain the recognition that comes from degrees,
titles, positions and so on
__ Often think I am more humble than others
__ Other ways I may have thought more highly of myself than
I should

It's important to allow people to take whatever time is needed, but they
shouldn't feel they have to explain their pasts for your benefit. Subjective
people may have difficulty here as with the other lists, debating whether
they should check an item or not, seeming incapable of deciding. Help them
stay focused by reading a statement, and then encourage them to go with
their first impressions, trusting God in the process.

When they have finished checking the issues that apply to their lives, ask
them to pray the short prayer that follows, committing those areas of pride
to God. As before, they may pray the prayer only once. When they come
to the blank, they should read the list of things they checked, and then complete the prayer.

Lord, I agree I have been prideful in the area of _____.
Please forgive me for this pridefulness. I choose to humble
myself and place all my confidence in You. Amen.

HEALING FOLLOWS HUMILITY

The following letter, which we received from a man who was caught in a
sexual addiction, is a powerful illustration of the truth of James 4:6, "God is
opposed to the proud, but gives grace to the humble." It is a humbling thing
to share such personal problems, but he wasn't about to let pride keep him
from his freedom. He wrote:

Realizing that I needed to be accountable to someone and to
bring these urges to "light," so as to break their power over me,
I shared these feelings with my wife and the men in my Bible

study group, so they could pray for me and hold me accountable.

They were all very supportive, though a little shaken that someone in ministry would share such a personal matter with them. I expressed that I am only a brother in Christ and not superior to them in any way, and that if we were ever to be of one mind and one accord, we would need to be open with one another.

I must admit that it was easy to be open, because *I know who I am in Christ*. I believe now that this temptation will soon be a thing of the past. My past no longer has a hold on me. I am accountable to others, and I have prayer partners. Victory is mine!

CHAPTER TWELVE

BREAKING THE CHAINS

STEP SIX: BONDAGE VERSUS FREEDOM

Suppose you were a guardian angel and could see the spiritual battle going on for the souls of mankind. In your observation, you see a brooding angelic figure of the other kind lurking outside the door of a young Christian named Danny.

Brilliantly disguised as an angel of light, this demon subtly suggests that Danny open the door to sin: *Why don't you take a peek at that* Playboy *magazine? You know you want to. You will get away with it. Who would know? Everybody else does it.*

The Spirit of God within Danny brings immediate conviction and offers a way of escape. Also within Danny is an appetite for food and sex, as well as preprogrammed thought patterns, which operate independently of God. The flesh or old nature in Danny wants to be satisfied and offers an argument against the Spirit of God: *What's wrong with looking at pornography anyway? After all, who created me to have all these desires? Wasn't it God? How could He create me a certain way and then condemn me for it?*

The battle in the mind is intense, "For the flesh sets its desire against the Spirit, and the Spirit against the flesh; for these are in opposition to one another" (Gal. 5:17). But Danny failed to take the way of escape by "taking every thought captive to the obedience of Christ" (2 Cor. 10:5). At first, the pictures are a delight to the eyes, and the body responds with a euphoric explosion of feelings. But the pleasure is only for a moment, because "each one is tempted when he is carried away and enticed by his own lust. Then when lust has conceived, it gives birth to sin; and when sin is accomplished, it brings forth death" (Jas. 1:14,15).

CONSEQUENCES TO WRONG CHOICES

The brooding figure takes advantage of the open door, because Danny acted independently of God by choosing to sin. Satan's role as the tempter changes immediately to the role of the accuser: "You will never get away with this. How can you call yourself a Christian and do what you do? You're pathetic!"

With a conscience that is overcome by guilt, Danny cries out to God, "Lord, forgive me, I'll never do it again." Two days later, Danny sins again, which precipitates another cry for forgiveness. As the downward spiral of sin, confess, sin, confess and sin again continues, another pathetic event takes place. Danny is caught in his sin by another "Christian," who knows nothing of compassion.

Instead of responding as a minister of reconciliation, he joins with the brooding figure in a "ministry" of condemnation.

"You're sick!" he says to Danny. "How can you do that and call yourself a Christian? You're an embarrassment to the Church. You better confess it and beg God's forgiveness."

Little does he know that Danny is already forgiven by God and that he has asked for forgiveness a hundred times before. His merciless and insensitive response will only drive Danny to greater depths of despair. The world, the flesh and the devil have brought another saint to his knees. How does one break this cycle of defeat? Is confession enough?

To confess means to agree with God or to walk in the light as He is in the light (see 1 John 1:5-9). It is the critical first step in repentance. We must agree with God and face the truth, but that alone will not deal with sin's entrapment. You have submitted to God, if the confession was genuine and accompanied by a commitment to do His will, but you haven't yet resisted the devil (see Jas. 4:7).

Complete repentance means to submit to God, resist the devil and close the door. The door will be closed when all the bondages have been broken and all the mental strongholds have been torn down. The latter includes renouncing the lies we have believed that contributed to the sinful behavior, and then choosing the truth. This Step is intended to break the bondages and tear down the strongholds, making possible the process of renewing their minds.

RESPONDING TO THOSE CAUGHT IN SIN

I wish I could say that the Church has not committed the same tragic error of the insensitive person who accused Danny. How we should respond to those who are caught in sin is spelled out in 2 Corinthians 5:16-20:

> Therefore from now on we recognize no man according to the flesh;....Therefore if any man is in Christ, he is a new creature; the old things passed away; behold, new things have come. Now all these things are from God, who reconciled us to Himself through Christ, and gave us the ministry of reconciliation, namely, that God was in Christ reconciling the world to Himself, not counting their trespasses against them, and He has committed to us the word of reconciliation. Therefore, we are ambassadors for Christ, as though God were entreating through us; we beg you on behalf of Christ, be reconciled to God.

Several critical issues stand out from this passage. First, these people are new creatures in Christ; they are children of God. They are supposed to consider themselves "to be dead to sin, but alive to God in Christ Jesus" (Rom. 6:11). But they almost never do. Their perceptions of themselves are extremely negative, and they are ignorant of their positions in Christ.

I asked a middle-aged lady, "How do you perceive yourself?"

"I'm evil," she said.

"You're not evil," I responded. "You are a child of God."

Others have said, "I just hate myself" or "I'm no good." These people have been victimized by the accuser of the brethren.

I become deeply troubled when I see self-righteous (pharisaic and legalistic) "Christians" going after another brother or sister in Christ. Why are we joining ranks with the accuser of the brethren when, in fact, Romans 8:1 says, "There is therefore now no condemnation for those who are in Christ Jesus"? Why are we counting their trespasses against them when even Jesus doesn't? What sickness lies within us that wants to expose the sins of others, when Scripture says, "Hatred stirs up strife, but love covers all transgressions" (Prov. 10:12)?

The fact that the Christian's ministry is reconciliation, not condemnation, is the second gem that must be mined from the 2 Corinthians passage. Notice the first practical application that follows after the admonition to live the Spirit-filled life: "Let us not become boastful, challenging one another, envying one another....Brethren, even if a man is caught in any trespass, you who are spiritual, restore such a one in a spirit of gentleness; each one looking to yourself, lest you too be tempted" (Gal. 5:26—6:1). The ministry of a spiritual Christian is reconciliation and restoration. If that is not your motive in confronting another person in regard to sin, then it is best that you do nothing at all.

The charge to be ambassadors for Christ is the third nugget that must be panned from the above passage. We don't speak or minister to others on our own behalves; we do so as representatives of Christ, "as though God were entreating through us" (2 Cor. 5:20).

The fact that Jesus dined with sinners brought judgment upon Him from the religious community. Have you ever noticed from the gospels that sinners loved to be around Jesus, and He waged war against the hypocrites? Today, the Church is accused of being full of hypocrites, and sinners stay away. That is not totally true in most cases, but there is enough truth in the statement to cause us to weep before God. Only an ambassador for Christ whom God can work through will be effective in helping people through this Step.

THE EFFECTS OF ADDICTION

People caught in addictive and immoral patterns of behavior are subjected to some of the cruelest harassment of the enemy. First, Satan tempts them to sin, then he mercilessly condemns them for sinning, and then he attacks their senses of worth. A common statement heard in recovery groups is, "Don't pay attention to that committee in your head." If you are working with those who are in bondage to sex, alcohol or drugs, I strongly encourage you to read *A Way of Escape* and my forthcoming book on recovery in Christ. These two books give the biblical basis for breaking the bondages and tearing down the strongholds of sex and substance abuse, and they include many illustrations and practical applications.

Sincere Christians who are unable to break free from their sins often question their salvation, wondering if they really are new creations in Christ and if the Holy Spirit really does live within them. But if they weren't Christians, why would these moral issues even bother them, and why would they be seeking help from the Church? But many think they have committed the unpardonable sin.

If they have never been exposed or caught, their sins remain dark secrets that even their closest companions may not know (perhaps having had an abortion, homosexual tendencies, child abuse, incest or molestation). They attempt to cope by living lies and remaining in continual states of denial, disregarding the gravity of their sins and the power the sins have over them. Some have rationalized their sins for years. Some alcoholics say to themselves, "I can stop any time I want to." But the only way they could prove it to anybody else is by stopping. Some are leaders in churches or communities. The possibility of exposure is very threatening to them. They believe there is too much to lose to walk in the light, so they live with the deception that it is more painful and damaging to tell the truth than to maintain a lie. Some are so discouraged that they have resigned themselves to live in bondage, hang on until the rapture and hope God's forgiveness will prevail in the end. In desperation, many ask the question Paul raised: "Who will set me free from the body of this death?" (Rom. 7:24). Paul answers his own question in the next verse: "Thanks be to God through Jesus Christ our Lord!" There *is* hope and a way of escape for the person who is willing to face the truth and walk in the light.

No Condemnation

These people do not need any more condemnation! Most really want to be free. Nobody likes to live in bondage, but they are desperately fearful of rejection. Church leaders fear losing their positions or their credibility.

As you help people through the Steps to Freedom, you'll find that this Step is the most difficult for people to be totally honest about and the most embarrassing. So it is important not to register shock or come across with a judgmental attitude.

After coming to terms with one sexual sin after another, one lady said, "Oh, I forgot you're here. What do you think of me?"

I said, "I love you for what you have just shared."

What a relief it was for her—and everyone—to discover that she had finally found a safe place where she could deal with hidden sins without the fear of rejection. What a joy it is for us to see the hope in people's faces when they begin to understand that resolution is possible, and they no longer have to be mastered by sin.

It is important to emphasize again that as you go through the Steps, it is not simply saying the words and praying the prayers that brings freedom. It is what the individuals do in their relationships with God during the process. Jesus is the Bondage Breaker who brings freedom as they honestly connect with Him.

Going Through Step Six

You can introduce this Step simply by reading the material preceding the opening prayer. The person you are helping should then pray this prayer aloud:

Dear heavenly Father,

You have told us to "put on the Lord Jesus Christ, and make no provision for the flesh in regard to its lusts" (Rom. 13:14). I acknowledge that I have given in to fleshly lusts that wage war against my soul (1 Pet. 2:11). I thank You that in Christ my sins are forgiven, but I have transgressed Your holy law and given the enemy an opportunity to wage war in my members (Rom. 6:12,13; Jas. 4:1; 1 Pet. 5:8). I come before Your presence to acknowledge these sins and to seek Your cleansing (1 John 1:9) that I may be freed from the bondage of sin. I now ask You to reveal to my mind the ways that i have transgressed Your moral law and grieved the Holy Spirit. In Jesus' precious name I pray. Amen.

We don't try to dig up old dirt that has been dealt with before. The conviction of God has been there all along. What we are looking for is habitual sins or ones that have not been dealt with. Some have opened their Bibles to Galatians 5:19-21, which lists the sins of the flesh. Generally, I trust the Holy Spirit to bring conviction, but sometimes it is helpful to ask some questions when you sense the Lord is prompting you, such as: "Have you ever struggled with telling the truth?" or "Are there any issues that you are just too ashamed to admit before God or before me?"

They need to know that God is "able to judge the thoughts and intentions of the heart. And there is no creature hidden from His sight, but all things are open and laid bare to the eyes of Him with whom we have to do" (Heb. 4:12,13). God knows all about us, and yet He loves us. He is not out to get us; He is out to restore us if we will just let Him by being honest.

UNDERSTANDING SEXUAL BONDAGES

Space won't permit me to outline here the material included in *A Way of Escape*, but permit me to point out the essential passages and truth we must know to help people break sexual bondages. One such passage is 1 Corinthians 6:15-20:

> Do you not know that your bodies are members of Christ? Shall I then take away the members of Christ and make them members of a harlot? May it never be! Or do you not know that the one who joins himself to a harlot is one body with her? For He says,

"The two will become one flesh." But the one who joins himself to the Lord is one spirit with Him. Flee immorality. Every other sin that a man commits is outside the body, but the immoral man sins against his own body. Or do you not know that your body is a temple of the Holy Spirit who is in you, whom you have from God, and that you are not your own? For you have been bought with a price: therefore glorify God in your body.

Scripture does place sexual sins in a category by themselves, classifying every other sin as being outside of the body. Why this is so I'm not totally sure, but I do know that it is my responsibility to not let sin reign in my mortal body and not to obey its lusts (see Rom. 6:12). The next verse tells me what I must and must not do in reference to the use of my body. "Do not go on presenting the members of your body to sin as instruments of unrighteousness; but present yourselves to God as those alive from the dead, and your members as instruments of righteousness to God" (v. 13).

There is no way that you could commit a sexual sin and not use your body as an instrument of unrighteousness. If you do, you will allow sin to reign in your mortal body, according to Scripture.

I have learned that helping someone accomplish complete repentance requires that he or she pray and ask the Lord to reveal every sexual use of his or her body as an instrument of unrighteousness. Then the person must renounce every sexual use of his or her body that God brings to mind. Finally, I have the person present his or her body to the Lord as a living sacrifice. Is that biblical? We are urged by the mercies of God to do that, as mentioned in Romans 12:1.

SEXUAL BONDING

Bonding takes place when unholy sex is committed. The person has become one flesh with his or her partner. Tragically, that is true even in the case of incest or rape. The body is used as an instrument of unrighteousness. The temple is violated. But that isn't fair! Of course it's not fair, and I can't promise that it won't happen to you or anyone else. But I can tell you how to resolve it in Christ so that you don't have to stay in bondage to the sexual abuse. We have observed that if there is voluntary compliance with the sexual abuser, the victim usually will become very sexually active, apparently looking for affirmation. If it is forced against his or her will, the individual usually shuts down sexually.

We are warned emphatically to flee from any form of immorality, because it is a self-destructive sin that we commit against our own bodies. God and Satan both know our weakness to sexual passions. Satan plays on that weakness, but God provides a way of escape. In truth, we have already died to sin, and our lives are hidden in Christ (see Col. 3:3). But it is necessary to affirm the truth that our bodies are temples of the Holy Spirit and that in Christ we are free from the bondage of sin.

People may be willing to share one or two sexual struggles, but when they pray that prayer, you are about to hear many other experiences. You will hear comments such as "That would be embarrassing," "You'll think I'm a terrible person," or "I can't even remember a lot of them. I was bombed most of the time." Try encouraging them by saying something like the following:

> You are not going to cause me to think less of you because of anything that you have done. There's no condemnation in this room. The details of your life may be different from mine, but we are all just people who need Jesus. I'm only interested in your freedom. The Lord wants you free—that is why He is bringing all these experiences to your mind. For your sake, be sure to be totally honest about every sexual sin from your past or present that may keep you in bondage. Wouldn't you love to leave this room with all of that behind you?

BREAKING SEXUAL BONDING

A young woman with a desire for God and wanting to find freedom came to one of our conferences. She was living with a man, and they were not married. She wanted to break the relationship, but even after six months of counseling she was not able to do it. She came with her counselor for an appointment. While going through Step Six, she revealed a sexually promiscuous lifestyle, and renounced and broke bonding from 40 or more sexual relationships. Two days later, she joyfully told us that the man she had been living with was out of her home, and she was free!

Another young woman had prayed for a Christian husband. In college she met a fellow student whom she thought to be God's answer to her prayer. There was talk of marriage, and while they did not have intercourse, there was heavy petting. Then he revealed that he had homosexual interests, and their relationship began to change. After months of struggle, she felt she no longer loved him but somehow still felt compelled to marry him. Her parents and friends tried to convince her that she didn't have to, but she felt bound. After going through the Steps, she knew she was free from that bond and no longer felt obligated to marry him. Even without intercourse, when the body is given to, or violated by, another in intimacy, bonding can occur.

Some have bought into the lie that their acts of adultery or abortion were justified. To illustrate, one person said that he and his wife were virgins when they were married, giving the impression that there had been no sexual involvement. But when his wife went through the Steps later, she indicated that there had been oral sex. That may have been a deliberate intent to be deceptive on the husband's part, or he may have actually been blinded in believing that oral sex is not a sexual use of another person's body in the same way as intercourse.

Many married couples have been involved in premarital sex, either with each other or other partners, and that has robbed them of the joy of their relationship in marriage until the past experiences were renounced. We have also seen people helped who could not consummate their marriages even after therapy and medical treatment. The problem was solved after dealing spiritually with past situations by going through the Steps to Freedom. This further illustrates how the spiritual dimension of our problems affects the whole person: the body, soul and spirit.

DEAL WITH SPECIFIC ISSUES

After a brief explanation of sexual bonding, ask the person to pray:

> Lord, I ask You to reveal to my mind every sexual use of my body as an instrument of unrighteousness. In Jesus' precious name I pray. Amen.

Then help the person to begin by saying, "As the Lord brings to your mind every sexual use of your body, whether it was done to you (rape, incest or any sexual molestation) or willingly by you, renounce every occasion by praying this prayer":

> Lord, I renounce (name the specific use of your body) with (name the person) and ask You to break that bond.

The person prays that prayer for each person and/or activity as God brings it to mind. An example would be: "Lord, I renounce having sex with

George and ask You to break that bond," or "Lord, I renounce the molestation by my uncle and ask You to break that bond."

If the person cannot remember the names of the individuals, he or she should just say "the guy in the bar," or even "that girl whose face I see in my mind"—whatever would identify the experience. It is not a matter of admitting something to God that He is not already aware of, but to bring into the light something performed in secret in order to break the bondages.

A number of deviant sexual behaviors may surface at this time. Because of the sensitivity of this area, when the individual tells his or her past history, he or she may not readily share involvement in activities such as: pornography, voyeurism, bestiality, anal or oral sex, transvestitism, cross-gender dressing or transsexuality. Encourage the person to deal with whatever the Lord surfaces by renouncing it specifically.

You do not want to usurp the Holy Spirit's ministry here, but because of what you have already heard of the person's life, you may want to give suggestions if they appear to be needed. The types of unrighteous sexual uses of the body that should be renounced would include:

- Premarital sexual activity;
- Extramarital affairs;
- Homosexual behavior;
- Pornography (books, magazines, movies, videos);
- Sexual perversions and compulsive behavior (inordinate sexual appetite, masturbation, sexual fantasies, anal or oral sex, devices);
- Prostitution (heterosexual and homosexual);
- Sexual perversions (bestiality, sadomasochism, transvestitism, transsexuality);
- Pedophilia (sexual preoccupation with young children);
- Rape (any sexual use of one's body by someone without consent);
- Child sexual abuse or incest (molestation);
- Abortion;
- Sexual spirits (*incubi* and *succubi*).

FORMS OF INTERFERENCE

If a person has had a sexually active past, there may be deception in the form of lying to save face. Emphasize that it is truth that sets us free. You may never know whether he or she has been totally open or not. You can only do your best and make sure that you have not been a barrier to honesty by exhibiting a judgmental attitude.

Some may argue that those sins were in the past and don't need to be dredged up anymore. That is typically a dodge to save face. Others may sincerely say that they have already confessed their sexual sins. That may be true, but as we noted earlier, simple confession is only the first step toward repentance. This is especially true with people caught in addictive sin. I can certainly see why some wouldn't want to share their sexual sins. It is embarrassing, but I think we should pay heed to James 5:16: "Confess your sins to one another, and pray for one another, so that you may be healed. The effective prayer of a righteous man can accomplish much." They need to follow James's two-fold instruction: to confide in a trusted and compassionate person who can help them, and to have spiritually mature people pray for them.

Don't be curious and press for vivid details. That is nothing more than voyeurism. Specific actions *must* be renounced, but discourage the kind of description that could give any platform to the enemy. On rare occasions, you may encounter a person who seems to enjoy recalling sexual experiences in graphic detail. You should control that by saying kindly, "You don't need to give that kind of detail. Just stay focused on the issues that you need to renounce." If necessary, you could lead him or her in a renunciation, such as: "I renounce the influences of Satan and sexual spirits that would cause me to want to relive and exploit my past sexual experiences. I announce the truth that my body is a temple of the Holy Spirit and that You, Lord, want my entire mind and body to be clean. I again commit myself to You for the renewing of my mind."

If you become sexually stimulated by the confession, there is a good chance that you have some issues yet to be dealt with. At least you should be warned by Galatians 6:1, "You who are spiritual, restore such a one in a spirit of gentleness; each one looking to yourself, lest you too be tempted."

LIES THEY BELIEVE

You may discern an area where a lie needs to be addressed, and further confirmation would be helpful. For example, a girl was told she was "special" by her abuser. After being sexually molested as a child, she chose to be sexually promiscuous. She was encouraged to say:

I renounce the lie that I need to give my body to someone so that I can be accepted and special. I announce the truth that I am accepted and loved by Christ just as I am.

When a person is molested as a child or teen, he or she often feels dirty or guilty, perhaps feeling a revulsion toward a legitimate sexual relationship in marriage. This could be renounced as follows:

I renounce the lie that I am evil or dirty as a result of my molestation. Thank You, Lord, that You know I was only a little child, and I needed love and acceptance. Therefore, I receive Your forgiveness for any way I might have cooperated, and I choose to forgive myself.

The following is appropriate for many to renounce:

I renounce all of the ways that Satan has perverted my attitude toward sex as a result of my past involvement. I specifically renounce (pornography, masturbation, oral sex, other forms of perverted sex, homosexuality, etc.). I announce the truth that I don't have to continue to be a victim of those past experiences. You are the God who makes all things new. I ask You, Lord, to renew my mind so that I am free to enjoy sex and my sexuality in the way You intended.

A PRAYER OF COMMITMENT AND AFFIRMATION

When the individual has finished dealing with the specific sexual issues from the past, ask the person to pray the next prayer. Or, you may choose to read it a phrase at a time and ask the person to pray it after you. Sometimes that may be appreciated and be more meaningful to him or her.

Lord, I renounce all these uses of my body as an instrument of unrighteousness and by so doing ask You to break all bondages Satan has brought into my life through that involvement. I confess my participation. I now present my body to You as a living sacrifice, holy and acceptable unto You, and I reserve the sexual use of my body only for marriage. I renounce the lie of Satan that my body is not clean, that it is dirty or in any way unacceptable as a result of my past sexual experiences. Lord, I thank

You that You have totally cleansed and forgiven me, that You love and accept me unconditionally. Therefore, I can accept myself. And I choose to do so, to accept myself and my body as cleansed. In Jesus' name. Amen.

After this prayer, one woman wept and said joyfully, "I have wished all of my life that I could say that."

SPECIAL PRAYERS FOR SPECIFIC NEEDS

The last portion of Step Six is a list of prayers covering other specific areas that may need to be confessed and renounced.

In most instances, having heard their stories, heard them pray through the Step on forgiveness and heard them pray through the above prayers regarding sexual sins, you will already know which of these special prayers will need to be prayed. But there may still be areas they have not revealed, and you will want to give them an opportunity to do that. There have been times when we were tempted to skip one of these prayers, and people interrupted, saying they wanted to pray it because it was an area of concern.

You can simply say: "Now we want to look at any special areas that need to be addressed." Then go down the list and give them an opportunity to pray any of the prayers that apply.

The prayers can be adapted or expanded to include any area of sin and the underlying deception that they may have believed as a result of being involved in the activity. For example, some may not have had eating disorders or cut on themselves, but they may have purposefully tried to punish themselves or cause pain by hitting themselves or pounding their heads against the wall. You could change the wording to:

Lord, I renounce the lie that my worthiness is dependent upon my appearance or performance. I renounce hitting myself, pounding my head against the wall, or purposefully trying to punish myself as a means of...

Renouncing the lie that their worthiness is dependent on performance is very important to many Christians. There was one woman whose entire life was characterized by drivenness. She believed that she needed to excel to compensate for her failures. Though she was a gifted person, she had never felt she was accepted by her parents. She was encouraged to pray, "I renounce drivenness and the compulsion to perform as a means of gaining approval or cleansing myself of evil, and announce the truth that I am totally accepted by Christ just as I am." Afterward, she felt as though a weight had been lifted from her.

The lies of Satan are subtle. Many people believe that they must be their own saviors and make themselves acceptable. Go ahead and hang yourself on the Cross if you want, but it won't do you any good; there was only room for one. The truth is, we are already accepted, approved and forgiven through the shed blood of Christ.

CONCLUDING THIS STEP

Once you have dealt with all of the areas covered by these prayers, you are ready to conclude this section. In summary, the following illustration has been meaningful to many:

> You've heard of the expression, "A skeleton in the closet." Well, suppose I have a skeleton in my closet—something that I've done wrong that I have never made right with God. What does the liar, the deceiver, the accuser of the brethren do? He knocks at my door and says, "I want to talk with you about the skeleton in your closet." Immediately, I feel anxiety, guilt and condemnation, because I know there is a skeleton there. If I opened the door, everyone would be able to see it.
>
> Now suppose that I have completely repented of my sin. There is no longer a skeleton in my closet. The Bible tells me that God totally cleanses and forgives me, and that He will never again bring up that sin and use it against me. But Satan doesn't give up easily; he continues to knock at the door and tell me that he wants to talk about the skeleton in my closet. This time, however, I don't feel the same anxiety and guilt. I still remember that there used to be a skeleton in the closet, but I know it's not there anymore.
>
> There is a big difference between an unresolved conflict from our pasts and only the memory of the conflict. On the basis of Scripture, what you have done in going through the Steps is to reduce those experiences to memories. You are free from the past and the sin that so easily entangles us. It no longer has any hold on you.

After using that illustration, you may sense God's leading to ask, "Are there any skeletons in your closet that we have missed?" Sometimes the Lord prompts people to name something, such as lying, cheating or stealing. But one person exclaimed, "The door is open, the light is on and the closet is empty!"

When they are ready, they pray the final prayer of Step Six:

> I now confess these sins to You and claim through the blood of the Lord Jesus Christ my forgiveness and cleansing. I cancel all ground that evil spirits have gained through my willful involvement in sin. I ask this in the wonderful name of my Lord and Savior Jesus Christ. Amen.

INSIGHT INTO OTHER AREAS OF BONDAGE

The following comments on the other prayers are for your information. It usually isn't necessary to give all of these explanations to the person you are helping.

Homosexuality

Homosexual behavior, or sexual desire or contact with someone of the same sex, may begin at a young age because of sexual molestation or for other reasons. A person may have "always" felt different sexually and be angry or confused about it. We want to help them realize that there is homosexual behavior but that God created us male and female in His image (see Gen. 1:27), to relate sexually with the opposite sex. These people have usually condemned themselves for years, trying to find a place of love and acceptance where they can be helped. They need to be reminded that God is not only the Creator, but He also re-creates, heals and restores.

Abortion

Since God entrusts parents with the life of the child they conceive, He expects them to assume responsibility for the protection and care of that child. Most women have remorse over abortions they've had, and some continue grieving for years. Sometimes they need to forgive the person who coerced them into getting the abortion. Sometimes praying the prayer and forgiving themselves (actually receiving God's forgiveness) gives great relief, and the final closure of entrusting that child to God may be very tearful and meaningful.

Abortions do not apply only to women. If you are helping a man who parented a child and did not assume responsibility for that life, he would need to confess and pray the abortion prayer as well. Many people have repeatedly asked forgiveness for an abortion but have never felt a final resolution. Resolution comes through choosing to accept God's forgiveness, by forgiving oneself and committing the child to God for His care in eternity.

Suicidal Tendencies

This includes both actual attempts to commit suicide as well as suicidal thoughts, such as wishing to die because of feelings of condemnation or wanting to drive his or her car into another car, and so on. Suicide is the final expression of control over one's own life. The deception is the belief that death is the solution, escape or end of everything. The prayer is a paraphrase of John 10:10 and rightly describes Satan as the thief, liar and destroyer he actually is. It also gives the person the opportunity to announce aloud his or her decision to choose life in Christ and trust Him to bring beauty from ashes (see Isa. 61:3).

Eating Disorders, or Cutting on Oneself

Eating disorders and other forms of self-abuse are an attempt to cleanse oneself of evil. Eating disorders have virtually nothing to do with food. People caught in this bondage are overwhelmed by condemnation and crumble under negative criticism. Their identities and senses of worth are based on their appearances and performances. After finding their freedom in Christ, many will say, "I can't believe the lies I have believed." These practices become secret, personal rituals unconsciously designed to rid themselves of evil for the purpose of gaining senses of worth.

The behavior may be expressed by frequent overconsumption of food that results in obesity as a means of insulating themselves from others or comforting themselves. Some have believed the lie that if they get too attractive, men will take advantage of them. It might involve self-denial of food because they see themselves as being too fat and thereby imperfect. They may binge on food and then purge their bodies from the guilt with laxatives or vomiting. They may cut on themselves with razor blades, knives or other sharp objects. All of these conducts (defecating, purging, cutting or punishing themselves) should be renounced as a symbolic means of cleansing, and the person should announce that only the blood of the Lord Jesus Christ cleanses from sin.

Substance Abuse

Denial is the most common defense of an addict. All people with addictive behaviors lie both to themselves and others. Many are tired of living lies and would love to walk in the light. The dysfunctional use of substances such as alcohol, drugs (either street or prescription), nicotine, caffeine and food becomes a means of coping and escape for them, and usually controls their time, money and relationships.

Assuming responsibility by confessing those self-destructive behaviors and renouncing the lies they've believed will free them so they can begin to respond to life in a healthy way. Obviously, the recovery process for substance abusers is complex.

STAYING FREE

We don't want to leave people with the belief that they have now completely dealt with every issue and will never again need to look at a particular area. Other occult issues may be remembered that need to be dealt with in accordance with Step One. Other names may come to minds of people who need to be forgiven, as in Step Three. The same would apply to this Step. The following testimony illustrates this point:

> A church leader had been faithful to his wife for more than 30 years. However, he had been deeply involved in sexual activity during his time as a bachelor in the military many years earlier. He dealt with some of the sexual memories when he took himself through the Steps.
>
> Then about a year later, during prayer, his sordid past came back again, and he felt great remorse. It took three hours for him to list every name and wrongful sexual act he could remember. He acknowledged before God all that he willfully sinned against Him and renounced each name and event. Then he not only claimed God's forgiveness, he also forgave himself. He later reported that certain sexual fantasies that had plagued him all his married life immediately disappeared and that his intimacy with his wife improved dramatically.

Because of the addictive nature of these sins, freedom won here must be maintained. Some may need ongoing help to solidify the gains made. This is not to undermine or minimize the freedom they will have received by going through Step Six. Mountains of anger, guilt, condemnation and hopelessness will be replaced with resolution, joy and freedom. But it is one thing to get free; it's another thing to stay free. This applies particularly in the sexual and other addictive areas. There are many lifestyle issues that should be worked out in a good follow-up program.

If they have addressed deep issues in this Step, you need to alert them to the fact that the enemy tempts people in their areas of weakness, trying to entice them back into bondage again. Remind them that they are not victims, and they are not powerless. They would be wise, however, to have a friend to whom they can be accountable and count on for prayer support. All of us need to be a part of a support group for regular encouragement and prayer support. As mentioned in Step Five, "We absolutely need God, and we *desperately* need each other."

CHAPTER THIRTEEN

LIVING AS A
NEW CREATURE

STEP SEVEN: ACQUIESCENCE
VERSUS RENUNCIATION

This last Step to Freedom deals with ancestral sins that are passed on from
one generation to another and the spiritual attacks that come from the
enemy. This is a crucial turning point for those people who come from
dysfunctional families or families involved in cults or the occult. It is
breaking the final links of bondage that have chained them to their past.
We cannot passively take our places in Christ; we must actively choose to
accept ourselves as new creations in Christ and take our places in the family of God.

After a conference, I noticed one of my seminary students sitting rather
dazed in his chair.

"Are you all right?" I asked.

"Yes," he responded.

"You look rather perplexed. What happened when you went through this
last Step?" I asked.

"I had to literally hang on to my chair to keep from running out of here,"
he said. It turned out that his mother was a psychic.

There may be some interference in this last Step if there have been cult
or occult experiences in a person's family heritage. An ex-Mormon I was
helping suddenly stopped in the middle of the declaration in total fear.

"What's going on in your mind?" I asked.

She cried out, "You mean you don't see him there?"

"Who?" I asked.

"My father, standing right there," she said, pointing her finger at the space beside me.

I didn't bother to look because I knew I wouldn't see anything. So the image wasn't real? Oh, yes, it was, but the problem was not in the room; it was in her mind.

"Tell me about your father," I continued.

"I'm responsible for my father," she said.

I told her that was a lie. We have a responsibility *to* one another, but not *for* one another. So she renounced the lie and picked up where she had left off. This time her grandmother showed up! Please understand that these appearances were not her father nor her grandmother but a deceptive battle for her mind.

The story of the rich man and Lazarus in Luke 16:26 clearly teaches that this is a present-day impossibility: "Between us and you there is a great chasm fixed, in order that those who wish to come over from here to you may not be able, and that none may cross over from there to us."

THE INFLUENCE OF HERITAGE

Acquiescence is passively giving in or agreeing without consent. Unless we make concerted efforts to do otherwise, we will remain products of our pasts. We will discipline our children the way we were disciplined. The families we were born into and the way we have been raised will shape our present beliefs and behaviors. Some of those family traits can be very good, others not so good.

Why are people prone to continue in the sins of their fathers, and how are they passed on? The cycle of abuse is one of the more attested social phenomena. Is it passed on genetically, environmentally or spiritually? The answer, I believe, is: "Yes! All three."

First, I believe that we can be genetically predisposed to certain strengths and weaknesses. For instance, it is well accepted that some people are more prone to become alcoholics than others. The average person may drink socially for many years and never develop an addiction, while others can be hooked in just a few months, maybe even weeks. That doesn't mean they were born alcoholics. They became addicted to alcohol by choosing to drink as a means of partying or coping.

In a similar fashion, some boys have higher levels of testosterone than others. They will develop beards by the time they are 14 years old, and others won't have full beards until they are 21 years old. Having lower levels of the male hormone does not make a boy a homosexual, but it may make him more vulnerable. Boys who develop late may experience more teasing, which may affect their self-perceptions.

Second, the environment we were raised in is the biggest contributor to our development. Values and attitudes are more caught than taught. If you were raised in a home where pornography was left around the house, you will struggle more with lust than the person who was raised in a morally responsible home. Mental strongholds are formed primarily from the environments in which we were raised. By environment, I mean the friends we had, the neighborhoods we played in, the churches we went to (or didn't go to) and the parents (or single parent or guardian) who raised us.

The third possibility is spiritual. In giving the Ten Commandments, God said, "You shall not make for yourself an idol, or any likeness of what is in heaven above or on the earth beneath or in the water under the earth. You shall not worship them or serve them; for I, the Lord your God, am a jealous God, visiting the iniquity of the fathers on the children, on the third and the fourth generations of those who hate Me, but showing lovingkindness to thousands, to those who love Me and keep My commandments" (Exod. 20:4-6).

CAN SIN BE INHERITED?

Some Christian leaders respond negatively to the teaching that we can inherit spiritual problems from our ancestors. Let me respond by saying that we are not guilty for our parents' sins, but because they sinned, we are vulnerable to their areas of weakness. Jeremiah 32 offers more insight: "Ah Lord God! Behold, Thou hast made the heavens and the earth by Thy great power and by Thine outstretched arm! Nothing is too difficult for Thee, who showest lovingkindness to thousands, but repayest the iniquity of fathers *into the bosom* of their children after them, O great and mighty God. The Lord of hosts is His name" (vv. 17,18, emphasis added).

Whatever is being passed on intergenerationally is not due to the environment, because it occurs in the bosom of the next generation. That could make it a genetic factor for those who insist upon a natural explanation for everything, but I don't think so.

Leviticus 26:38-40 offers some valuable insight: "'But you will perish among the nations, and your enemies' land will consume you. So those of you who may be left will rot away because of their iniquity in the lands of your enemies; and also because of the iniquities of their forefathers they will rot away with them. If they confess their iniquity and the iniquity of their forefathers, in their unfaithfulness which they committed against Me, and also in their acting with hostility against Me." Confessing the iniquity of my father will not have any affect on me genetically

THE NEED FOR REPENTANCE

A story I saw recently on television is a modern-day illustration of this. A high school girl in a small hamlet in Southern Germany decided to do a report on the role her town played in World War II. She had always been told that her town had resisted Hitler and that the Catholic Church had instructed its people not to pray for him.

What she discovered in the local library was just the opposite. The town had acquiesced to Hitler's regime. Her report brought quick disclaimers from town leaders and warnings not to dig up any more dirt. She felt betrayed by her ancestors and did much more extensive research. The whole town turned against her when she reported her findings. Her husband left her, her family deserted her and she was eventually run out of town.

Now we wonder why white supremacy has risen again in Germany. How can this be? Haven't they learned anything from their past? How could something so sinful be on the rise again? I submit that it can because there never was complete repentance. They covered it up. Some even deny the holocaust took place! Those who will not face the sins of their fathers may be doomed to repeat them.

After the nation of Israel split, every king in Israel continued in the sins of Jeroboam. I don't believe that any of them had to. Any one of them could have said, "Jeroboam was wrong, we should go back to Jerusalem and worship God the way He instructed David." But none did.

A mother with a child in her arms and a husband by her side approached me at a conference. She had read almost all of my books and worked through the Steps to Freedom on her own. She believed that one more issue needed to be resolved.

"My parents and their parents bad-mouthed every pastor in every church we ever went to, and I have done the same," she told me. "I don't want my child to repeat this same sin, so I am confessing my sin and the sin of my ancestors to you as a member of the clergy. Would you forgive me?"

What a courageous and marvelous thing she did for herself and for her child!

NEW CREATURES BUT PERSONALLY RESPONSIBLE

Some may still protest the need to do this because we are new creatures in Christ, and Jesus paid the penalty for all our sins. Indeed, He did, but when we were born again, were our minds instantly transformed? I can't imagine anybody believing more strongly than I do about our new position in Christ. It is the basis for all that I am, all that I do and all that I teach concerning evangelism and discipleship. Because we are new creatures in Christ, we can actively choose to confess and renounce the sins of our ancestors and stop the cycle of abuse. That is the final step in the process of repentance.

But regardless of how they originate, there are numerous kinds of bondages that can be environmentally, genetically and spiritually passed on because of the iniquities of our ancestors. These are the roots of sexual addiction and perversion, alcoholism and drugs, violent behavior and more. There may be family traits such as pride in achievement, success, intellectualism, prestige, independence, control or unforgiveness. It isn't our purpose to place blame or to categorize every root cause of problems. Many of these strongholds have already been dealt with in previous Steps, and the Lord will be faithful to complete His work.

What people need to know is that they can be free in Christ from inherited or acquired bondages linked to generational sin. We have new lives, because of the great work that Christ accomplished for us on the cross and in His resurrection.

ABOUT CURSES

Curses are blasphemous pronouncements, oaths or swearings intended to bring injury to a person. This is more common in the Third-World countries, but it is also present in North America, with people dabbling so commonly in the supernatural through witchcraft, New Age, and so on. A major purpose of satanic worship is to summon and send demons. If you have ever been abruptly awakened at a certain time of the night, like 3:00 A.M., you may have been targeted. Whether it is true or not, we often hear reports of witches and satanists who are praying for the downfall of Christians, especially pastors.

Predictions given by a medium, or even things unwisely said or done by a parent, may be *used* by Satan as a curse on a person's life. By playing games as "innocent" as the Ouija board or magic eight ball, a particular message or response may be imprinted on a person's mind so that it acts like a curse or

assignment. The person may, either consciously or unconsciously, feel help-
lessly bound to that assessment or prediction. (Hopefully, this was dealt
with in Step One.)

Unless the Lord specifically brings something to the minds of people we
are working with, we don't deal with any specific curses, hexes or pronouncements. We encourage them to take their places in Christ, put on the
armor of God and stand against all assignments and weapons formed
against them. Christ is our defense. Don't ever let the devil set the agenda.
We want those we are helping to come under the protection and authority
of Christ, and by the grace of God to break any link to the bondages of
generational sins and curses. They don't have to be victims of their pasts
anymore.

GOING THROUGH STEP SEVEN

You can begin this Step by reading the opening paragraphs or using your
own words to explain what has been covered above. We often have people
read the declaration quietly by themselves first to see if they have any questions. We want them to know the authoritative stand they will be taking
when they read the following declaration aloud:

> I here and now reject and disown all the sins of my ancestors. As
> one who has been delivered from the power of darkness and
> translated into the Kingdom of God's dear Son, I cancel out all
> demonic working that has been passed on to me from my ances-
> tors.
>
> As one who has been crucified and raised with Jesus Christ
> and who sits with Him in heavenly places, I renounce all satanic
> assignments that are directed toward me and my ministry, and I
> cancel every curse that Satan and his workers have put on me. I
> announce to Satan and all his forces that Christ became a curse
> for me (Gal. 3:13) when He died for my sins on the cross. I
> reject any and every way in which Satan may claim ownership
> of me.
>
> I belong to the Lord Jesus Christ who purchased me with His
> own blood. I reject all other blood sacrifices whereby Satan may
> claim ownership of me. I declare myself to be eternally and
> completely signed over and committed to the Lord Jesus Christ.
> By the authority that I have in Jesus Christ, I now command

every familiar spirit and every enemy of the Lord Jesus Christ
that is in or around me to leave my presence. I commit myself
to my heavenly Father to do His will from this day forward.

DEALING WITH SPECIFICS

A person may not be aware of overt demonic activity or curses, but may be
concerned about some known behavior of his or her ancestors. You may
choose to have the person pause after the second sentence, which ends with
the words "...passed on to me from my ancestors." At that point you could
encourage him or her to pray, "And I specifically renounce (*let him put in whatever it is that has been of particular concern—unforgiveness, pride, incest, etc.*)." Then
have him conclude the declaration.

When the individual has finished the declaration, have him pray:

> Dear heavenly Father,
> I come to You as Your child, purchased by the blood of the
> Lord Jesus Christ. You are the Lord of the universe and the Lord
> of my life. I submit my body to You as an instrument of right-
> eousness, a living sacrifice, that I may glorify You in my body. I
> now ask You to fill me with Your Holy Spirit. I commit myself
> to the renewing of my mind in order to prove that Your will is
> good, perfect and acceptable for me. All this I do in the name
> and authority of the Lord Jesus Christ. Amen.

The person has just completed a fierce moral inventory. The impact on
some is dramatic. He or she actually looks different. I have encouraged
many to freshen up in the rest room and take a good look at themselves in
the mirror.

"Why? Do I look that bad?" some have asked, because they probably felt
emotionally drained.

"On the contrary, you look that good," I respond.

I usually have people close their eyes and share with me what is going on
in their minds. Many experience a peace and quietness that they have never
known before. One lady said, "How did you know that would happen?"
Another one said, "I'm normal!" There really is a peace of God that passes all
understanding that will guard our hearts and our minds (see Phil. 4:7).

A good way to launch people in their walks of freedom is to read the final
paragraphs, which follow the prayer. They need to know how to maintain

the freedom they have gained. They have submitted to God and resisted the devil in a comprehensive way. Now they must understand that staying free is a lifelong process.

DEALING WITH LINGERING CONCERNS

If people do not sense complete resolution, we encourage them to pray and ask the Lord to reveal what it is that is still keeping them in bondage. Allow them to sit in quiet deliberation for a few minutes. After that you might ask, "What is the *first thing* that came to your mind?" We have often seen God bring to mind something specific that still needed to be addressed.

Rarely, a person may say, "It is almost completely quiet, but there are voices way off in the distance," or "I hear laughing in the background." You can help him or her learn to walk in the authority of Christ by leading the person to say: "In the name of the Lord Jesus Christ, I command you to leave my presence. I am a child of God and the evil one cannot touch me." When he or she has done this, the person usually exclaims, "It's quiet!"

If you are working with severe cases of satanic ritual abuse (SRA), there is a good chance the person will have a multiple personality disorder. In such cases, the person may hear the voices of other personalities, but he or she will sense a great difference, even though there may be much more work to do before total integration will take place.

If the person had difficulty working through a certain section of the Steps, you may want to have him or her turn to that portion again. This is particularly true of the Doctrinal Affirmation in Step Two. Many experience difficulty reading through it the first time, but they immediately sense an amazing difference between the two readings. When they experience this difference, they will often have a sense that something significant really happened.

EVALUATING FREEDOM

Highly subjective people are the most difficult people to work with. They struggle with assuming responsibility for their own thoughts. They are easy targets for deceiving spirits, because they flow with whatever comes along. Passive people are that way because they expect something to be done *for* them. They are looking for some elusive experience or emotional high, rather than assuming their own responsibility to think and take action. They often lack the assurance that their resolution is complete. If this is the case, neither you nor the person should trust his or her feelings. We walk by faith according to what God says is truth. You may want to say:

> We know that God answers prayer. If you were honest and sincere as you went through the Steps, then I believe that God has answered the prayers you have prayed today and that many personal and spiritual conflicts have been resolved.
>
> When you leave today, don't trust your feelings; choose to believe what God says is true. Remember that the battle is for your mind. Saturate your mind with scriptural truth about God's character and His love for you. Don't get bogged down with what didn't happen. Rejoice in what did happen. You have faced and worked through a lot of issues today. Learn to recognize the lies you are believing that cause you to doubt. Take every thought that comes in your mind captive to the obedience of Christ. That means evaluate what you are thinking according to the Word of God. It is His truth that sets you free (see John 8:32).

We are thankful for the hundreds of testimonies that we receive, and we're grateful that the Lord allows us to be used to help others. You will receive some letters as well as you gain experience in helping others. None, however, are more rewarding than those we get from the survivors of SRA. The following testimony was very special:

> I waited a while to write to be sure that my freedom didn't "wear off." That doesn't sound like I was trusting God, but *He* understood that I wanted to write you at the proper time. Then, too, my Christian therapist said, "I'll give you one to two weeks to be back where you were! And if you are, don't beat yourself up for a lack of faith."
>
> God had great things in mind, however, for my therapist and me. She is now using your Freedom in Christ materials, as she has seen wondrous changes in several of her patients! We now pray together as I continue to remember the details of my incest and ritual abuse.
>
> I am awakening less now at 3:00 A.M. than before and have had the tools of God's Word to combat the demonic voices. Twice these battles literally wore me out, but at the end of them,

God gave me a song of praise on my lips...actually a "joyful noise" since I'm tone deaf. The joy of knowing the depth of my identity "in" Christ is hard to explain. I pray that it will show on my face and lead others to Him

CHAPTER FOURTEEN

In Closing

Stephanie looked like a rag doll, but her eyes revealed the truth of her new-found freedom. She had just completed a marathon session through the Steps to Freedom with tremendous resolution.

"I'm exhausted!" she said.

"You should be," I responded. "You have just emerged from an incredible war, and you won. Congratulations."

"Thanks," she said, "but what will I do next week if I have a problem? You will be out of town!"

Many people think they can't make it through the next week—or month, or year—without their encourager or helper. I asked Stephanie, "What did *I* actually do? You were the one who did all the work, and it was God who set you free."

Every pastor and counselor has limited time and resources, but God doesn't. People can call upon Him 24 hours of every day for the rest of their lives. "God is our refuge and strength, a very present help in trouble. Therefore we will not fear" (Ps. 46:1,2).

We don't want these people to be dependent upon us; we want them to be dependent upon God. He is their Deliverer. He is the wonderful Counselor. Only He can set them free and give them the grace to continue on. Walking through the Steps to Freedom doesn't just resolve present and past conflicts—it teaches them how to stand and resolve issues that will surface later.

Varying Responses

What can you expect at the close of your appointment? How will the person feel? How much freedom will have been gained? Where will he or she go from here? There is certainly no set answer to any of these questions. Those you take through the Steps will have differing life experiences, problems, personalities, biblical knowledge, spiritual maturity and levels of commitment. The one constant is our faithful God, who does hear and answer prayer.

Hopefully, every person will be further along in their walks with God. They did a thorough housecleaning. The least you can expect is that they are really going to be ready for communion next Sunday. The chances of somebody getting hurt is minimal unless you lose control in the session. Stay on track, and stay away from controversial issues. If you let the person's subjectivity or the devil set the agenda, you will go down a thousand and one rabbit trails.

Some people feel let down because they don't experience the dramatic changes that others do. Some come with unrealistic expectations. They think, *I'm going to go through these Steps and then everything will be perfect.* Try not to make any promises about what will happen in the session. There is no way to know for certain that everything from the past will be covered. Other things may surface later and will need to be addressed, so you should never promise a total resolution beforehand. There's a delicate balance between offering legitimate hope before and during the session, and making promises that can't be kept.

Many people ask about their medications. Unless you are a doctor, do not give medical advice. I suggest that they, with their doctors' approval and monitoring, work on plans to gradually reduce their medications or treatments if that is what the doctors advise. People develop a tolerance to certain prescription drugs, and they will have severe side effects if they go off too suddenly. I suggest that you buy an inexpensive "pill book" at any major bookstore. It will tell you the names of every prescription drug, what the drug is used for, what side effects it will have, and if there are any dangerous combinations with other drugs. Then you will know what they are being treated for.

In the vast majority of cases, people sense tremendous help and freedom after completing the Steps. Some may not be aware of how much was really accomplished until they gain perspective by looking back sometime later and seeing how much their lives have changed.

A pastor thanked me for the time we spent together. It didn't seem like an overwhelming experience to either of us. Two weeks later, however, his wife told me she had a totally new husband. There were no more outbursts of anger, and he seemed to have a new love for her and for life in general.

Incomplete Resolution

Occasionally there will be those who have gone through the Steps to Freedom who come back later and say they are still not free. Typically, a person might continue to struggle for two reasons:

1. *The person did not carefully and thoroughly walk through the Steps.* If you did not take the person through the Steps yourself, find out who did, whether the process was completed and how long it took. You need to discern whether the person needs to go through the entire set of Steps again or whether you only need to help with some specific issues.

For example, if the person took himself or herself through the Steps, or if someone else did but only took an hour, you would go through all of the Steps again. This is not to negate anything that was resolved earlier, but you are making sure that nothing was overlooked. Generally, it will take three or four hours to go through the Steps thoroughly. And if a person takes himself or herself through, there is a good possibility that he or she was not able to be complete or objective.

At one conference, a pastor's wife who had taken herself through the Steps four times came for help because she *knew* she was still not free. One of our staff members walked her through as though it was her first time. When they were through, this woman knew that she was free. Some people just need the support and objectivity of a spiritually sensitive person to help them.

The most difficult issue for people to process on their own is forgiveness. What some may attempt to do in five minutes on their own may take an hour in your session. However, I don't want to give the idea that people can't process this on their own. Many do. We have received letters from people all over the world who have found their freedom just from reading the books and taking themselves through the Steps.

2. *Specific issues need more attention.* If you know the issue that is still troubling the person, go back to the appropriate Step (usually the first, third or sixth), and make sure the issues involved are clearly understood. If there are any questions or misunderstandings, it won't do any harm to go through that Step again.

A pastor had read all my books and taken himself through the Steps, but something wasn't complete. He approached me after a leadership conference; however, time didn't permit me to take him through the Steps myself. He briefly shared his story with me. I then encouraged him to pray, asking the Lord to reveal what was still keeping him in bondage. After several minutes of silence, he said, "The only thing I can think of is my perfectionism."

I had him renounce the lie that his worth was based on his ability to perform and announce the truth that his identity and sense of worth comes from who he is as a child of God.

I also learned from his story that he had a verbally abusive father. So I had him renounce the curses of his father and receive the blessings of God. Whenever I do a shortened version like that, I always close with the declaration and prayer of Step Seven, and then have the person read the list of who they are in Christ. This pastor took 10 minutes to read through that list because of the tears that were flowing down his cheeks.

One woman went through the Steps and had what seemed to be total resolution. Near the end of the conference, she came to one of our staff members and said that as I was teaching on spiritual conflict she felt an oppression. Our staff person stepped into a side room with her and asked her to pray as described above. As she did, she was flooded with memories of an experience that she had as a child. They dealt with the new memory, and the oppression was gone.

If there is any difficulty in identifying a specific issue to resolve, it is generally best to go back and review all of Steps One, Three and Six. Those are the areas that most often require another layer to be removed. There may be some renouncing and forgiving to do, but basically it is usually an identity issue associated with one of those Steps. Somewhere they may still be believing a lie. We will often go back to the concept of the identity chart and work through the troubling issues with them, identifying the lies and repudiating the lies with the truth of Scripture.

After identifying identity issues more deeply, one person wrote:

> Thank you so much for taking me through the Steps to Freedom yesterday. It really helped me to get an objective view of where the battle line is in my life. I knew that what I believed about my identity was out of alignment with truth, but I just couldn't practically apply it to my life by myself.
>
> When I had gone through the Steps by myself a few years ago, I had such a radical freedom experience. I really thought I could maintain it myself forever, and I planned to. But I didn't realize that I still hadn't dealt with some of the real underlying emotions. I had certainly gotten in touch with my hurt and anger during times of forgiveness before, but I hadn't realized how it had affected my core identity. Because I felt rejected and unworthy, I believed that I needed to "perform" in order to be accepted.
>
> Thanks for your acceptance and love. It helped me to be real

and transparent about my struggles with others. It was important for my own growth, but also in the ability to help others. I have more honest compassion for others now. It is amazing that going through the Steps allowed me to share all my skeletons in only a few hours. In all my years of Christian counseling, I had only started to approach talking about the really painful things. During the Steps, it all comes out and gets resolved with no guilt or remorse.

I've already started looking up Scriptures to counter all the lies I believed about myself. Thanks especially for seeing in me something of value worth devoting time to. I've spent my entire life trying to act like everything was all right and trying to figure out how to do the right thing so I wouldn't get in trouble or be rejected. Now I just want to be the person God wants me to be, and let the doing come naturally.

CONTINUING THE FREEDOM WALK

Many have won major battles, but they need to know that there will be others. They will walk out the door with the rest of their lives to live. There are more skirmishes ahead, but they are more winnable now because of the bondages that have been broken and a greater sense of God's presence in their lives. I always ask people before they leave, "What would you do if you heard a little voice in your head say, 'I'm back' or 'It didn't work'?" The battle goes on, and they need to be aware of that. There will never be a time when we don't need to submit to God, resist the enemy and put on the armor of God (see Eph. 6:10-20; Jas. 4:7). Hopefully, they are more aware of who the enemy is, what his weapons are, what his plan is and how they can stand against him.

To walk in freedom they must continue doing what they did when they went through the Steps: renounce lies, choose truth, confess, affirm, forgive and so on. All thoughts should be passed through the grid of Philippians 4:8 to see if they are true, pure, acceptable and pleasing to God. We must assume responsibility for our own mind and choose to take "every thought captive to the obedience of Christ" (2 Cor. 10:5). Remember, we are not called to dispel the darkness; we are called to turn on the light. The way you overcome the lie is by choosing the truth. Christ is the Prince of Peace, and the mind *can* be a quiet sanctuary under *His* Lordship (see Phil. 4:7).

Most of the time, the people you help will be able to apply what they have learned and continue to walk in freedom. When they encounter difficulties, they can seek out friends who understand spiritual conflict and who will agree with them in prayer. As James says, "Therefore, confess your sins to one another, and pray for one another, so that you may be healed. The effective prayer of a righteous man can accomplish much" (5:16). Every Christian needs at least one friend who will stand with him or her in this way. You can help people greatly by encouraging them to find such friends for sharing and accountability.

Follow-up begins in the appointment itself. While going through the Steps, people are already learning how to resolve their conflicts and stand firm. Here are a few specific helps you can give at the close of the session:

1. Use the first few paragraphs of the After Care section to emphasize the fact that freedom must be maintained.
2. Also from the After Care section, briefly point out the specific suggestions for maintaining freedom, the special prayers and the "Who I Am in Christ" list. This can be skimmed briefly, because we always encourage them to read the Steps more thoroughly at home later.
3. Explain that the most important thing they can do at this time is to review and reinforce what they have learned from *Victory over the Darkness* and *The Bondage Breaker*, the conference tapes or videos, and from going through the Steps.

   Earlier it was emphasized that these books should be read before going through the Steps. If the person wasn't able to go through the material before, he or she would profit greatly by doing so now.
4. Encourage those you have helped to identify a friend with whom to meet regularly for prayer over a period of weeks, and also to get into a small group, preferably one using a teaching guide that accompanies the Steps. They need that fellowship, encouragement, prayer support and accountability.
5. Suggest that they read *Living Free in Christ*, which contains a separate, short chapter on each of the 36 statements of who we are in Christ. There comes a time when we all need to stop figuring out what is wrong about us and find out from Scripture what is right about us. I wrote *Living Free in Christ* to explain from Scripture how Christ meets the most critical needs of our lives, which are the "being" needs (life, identity, acceptance, security and significance). Each chapter ends

with an opportunity to pray. It is a means for them to renew their minds to a true knowledge of who they are in Christ.

6. Encourage them in the areas where they are weak, based on your observations while going through the Steps. Give a lot of affirmation for what they did, such as, "Thank you for being so honest. I know it must have been hard to share that with me." Others need to be apprised of the "onion layer effect." They have dealt with all they know, but they may not be finished. God has required us to be good stewards of what He has entrusted to us. When we have shown ourselves faithful with that, He may reveal another layer of the onion (see 1 Cor. 4:1-5).

7. Encourage them to daily read *aloud*: The Doctrinal Affirmation from Step Two, the Daily and Bedtime Prayers at the back of the Steps, and the "Who I Am in Christ" list for the next several weeks. This reinforces what they have done and renews their minds to the truth. I know of nothing in the Scripture that indicates that Satan can read our minds, so reading aloud announces our stand to the spirit world, and affirms the truth about our relationship to God.

8. In some cases you may sense the need to recommend that they seek professional help for ongoing lifestyle issues. Every church should have a professional referral list that has been thoroughly checked out. However, you can refer to the wrong person who will undo in a short time all that God has done through you. Someday the Christian community is going to take seriously Psalm 1:1,2 "How blessed is the man who does not walk in the counsel of the wicked, nor stand in the path of sinners, nor sit in the seat of scoffers! But his delight is in the law of the Lord." I have never felt comfortable turning the minds of our Christians over to professional scoffers. It is even worse for the person to go back to some self-help group where he or she may only wallow in the past, and where he or she knows nothing of Christ, much less His plan for recovery.

9. Close the session by asking the person to read aloud the "Who I Am in Christ" list. But before you do, this would be an excellent time to explain the identity chart you made while he or she prayed through his or her forgiveness list (Step Three), if you did not review it at that time.

During the forgiveness process, you may have written a list of words they used to describe the pain they forgave. If you did that, the left column of the chart will be filled in under the title "Birth and Before Freedom Identity." Now you can suggest a meaningful, personalized Bible study using that identity chart. For example, under "Birth and Before Freedom Identity," they may have said "unloved." Across the chart under "In Christ Identity," they could write "Jeremiah 31:3: 'I have loved you with an everlasting love; therefore I have drawn you with lovingkindness.'"

Another suggestion would be to write one of their feelings (such as fear) at the top of an index card and the Scripture chosen (perhaps 2 Tim. 1:7), and then carry that card with them, or put it in a prominent place. They could refer to it often, until it's programmed into their minds. If you assign this as a personal re-identification project you could explain:

> You are not primarily a product of your past, nor are you the person you were before Christ. You are a product of the work of Christ on the cross. Second Corinthians 5:17 declares that you are a new creation in Christ, but the memories in your mind were not erased. All the old programming from the past is still there. Thought ruts and old habits take time and persistence to break. Romans 12:2 instructs us, "Do not be conformed to this world [or false input from your past or present], but be transformed by the renewing of your mind." How do you do that? By "taking every though captive to the obedience of Christ" (2 Cor. 10:5), and thinking about what is true (see Phil. 4:8). You cooperate with God in your transformation by recognizing lies and choosing truth about who you are and who He is.

COMPARING IDENTITIES

You may want to briefly read the left column of their identity charts, listing the most repeated lies they've believed as a result of their past experiences. Or you may choose to have them read the list. Then ask them to read who they are in Christ on the "Who I Am in Christ" page in the back of this book. The two lists read in opposition to each other have a forceful impact.

Before you finish in prayer, have the person close his or her eyes and relax. Then do as I suggested in the last chapter by asking: "What's going on in your mind right now?"

This is often a deeply moving moment. You may hear comments like: "It's peaceful, and the voices are gone"; "It's quiet and I feel like my mind is my own"; "I'm in a beautiful field of flowers, and the sun is shining"; or "It's light, and I feel free." Sometimes they go on and on, sharing descriptive thoughts. However, one young woman said, "I just feel so tired."

"But is it quiet and peaceful?" I asked.

"Yes, but I actually feel very flat and tired."

At the conference that night, she came up to our staff with a sparkle in her eyes and full of excitement. She said, "I was so tired when I left the session that I went home and took a nap. When I woke up, I had such a feeling of joy. I felt like I was walking three feet off the ground."

GROWTH GROUPS

Many Christians have said that after going through the Steps to Freedom, they felt just like they did when they first received Christ, and they earnestly desire to maintain their freedom. As with new Christians, these renewed Christians need a place where they can be nurtured. It's difficult to overemphasize the value of a small-group discipleship experience to establish them in truth and freedom.

Properly conducted, small groups offer safe environments where people feel love and acceptance, receive nurture and encouragement, and can mature. The maturity of the leader, the variety of people involved, and the insights of others all contribute to growth. Our ministry has prepared materials that can be used for both adult and youth groups. There are youth additions for the following material as well as professionally recorded video and audio series.

The study guides for *Victory over the Darkness* and *The Bondage Breaker* offer a question-and-answer approach in which each person in the group has a workbook and comes to the small-group session ready to discuss the insights gained.

Breaking Through to Spiritual Maturity is a curriculum guide for the leader of a small group or larger class. The study reviews the content of both *Victory over the Darkness* and *The Bondage Breaker* and can be used in either a 13-week or 26-week format. There are pages that can be duplicated and distributed to every member of the group for recording highlights of the group discussion. There is optimum benefit if each member of the group has a copy of both *Victory over the Darkness* and *The Bondage Breaker*, because they can read ahead each week and be prepared for the discussion time.

Any encourager/leader would be quickly overloaded trying to take people through the Steps and doing all of the follow-up and small-group ministry personally. This requires a team effort, and that is why there is great benefit to incorporating this ministry into a local church. Some may be more comfortable and called to taking people through the Steps; others may be more gifted in small-group ministry. But all who are a part of the ministry need to be thoroughly familiar with the teaching on the identity and authority of the believer and know that they are free in Christ.

A FREEDOM MINISTRY

One church put together a "freedom ministry" after I had conducted a conference in its facilities. A year and a half later, they had led more than 500 people to freedom in Christ, and 95 percent of it was done by lay people. How you can establish that kind of ministry in your church is spelled out in the inductive study for this book.

After working with thousands of people and hundreds of churches, I have become aware of the fact that many churches are in bondage. The idea of corporate bondage was a new idea to many, but nobody challenged it. Denominational leaders, pastors and lay people agreed that something was wrong with their churches, but nobody knew what to do about it. So Dr. Charles Mylander, a denominational leader with the Friends church, and I started to develop a means for leaders to resolve their corporate bondages. The result was our book *Setting Your Church Free*. The results and responses have been overwhelming.

Helping people find their freedom in Christ is not an end in itself. Neither is helping churches find their freedom in Christ. The real end is to fulfill the Great Commission. I believe that if we can get our people and our churches free in Christ, we can come together and reach our cities and this world for Christ. I want to close this book with a tremendous testimony of how one man was used of God to lead his church and its people to freedom in Christ.

> Dear Neil:
> In 1993, I purchased a set of your tapes. After listening to them, I began applying your principles to my problems. I realized that some of my problems could be spiritual attacks, and I learned how to take a stand. I won victories over some problems in my life.
> But that was only the tip of the iceberg. I'm a deacon and a lay preacher in a Baptist church. My pastor was suffering from depression and other problems that I was not aware of, and in

1994, he committed suicide. This literally brought our church to its knees. I knew some of the pastor's problems, and I felt they were spiritual in nature. But I didn't know how to relate my insights to the people.

The church elected me as their interim pastor. While in a local bookstore, I saw a book entitled *Setting Your Church Free*. I purchased it and read it. I felt with all the spiritual oppression that was in our church, this was the answer. Only one problem: getting the rest of the church to believe. After a few weeks of preaching on spiritual things, I knew we had to act on "setting our church free." The previous pastor (who had killed himself) hadn't believed your material. He would never read or listen to your message.

Slowly, very slowly, the people accepted my messages and I was able to contact one of your staff members. He flew to our town and led the leaders of our church through *Setting Your Church Free*. The leaders loved it. I felt Step One was past. Next I wanted to take all the people through the Seven Steps to Freedom. Six weeks later, I was able to do so. I really don't understand it, but we were set free from the spiritual bondage of multiple problems.

During all of this, one of my middle-aged members, who used to be an evangelist, was set free, learned who he was in Christ and is back in the ministry. Praise the Lord! I saw the children of the deceased pastor set free, and they were able to forgive their father. They were then able to go on with their lives. (At one point, one of the children had even contemplated suicide.)

This is a new church. God is free to work here! We formed a pulpit committee. Our church voted 100 percent for our new pastor. That has never happened in our church before, and we are an independent fundamentalist church.

Well, when you do things God's way, you get God's results!

APPENDICES

Appendix A: Seeking Forgiveness
Appendix B: Statement of Understanding
Appendix C: Identity Chart
Appendix D: Dealing with Abuse and Harassment
Appendix E: Confidential Personal Inventory
Appendix F: Steps to Freedom in Christ
Scripture List: Who I Am in Christ

Please Note: Permission to copy appendices
A through F, as well as the "Who I Am in Christ"
Scripture list at the end of the book, is granted for
individual counseling and church use only.

SEEKING FORGIVENESS

The most important forgiveness we can have is God's forgiveness. This comes only through our relationship with Christ, "in whom we have redemption, the forgiveness of sins" (Col. 1:14). Salvation assures us that our sins are forgiven, past, present and future. "There is therefore now no condemnation for those who are in Christ Jesus" (Rom. 8:1).

It is important to distinguish between issues that define what constitutes a relationship and those issues that define how we are to live in harmony with those to whom we are related. When we are born physically, we are related by blood to our fathers. Nothing can change that fact, and we will be blood related regardless of our behavior. Once born, however, we will live in harmony with our fathers if we obey them. If we disobey our fathers, fellowship will be broken. But the fact that we are related has not been affected.

When we are born again spiritually, we are related to God the Father through the blood of the Lord Jesus Christ (see Heb. 10:19-22; 1 Pet. 1:17-23). Nothing can change this (see Rom. 8:31-39). We are His children, and we will remain His children. We entered into that relationship by our beliefs, not by our behavior (see Eph. 2:8,9; Titus 3:4-7). We will live in harmony with our heavenly Father if we are obedient to Him and walk by faith in the power of the Holy Spirit. Many people confuse these two issues, thinking that an act of disobedience will result in the loss of salvation.

Every child of God is already forgiven by his or her heavenly Father. Confession of sins, however, is essential if a person desires to draw near to God and live in harmony with Him.

Many people have found it helpful to make a list of their sins (sins of both commission or omission). Ask God to guide you. Then go through the list by confessing, "I did...(name the specific sin)." There is a major difference between confessing and asking for forgiveness. Confessing is acknowledging what you have said or done. It is extremely hard for some people to say, "I did it." It is easier if they know they are already forgiven. Refusing to acknowledge our sins before God is to choose to live barren and fruitless lives. Once you have confessed to all the sins on your list, write 1 John 1:9 across it and destroy it.

To be completely right with God, we need to seek the forgiveness of others. Our relationships with God are inextricably wound up with how we relate to others. The following is an exercise to help you understand why we are to seek the forgiveness of others and how we can do it:

1. The motivation for seeking forgiveness:

Read Matthew 5:23-26 and comment on the following sentences:

The worshiper coming before God to offer a gift "remembers" that someone has something against him. The worshiper is the offender.

This does not mean the worshiper is to become introspective, probing into his own soul. It means an awareness of another's feelings toward him is to be the motivating key. This remembrance is the working of the Holy Spirit.

An exception (where the offended is unaware) would be when restitution has to be made (e.g., something stolen to be returned, something broken paid for and so on). Concerning restitution, comment on the following verses:

Luke 19:8: _____
Leviticus 6:5: _____
Numbers 5:7: _____
2 Samuel 12:6: _____

2. The urgency of seeking forgiveness:

Christ says that as soon as the worshiper senses his need, he should go and be reconciled. This is a prerequisite to acceptable worship of God. Put another way, our worship is unacceptable to God if we have not made right an offense against another.

3. The process of seeking forgiveness:

A. Regarding people from whom you need forgiveness, clearly identify to yourself the offenses committed. Write them out, including the attitude behind the wrong or offensive actions.

B. Make sure you have already forgiven them for any wrongs on their part.

C. Think through the precise wording you will use as you ask forgiveness.
   1. Label your action as "wrong."
   2. Go into only as much detail as necessary for the offended person to understand what you are confessing.
   3. Make no defenses, alibis or excuses.
   4. Do not project blame. Never confess *for* another.
   5. Your confession should lead to the direct question: "Will you forgive me?"

D. Seek the right place and the right time to approach the offended person.

E. Make your quest for forgiveness in person with family members or persons whom you can talk to face-to-face with the following exception: where there has been action of an immoral nature, DO NOT seek to deal with this alone and face-to-face. For instance, if incest was involved, have a minister or counselor present for your face-to-face conversation.

F. Except where no other means of communication is possible, DO NOT write a letter, because:
   1. A letter can be easily misread or misunderstood.
   2. A letter can be read by the wrong people, those having nothing to do with the offense or action.
   3. A letter can be kept when it should have been destroyed.
   4. Your confession does not need to be "documented."

G. Make restitution when the situation requires it.

H. Once you sincerely seek forgiveness and have made necessary restitution, you are free.

I. If forgiveness is refused, and there seems to be no hope of change on the part of the offended person, then prayerfully and humbly commit your case to "the judge" (God, our heavenly Father) and leave it there (see Matt. 5:25; 1 Pet. 2:21-23).

STATEMENT OF UNDERSTANDING

The following is a suggested Statement of Understanding. If you do plan to use it, please adapt it to your own church ministry by using your own letterhead. Also, this statement is not endorsed by us as being legally adequate for your ministry. You may choose to create your own statement in consultation with your church's leadership.

STATEMENT OF UNDERSTANDING

(Adult Consent Form)

I understand that the staff of _____ and those associated with them are not professional or licensed counselors, therapists, medical or psychological practitioners, unless otherwise indicated.

I deem the persons leading these sessions to be "encouragers" in the Christian faith, who are helping me assume my responsibilities in finding freedom in Christ. I am also aware that my encourager may need to intervene if he or she suspects that a child (under the age of 18) or an elder (over age 65) is currently endangered by abuse or if I am a danger to myself or others.

I understand that I am not being advised to alter any prescription medication I am currently taking. This is a matter between myself and my physician/therapist.

I understand that I am free to leave at any time and am here voluntarily. I understand that I am under no financial obligation. I am also aware of my right to ask for clarification of any part of this statement of understanding.

(PLEASE PRINT)

Name_____Date_____

Address_____

City_____State_____ Zip_____

Phone (H)(_____)_____(W)(_____)_____

Signed_____

IDENTITY CHART

Birth and Before Freedom Identity	In Christ Identity
Lies—Romans 3:4	Truth—Romans 12:2; 2 Corinthians 5:17; 10:5
Rejected	
Abandoned	
Victim	
Fearful	
Dirty	

I am no longer just a product of my past. I am primarily a product of the work of Christ on the cross.

DEALING WITH ABUSE AND HARASSMENT

There are times when husbands, wives or parents violate the laws of civil government that are ordained by God to protect innocent people against abuse that threatens their well-being. Abusive behavior comes in a variety of forms, such as physical, sexual, spiritual, mental and emotional.

If counselees confide that they are experiencing abuse, counsel them as follows:

1. Stop the abuse. In the case of spousal abuse, women are often confused (deceived) concerning the biblical admonition of Ephesians 5:22: "Wives, be subject to your own husbands, as to the Lord." Likewise, children are often confused (deceived) concerning the commandment, "Honor your father and your mother" (Exod. 20:12).

There is *no* biblical mandate for a person to continue to submit to abuse. These passages are not addressing issues of abuse; instead, they are guidelines for God's normal and ordained pattern for domestic life.

2. Seek legal protection. When necessary, appeal to civil authority, public safety officers or a child protective service. This allows God to place direct pressure on abusers to conform to justice. If an offender will not control his or her own behavior, then legal authorities should intervene. Encourage a person to speak the truth and to be willing to expose secrets when necessary to those who will provide the greatest protection and support. Hot lines and shelters are listed in the front of a local telephone book, or the church staff members could be consulted for other resources.

3. Seek counsel from a local church pastor. If the person has a trusted and supportive pastor, he or she should be urged to immediately seek help through that church. In some states, a lay counselor or pastor may not be legally bound to report abuse, but even if there is no legal mandate, a moral obligation exists to attempt to protect an individual (whether an adult or child) from known harm. Enlisting the support of a church also broadens the support base for the abused person.

If you are a helper working with a local church pastor, which is highly recommended, seek counsel from your own pastor. This should be done with the knowledge of the person you are helping and is not a breach of confidentiality, especially if you have used the release form, which declares that intervention will take place if there is a danger of abuse to the person or others. (See appendix B.)

4. *Seek a Christian support/care group.* Victims of abuse can be greatly helped by carefully guided support groups that deal with their specific problems. Care should be taken, however, that the support group does not deal with the issues in an unbiblical manner, such as justifying anger and rage as a proper way of coping with the abuse. Seeking out a special care group does not replace fellowship in a local church body. Encourage abused persons to form as many avenues of healthy Christian relationships as possible.

DEALING WITH HARASSMENT

There are times when employers or fellow employees violate the laws of civil government and ordinary decency ordained by God to protect innocent people against degrading behavior. Submitting to the authority of an employer *does not* mean being obligated to degrading behaviors.

The principles for dealing with sexual harassment (e.g., in the workplace) are the same as those for dealing with abuse. The person must distinguish between forgiving the offender and responsibly reporting inappropriate behavior. Encourage the person to appeal to a higher authority, such as the company's employee-relations officer or the local government department that deals with these issues.

CONFIDENTIAL PERSONAL INVENTORY

I. Personal Information

Name: _____ Age: ____ Telephone: _____

Address: _____

Church Affiliation   Present: _____

                      Past: _____

Education: Highest grade completed: _____

             Degree(s) earned: _____

Marital Status: _____

Previous History of Marriage/Divorce: _____

Vocation Present: _____

          Past: _____

II. Family History

A. Religious

1. Have any of your parents, grandparents or great-grandparents to your knowledge ever been involved in any occultic, cultic or non-Christian religious practices? Please describe.

2. Briefly describe your parents' Christian experience (i.e., if they were believers, did they profess and live their Christianity?).

B. Marital Status

1. Are your parents presently married or divorced? Explain.

2. Was your father clearly the head of the home or was there a role reversal where your mother ruled the home? Explain.

3. How did your father treat your mother?

4. Was there ever an adulterous affair to your knowledge with your parents or grandparents? Any incestuous relationships?

5. Were you adopted or raised by foster parents or legal guardians?

C. Sibling Data

1. Please identify the sex and age of your siblings(s) and place yourself in birth order.

2. Please describe the emotional atmosphere in your home while you were growing up. Include a brief description of your relationship with your parents and siblings(s).

D. Health

1. Are there any addictive problems in your family history (alcohol, drugs, etc.)?

2. Is there any history of mental illness? Please describe.

3. Please indicate if you have any history of the following ailments in your family:

___ Tuberculosis   ___ Cancer   ___ Other(s)
___ Heart disease   ___ Ulcers
___ Diabetes   ___ Glandular problems

4. How would you describe your family's concern for:
   a. Diet: _____

   b. Exercise: _____

   c. Rest: _____

E. Moral Climate

Rate the moral atmosphere in which you were raised during the first 18 years of your life.

	Overly Permissive	Permissive	Average	Strict	Overly Strict
Clothing	5	4	3	2	1
Sex	5	4	3	2	1
Dating	5	4	3	2	1
Movies	5	4	3	2	1
Music	5	4	3	2	1
Literature	5	4	3	2	1
Free will	5	4	3	2	1
Drinking	5	4	3	2	1
Smoking	5	4	3	2	1
Church Attendance	5	4	3	2	1

III. History of Personal Health
A. Physical

1. Describe your eating habits (i.e., Do you lean toward eating only junk food or only eating healthy food? Do you eat regularly or sporadically? Is your diet balanced? etc.).

2. Do you have any addictions or cravings that cause you to find it difficult to control sweets, drugs, alcohol, food in general, etc.?

3. Are you presently under any kind of medication for either physical or psychological reasons? Explain.

4. Do you have any problems sleeping? Describe your sleeping patterns (i.e., do you have restful sleep?). Are you having any recurring nightmares or disturbances?

5. Does your schedule allow for regular periods of rest and relaxation?

6. Have you ever experienced any type of trauma (i.e., physical, emotional or sexual history of abuse, involvement in a severe accident, death of family member, etc.)? Explain.

B. Mental

1. Describe briefly your earliest memory.

2. Do you have periods or blocks of time in your past that you can't remember? Please describe your experience.

3. Please indicate any of the following with which you have struggled or with which you are presently struggling:

___ daydreaming   ___ lustful thoughts   ___ inferiority
___ inadequacy   ___ worry   ___ doubts
___ fantasy   ___ obsessive thoughts   ___ insecurity
___ dizziness   ___ headaches   ___ compulsive
___ blasphemous thoughts   thoughts

4. Do you spend much time wishing you were somebody else or fantasizing that you were somebody else or possibly imagining yourself living at a different time, place or under different circumstances? Explain.

5. How many hours of TV do you watch per week? _____ List your five favorite programs.

6. How many hours do you spend a week reading?_____ What do you read primarily (newspaper, magazines, books, etc.)?

7. What type of music do you listen to, and what is the amount of time spent listening?

8. Would you consider yourself to be an optimist or a pessimist (i.e., do you have a tendency to see the good in people and life, or the bad?)?

9. Have you ever thought that maybe you were "cracking up," and do you presently fear that possibility? Explain.

10. Do you have regular devotions in the Bible? When and to what extent?

11. Do you find prayer difficult mentally? Explain.

12. When attending church or other Christian ministries, are you plagued with foul thoughts, jealousies, other mental harassments? Explain.

C. Emotional

1. Please indicate which of the following emotions you have or are presently having difficulty controlling:

___ frustration	___ fear of dying
___ anger	___ fear of losing your mind
___ anxiety	___ fear of committing suicide
___ loneliness	___ fear of hurting loved ones
___ worthlessness	___ fear of going to hell
___ depression	___ fear of abandonment
___ hatred	___ fear of _____

2. Which of the above-listed emotions do you feel are sinful? Why?

3. Concerning your emotions, whether positive or negative, please indicate which of the following best describes you:
___ readily express them
___ express some of my emotions, but not all
___ readily acknowledge their presence, but reserved in expressing them
___ tendency to suppress my emotions
___ find it safest not to express how I feel
___ tendency to disregard how I feel since I cannot trust my feelings
___ consciously or subconsciously deny them since it is too painful to deal with them

4. Do you know someone in your life with whom you could be emotionally honest right now (i.e., you could tell this person

exactly how you feel about yourself, life and other people)?

5. How important is it that we are emotionally honest before God, and do you feel that you are? Explain.

IV. Spiritual History

A. If you were to die tonight, do you know where you would spend eternity?

B. Suppose you did die tonight and appeared before God in heaven and He were to ask you, "By what right should I allow you into My presence?" How would you answer Him?

C. First John 5:11-12 says, "God has given us eternal life, and this life is in His Son. He who has the Son has the life; he who does not have the Son of God does not have the life."

1. Do you have the Son of God in you (see 2 Cor. 13:3)?

2. When did you receive Him (see John 1:12)?

3. How do you know you have received Him?

D. Are you plagued with doubts concerning your salvation? Please explain.

E. Are you presently enjoying fellowship with other believers and, if so, where and when?

F. Are you under the authority of a local church where the Bible is preached, and do you regularly support it with your time, talent and treasure? If not, why?

NON-CHRISTIAN SPIRITUAL EXPERIENCE INVENTORY

Check any of the following with which you or your ancestors have had any involvement. Place a check before each one in which you have participated in fun, out of curiosity or in earnest.

___ Psychic readings
___ Card laying
___ Crystal ball
___ Palm reading
___ Tea leaves
___ Tarot cards
___ Attended or participated in a séance
___ Attended or participated in a spiritualist meeting
___ Ouija board
___ Magic eight ball
___ Automatic (spirit) writing
___ Levitation
___ Table lifting
___ Read or follow the horoscope
___ Astrology
___ Clairvoyance
___ Telepathy
___ ESP
___ Speaking in a trance
___ Mystical meditation
___ Astral projection/travel
___ Magical charming
___ Fetishism (objects of worship/idols)
___ Cabala/kabala
___ Water witching

(dowsing) rod and pendulum
___ Materialization
___ Metaphysics
___ Self-realization
___ Witchcraft
___ Sorcery
___ Mental suggestion
___ Dream interpretation
___ I Ching
___ Been hypnotized
___ Practiced self-hypnosis
___ Other

___ Practiced yoga
___ Christian Science
___ Unity
___ The Way International
___ Unification Church
___ Mormonism
___ Church of the Living Word
___ The Local Church
___ Children of God
___ Worldwide Church of God (Herbert W. Armstrong)
___ Jehovah's Witnesses
___ Unitarianism

___ Masonic orders
___ Swedenborgianism
___ Other

___ Zen Buddhism
___ Hare Krishna
___ Bahaism
___ Rosicrucianism
___ New Age
___ Inner Peace Movement
___ Spiritual Frontiers Fellowship
___ Transcendental Meditation
___ EST/The Forum
___ Eckankar
___ Mind-control philosophies
___ Science of the Mind
___ Science of Creative Intelligence
___ Theosophical Society
___ Islam
___ Black Muslim
___ Hinduism
___ Other

___ Had a spirit guide.

___ Read or possessed occult literature, especially the Satanic Bible, Book of Shadows, Secrets of the Psalms, Sixth and Seventh Books of Moses.

___ Read or studied parapsychology.

___ Practiced black or white magic.

___ Possessed occult or pagan religious objects that were made for use in pagan temples or religious rites, or in the practice of magic, sorcery, witchcraft, divination or spiritualism.

___ Seen or been involved in Satan worship.

___ Sought healing (either as a child or as an adult) through magic conjuration, charming, psychic healing or New Age medicine.

___ Tried to locate a missing person or object by consulting someone with psychic powers.

___ Encountered ghosts or materializations of persons known to be dead.

___ Entered into a blood pact with another person.

___ Been the object of sexual attacks by demons (incubi, succubi).

___ Been involved with heavy metal or allied kinds of rock music.

___ Heard voices in your mind or had compulsive thoughts that were foreign to what you believe.

___ Have periods in childhood or the present when you cannot remember what happened.

1. Have you ever attended a New Age or parapsychology seminar, or consulted a medium, spiritist or channeler? Explain.

2. Do you or have you ever had an imaginary friend or spirit guide offering you guidance or companionship? Explain.

3. Have you ever heard voices in your mind or had repeating and nagging thoughts that were foreign to what you believe or feel, as though a dialogue was going on in your head? Explain.

4. What other spiritual experiences have you had that would be considered out of the ordinary (such as sensing an evil presence in your room at night as a child)?

5. Have you been a victim of satanic ritual abuse? Explain.

Forgiving Others

Forgiveness is the central issue in man's relationship to God, "For all have sinned and fall short of the glory of God" (Rom. 3:23), and "the wages of sin is death" (i.e., separation from God, 6:23). The purpose for the first coming of Christ was to take upon Himself our sins (see 2 Cor. 5:21) and to pay the penalty for it (see Heb. 9:22) that we may be forgiven (see Col. 1:14). It is also the basis for our relationships with other people. Comment on the following verses:

1. Matthew 5:23-26

2. Matthew 6:9-15

3. Matthew 18:21-35

   a. How does our debt of sin before a holy God compare to the debt others may owe us?

   b. How would knowing this enable us to forgive others (see Luke 7:47)?

   c. How often should we forgive others (see Luke 17:3-5)?

   d. Is this a question of faith or obedience?

   e. How does God feel toward those whom He has forgiven by sacrificing His only begotten Son when they will not forgive others?

   f. Should we, as God's children, see forgiveness as optional or required by God? The most common reason given for not forgiving another is the desire to seek revenge. "Justice must be served," "You'll pay for this," or "I'll get even," if not stated are certainly felt. Comment on the following verses concerning these inner thoughts and feelings:

1. Proverbs 24:17,18

2. Romans 12:19

3. 1 Peter 3:8,9

4. 1 John 4:19-21

5. What six responses stand in contrast to forgiveness in Ephesians 4:31? What are we to do?

a. _____	d. _____
b. _____	e. _____
c. _____	f. _____

Forgiveness is not forgetting. People who try to forget find they cannot. God says He will remember our sins no more (see Heb. 10:17), but God being omniscient cannot forget. What it means is that God will not take our past offenses and use them against us. "As far as the east is from the west, so far has He removed our transgressions from us" (Ps. 103:12).

Forgetting may be the result of forgiveness, but never the means of forgiveness. Forgiveness is also a hard choice because it pulls against the idea of justice. But our relationship with God is based on His mercy (see Titus 3:5), and so must it be with others (see Luke 6:35-38). Forgiveness is costly. We must pay the price of the evil we forgive by accepting the consequences of another person's sin upon ourselves. Consequently, it is substitutional. No one really forgives another without bearing the penalty of the other person's sin. This is forgiving others as Christ has forgiven us (see Eph. 4:32; Col. 3:13). You may say, "But I can't forgive them; they hurt me so bad." This is certainly true and, undoubtedly, nobody has really forgiven another without acknowledging the hurt and often the hate (see Prov. 14:10). The point is that they are still hurting you, and the hurt will continue to bind you until you release yourself from the past by forgiving. "But they are off the hook," the heart is quick to protest. Not really, for they will stand before God some day and give an account (see 2 Cor. 5:10).

STEPS TO FORGIVENESS

1. On a separate piece of paper, make a list of every person that has ever offended you. Face the specific wrong (i.e., rejection, deprivation of love, injustice, unfairness, physical and verbal abuse, betrayal, neglect).

2. Face the hurt and the hate. If you bury it, you bury the possibility of forgiving. It is not a sin to acknowledge the reality of these emotions.

3. Face the Cross. It is the Cross that makes forgiveness legal and morally right. Jesus died "once for all" when He took upon Himself all the sins of the world (1 Pet. 3:18).

4. Decide that you will bear the burden of their sins (see Gal. 6:2). This means that you will not retaliate (see Luke 6:27-34), nor use the information against them in the future, for "love covers a multitude of sins" (1 Pet. 4:8; see also Prov. 10:12). "He who covers a transgression seeks love, but he who repeats a matter separates intimate friends" (Prov. 17:9).

5. You are now ready to forgive or not forgive. Forgiveness is a crisis of the will, a choice to let the other person off the hook and free yourself from the past. Your feelings will follow in time. You need to release the desire to hate and seek revenge.

6. If bitterness has been present for some time, you may want to find a righteous and trusted counselor friend who will pray with you and for you (see Jas. 5:16). Otherwise, alone before God, go down the list and pray, "I forgive _____(name)_____ for ___(list the offenses)___."

7. Destroy the list and do not tell the offenders they are forgiven. Telling them you have forgiven them may create more conflict because the offenders may be projecting their problems onto other people. Your forgiveness of others is between you and God.

8 Do not expect that your choice to forgive will result in major changes in others. Instead, pray for them (see Matt. 5:44), so they may find the freedom of forgiveness in Christ (see Gal. 5:1,13-15). Try to understand them. They are victims also.

9. Remember that forgiveness is first a choice of the will in obedience to God. Some positive emotional results will come with time and include:

   a. The ability to pray for the person without feeling hurt, anger or resentment.
   b. The ability to revisit people and places without a negative reaction.

10. Thank God for the lessons learned and the maturity gained as a result of the experience (see Rom. 8:28,29).

11. Have you accepted your part of the blame for what happened and confessed it to God (see 1 John 1:9) and others (see Matt. 5:23-26)?

SEEKING FORGIVENESS

The most important forgiveness we can have is God's forgiveness. This can come only through our relationship with Christ "in whom we have redemption, the forgiveness of sins" (Col. 1:14). Salvation assures us that our sins are forgiven—past, present and future. "There is therefore now no condemnation for those who are in Christ Jesus" (Rom. 8:1). We may be out of fellowship with God, however, and this requires our confession (see 1 John 1:9).

It is very important to distinguish between relationship and fellowship. When we are born physically, we are related by blood to our fathers. Nothing can change that fact, and we will be blood-related regardless of our behavior. Once born, however, we will be in and out of fellowship with our fathers, dependent upon our behavior. If we obey our fathers, we will be in fellowship with them. Disobey, and fellowship is broken.

When we are born again, we are related to the Father through the blood of the Lord Jesus Christ (see Heb. 10:19-22; 1 Pet. 1:17-23). Nothing can change this fact (see Rom. 8:31-39). We are His children, and we will remain His children. We entered into that relationship by our beliefs, not our behavior (see Eph. 2:8,9; Titus 3:4-7). But the harmony of our relationship with God can be interrupted by disobedience, just as harmony with our parents was interrupted when we disobeyed them. When we obey God, we live in harmony with Him. When we don't, our relationship with Him is disturbed, and we feel miserable as a result.

The primary purpose for this exercise is to seek the forgiveness of others. But if you are knowledgeable of sin in your life, then make a list of sins whether by commission or omission (see Jas. 4:17). Ask God to guide you. Then go through the list by confessing, "I did/did not (and name the specific sin)." There is a major difference between confessing and asking for forgiveness. Confessing is acknowledging what you have thought, said or done. This is then followed by asking God to forgive you for the acknowledged sin. Refusing to acknowledge our sins before God is to choose to remain out of fellowship with Him and live a barren, fruitless life. The remaining portion of this exercise deals with our need to seek the forgiveness of others.

I. The Motivation for Seeking Forgiveness

Matthew 5:23-26 is a key passage on seeking forgiveness. Several points in these verses bear emphasizing.

The worshiper coming before god to offer a gift "remembers" that someone has something against him. The worshiper is the offender.

This does not mean the worshiper is to become introspective, probing into his own soul to "dig up dirt" to be confessed. It means that a remembrance of another's feelings toward him is to be the motivating key. This remembrance is the working of the Holy Spirit.

It is the offense known by the other party that needs to be dealt with. If you have had jealous, lustful or angry thoughts toward another, of which the other person is unaware, these are to be confessed to God alone.

An exception to this (where the offended is unaware) would be where restitution needs to be made (e.g., something stolen to be returned, something broken to be paid for, someone's name restored, etc.).

II. The Urgency of Seeking Forgiveness

Christ says that as soon as the worshiper senses his need, he should go and be reconciled. This is a prerequisite to acceptable worship of God. Put another way, our worship is **unacceptable to God** if we have not made right an offense against another.

III. The Process of Seeking Forgiveness

A. Regarding people of whom you need to ask forgiveness, clearly identify to yourself the offenses committed. Write them out, including the **attitude** behind the wrong or offensive actions.

B. Make sure you have already forgiven them for any wrongs on their part.

C. Think through the precise wording you will use as you ask forgiveness.
   1. Label your action as "wrong."
   2. Go into only as much detail as necessary for the offended person to understand what you are confessing.
   3. Make no defenses, alibis or excuses.
   4. Do not project blame. Never confess for another.
   5. Your confession should lead to the direct question, "Will you forgive me?"

D. Seek the right place and the right time to approach the offended person.

E. Make your quest for forgiveness in person with family members or persons with whom you can talk face-to-face, with the following exception. Where there has been action of an immoral nature, DO NOT seek to deal with this alone and face-to-face. If incest was involved, have a minister or counselor with you in your face-to-face confession.

F. Except where no other means of communication are possible, DO NOT write a letter.
   1. A letter can be very easily misread or misunderstood.
   2. A letter can be read by the wrong people, those having nothing to do with the offense or the confession.
   3. A letter can be kept when it should have been destroyed.
   4. You don't want to "document" your confession.

G. Once you sincerely seek forgiveness, you are free.

H. If forgiveness is refused, and there seems no hope of change on the part of the offended person, then prayerfully and humbly commit your case to "the Judge" (God, our heavenly Father) and leave it there (see Matt. 5:25; 1 Pet. 2:21-23).

I. After forgiveness, fellowship with God in worship (see Matt. 5:24).

Steps to Freedom in Christ

Preface

If you have received Christ as your personal Savior, He has set you free through His victory over sin and death on the cross. If you are not experiencing freedom, it may be because you have not stood firm in the faith or actively taken your place in Christ. It is the Christian's responsibility to do whatever is necessary to maintain a right relationship with God. Your eternal destiny is not at stake; you are secure in Christ. But your daily victory is at stake if you fail to claim and maintain your position in Christ.

You are not the helpless victim caught between two nearly equal but opposite heavenly superpowers. Satan is a deceiver. Only God is omnipotent (all powerful), omnipresent (always present) and omniscient (all knowing). Sometimes the reality of sin and the presence of evil may seem more real than the presence of God, but that is part of Satan's deception. Satan is a defeated foe, and we are in Christ. A true knowledge of God and our identity in Christ are the greatest determinants of our mental health. A false concept of God, a distorted understanding of who we are as children of God, and the misplaced deification of Satan (attributing God's attributes to Satan) are the greatest contributors to mental illness.

As you prepare to go through the Steps to Freedom, you need to remember that the only power Satan has is the power of the lie. As soon as we expose the lie, the power is broken. The battle is for your mind. The control center is in your mind. If Satan can get you to believe a lie, he can control your life, but you don't have to let him. The opposing thoughts that you may experience can control you only if you believe them. If you are going through the Steps by yourself, don't pay attention to any deception (i.e., lying, intimidating thoughts in your mind).

Thoughts such as, *This isn't going to work; God doesn't love me* and so on, can interfere only if you believe those lies. If you are going through the Steps with a trusted pastor or counselor or lay encourager (which we strongly recommend if there has been severe trauma in your life), then share any thoughts you are having that are in opposition to what you are attempting to do. As soon as you expose the lie, the power of Satan is broken. *You must cooperate with the person trying to help you by sharing what is going on inside.*

Knowing the nature of the battle for our minds, we can pray authoritatively to stop any interference. The Steps begin with a suggested prayer and declaration. If you are going through the Steps by yourself, you will need to change some of the personal pronouns (i.e., "I" instead of "we").

PRAYER

Dear heavenly Father,

We acknowledge Your presence in this room and in our lives. You are the only omniscient (all knowing), omnipotent (all powerful), and omnipresent (always present) God. We are dependent upon You for apart from Christ we can do nothing. We stand in the truth that all authority in heaven and on earth has been given to the resurrected Christ, and because we are in Christ, we share that authority in order to make disciples and set captives free. We ask You to fill us with Your Holy Spirit and lead us into all truth. We pray for Your complete protection and ask for Your guidance. In Jesus' name. Amen.

DECLARATION

In the name and authority of the Lord Jesus Christ, we command Satan and all evil spirits to release (name) in order that (name) can be free to know and choose to do the will of God. As children of God seated with Christ in the heavenlies, we agree that every enemy of the Lord Jesus Christ be bound and gagged to silence. We say to Satan and all his evil workers that you cannot inflict any pain or in any way prevent God's will from being accomplished in (name's) life.

PREPARATION

Before going through the Steps to Freedom, review the events of your life to discern specific areas that might need to be addressed.

Family History
    __ Religious history of parents and grandparents
    __ Home life from childhood through high school
    __ History of physical or emotional illness in the family
    __ Adoption, foster care, guardians

Personal History
    __ Eating habits (bulimia, binging and purging, anorexia, compulsive eating)
    __ Addictions (drugs, alcohol)
    __ Prescription medications (what for?)
    __ Sleeping patterns and nightmares
    __ Raped or any sexual, physical, emotional molestation
    __ Thought life (obsessive, blasphemous, condemning, distracting thoughts; poor concentration; fantasy)
    __ Mental interference in church, prayer or Bible study
    __ Emotional life (anger, anxiety, depression, bitterness, fears)
    __ Spiritual journey (salvation: when, how and assurance)

Now you are ready to begin. The following are seven specific Steps to process in order to experience freedom from your past. You will address the areas where Satan most commonly takes advantage of us and where strongholds have been built. Christ purchased your victory when He shed His blood for you on the cross. Realize your freedom will be the result of what you choose to believe, confess, forgive, renounce and forsake. No one can do that for you. The battle for your mind can only be won as you personally choose truth.

As you go through these Steps to Freedom, remember that Satan will only be defeated if you confront him verbally. He cannot read your mind and is under no obligation to obey your thoughts. Only God has complete knowledge of your mind. As you process each Step, it is important that you submit to God inwardly and resist the devil by reading aloud each prayer—verbally renouncing, forgiving and confessing.

You are taking a fierce moral inventory and making a rock-solid commitment to truth. If your problems stem from a source other than those covered in these Steps, you have nothing to lose by going through them. If you are sincere, the only thing that can happen is that you will get very right with God!

STEP 1: COUNTERFEIT VERSUS REAL

The first Step to Freedom in Christ is to renounce your previous or current involvements with satanically inspired occult practices and false religions. You need to renounce any activity and group that denies Jesus Christ, offers guidance through any source other than the absolute authority of the written Word of God, or requires secret initiations, ceremonies or covenants.

In order to help you assess your spiritual experiences, begin this Step by asking God to reveal false guidance and counterfeit religious experiences.

Dear heavenly Father,
I ask You to guard my heart and my mind and reveal to me any and all involvement I have had either knowingly or unknowingly with cultic or occult practices, false religions and false teachers. In Jesus name I pray. Amen.

Using the "Non-Christian Spiritual Experience Inventory," carefully check anything in which you were involved. This list is not exhaustive, but it will guide you in identifying non-Christian experiences. Add any additional involvements you have had. Even if you "innocently" participated in something or observed it, you should write it on your list to renounce, just in case you unknowingly gave Satan a foothold.

1. Have you ever been hypnotized, attended a New Age or parapsychology seminar, consulted a medium, spiritist or channeler? Explain.

   _____

2. Do you or have you ever had an imaginary friend or spirit guide offering you guidance or companionship? Explain

   _____

3. Have you ever heard voices in your mind or had repeating and nagging thoughts condemning you or that were foreign to what you believe or feel, like there was a dialogue going on in your head? Explain.

   _____

4. What other spiritual experiences have you had that would be considered out of the ordinary?

   _____

5. Have you been involved in satanic ritual of any form? Explain.

   _____

Non-Christian Spiritual Experience Inventory

(please check those that apply)

Occult
___ Astral projection
___ Ouija board
___ Table lifting
___ Dungeons and Dragons
___ Speaking in a trance
___ Automatic writing
___ Magic eight ball
___ Telepathy
___ Ghosts
___ Séance
___ Materialization
___ Clairvoyance
___ Spirit guides
___ Fortune-telling
___ Tarot cards
___ Palm reading
___ Astrology
___ Rod and pendulum (dowsing)
___ Self-hypnosis
___ Mental suggestions or attempting to swap minds
___ Black and white magic
___ New-Age Medicine
___ Blood pacts (or cutting yourself in a destructive way)

___ Fetishism (objects of worship)
___ Incubi and succubae (sexual spirits)
___ Other _____
_____
_____

Cult
___ Christian Science
___ Unity
___ Scientology
___ Witness Lee
___ The Way International
___ Unification Church
___ Mormonism
___ Church of the LivingWord
___ Jehovah's Witnesses
___ Children of God
___ Swedenborgianism
___ Herbert W. Armstrong (Worldwide Church of God)
___ Unitarianism
___ Masons
___ New Age
___ Other _____
_____
_____

Other Religions
___ Zen Buddhism
___ Hare Krishna
___ Bahaism
___ Rosicrucian
___ Science of the Mind
___ Science of Creative Intelligence
___ Hinduism
___ Transcendental Meditation
___ Yoga
___ Eckankar
___ Roy Masters
___ Silva Mind Control
___ Father Divine
___ Theosophical Society
___ Islam
___ Black Muslim
___ Other _____
_____
_____

When you are confident that your list is complete, confess and renounce each involvement whether active or passive by praying aloud the following prayer, repeating it separately for each item on your list:

> Lord, I confess that I have participated in_____.
> I ask Your fogiveness, and I renounce_____.

If there has been any involvement in satanic ritual or heavy occult activity (or you suspect it because of blocked memories, severe nightmares, sexual dysfunction or bondage), you need to state aloud the special renunciations that follow. Read across the page, renouncing the first item in the column on the Kingdom of Darkness and then affirming the first truth in the column on the Kingdom of Light. Continue down the page in that manner.

All satanic rituals, covenants and assignments must be specifically renounced as the Lord allows you to remember them. Some who have been subjected to satanic ritual abuse have developed multiple personalities in order to survive. Nevertheless, continue through the Steps to Freedom in order to resolve all that you consciously can. It is important that you resolve the demonic strongholds first. Eventually, every personality must be accessed, and each must resolve their issues and agree to come together in Christ. You may need someone who understands spiritual conflict to help you with this.

Special Renunciations for Satanic Ritual Involvement

KINGDOM OF DARKNESS	KINGDOM OF LIGHT
I renounce ever signing my name over to Satan or having had my name signed over to Satan.	I announce that my name is now written in the Lamb's Book of Life.
I renounce any ceremony where I may have been wed to Satan.	I announce that I am the bride of Christ.
I renounce any and all covenants that I made with Satan.	I announce that I am a partaker of the New Covenant with Christ.
I renounce all satanic assignments for my life, including duties, marriage and children.	I announce and commit myself to know and to do only the will of God and accept only His guidance.

KINGDOM OF DARKNESS	KINGDOM OF LIGHT
I renounce all spirit guides assigned to me.	*I announce and accept only the leading of the Holy Spirit.*
I renounce ever giving of my blood in the service of Satan.	*I trust only in the shed blood of my Lord Jesus Christ.*
I renounce ever eating of flesh or drinking of blood for satanic worship.	*By faith I eat only the flesh and drink only the blood of Jesus in Holy Communion.*
I renounce any and all guardians and satanist parents that were assigned to me.	*I announce that God is my Father and the Holy Spirit is my Guardian by which I am sealed.*
I renounce any baptism in blood or urine whereby I am identified with Satan.	*I announce that I have been baptized into Christ Jesus and my identity is now in Christ.*
I renounce any and all sacrifices that were made on my behalf by which Satan may claim ownership of me.	*I announce that only the sacrifice of Christ has any hold on me. I belong to Him. I have been purchased by the blood of the Lamb.*

STEP 2: DECEPTION VERSUS TRUTH

Truth is the revelation of God's Word, but we need to acknowledge the truth in the inner self (see Ps. 51:6). When David lived a lie, he suffered greatly. When he finally found freedom by acknowledging the truth, he wrote: "How blessed is the man...in whose spirit there is no deceit" (Ps. 32:2). We are to lay aside falsehood and speak the truth in love (see Eph. 4:15,25). A mentally healthy person is one who is in touch with reality and relatively free of anxiety. Both qualities should characterize the Christian who renounces deception and embraces the truth.

Begin this critical Step by expressing aloud the following prayer. Don't let the enemy accuse you with thoughts such as: *This isn't going to work* or *I wish I could believe this but I can't* or any other lies in opposition to what you are proclaiming. Even if you have difficulty doing so, you need to pray the prayer and read the Doctrinal Affirmation.

Dear heavenly Father,
I know that You desire truth in the inner self and that facing

this truth is the way of liberation (John 8:32). I acknowledge that I have been deceived by the "father of lies" (John 8:44) and that I have deceived myself (1 John 1:8). I pray in the name of the Lord Jesus Christ that You, heavenly Father, will rebuke all deceiving spirits by virtue of the shed blood and resurrection of the Lord Jesus Christ.

By faith I have received You into my life and I am now seated with Christ in the heavenlies (Eph. 2:6). I acknowledge that I have the responsibility and authority to resist the devil, and when I do, he will flee from me. I now ask the Holy Spirit to guide me into all truth (John 16:13). I ask You to "Search me, O God, and know my heart; try me and know my anxious thoughts; and see if there be any hurtful way in me, and lead me in the everlasting way" (Ps. 139:23,24). In Jesus' name I pray. Amen.

You may want to pause at this point to consider some of Satan's deceptive schemes. In addition to false teachers, false prophets and deceiving spirits, you can deceive yourself. Now that you are alive in Christ and forgiven, you never have to live a lie or defend yourself. Christ is your defense. How have you deceived or attempted to defend yourself according to the following?

Self-deception
___ Being hearers and not doers of the Word (see Jas. 1:22; 4:17)
___ Saying we have no sin (see 1 John 1:8)
___ Thinking we are something when we aren't (see Gal. 6:3)
___ Thinking we are wise in this age (see 1 Cor. 3:18,19)
___ Thinking we will not reap what we sow (see Gal. 6:7)
___ Thinking the unrighteous will inherit the Kingdom of God (see 1 Cor. 6:9)
___ Thinking we can associate with bad company and not be corrupted (see 1 Cor. 15:33)

Self-defense (defending ourselves instead of trusting in Christ)
___ Denial (conscious or subconscious)
___ Fantasy (escape from the real world)
___ Emotional insulation (withdraw to avoid rejection)
___ Regression (reverting back to a less threatening time)
___ Displacement (taking out frustrations on others)
___ Projection (blaming others)
___ Rationalization (defending self through verbal excursion)

For those things that have been true in your life, pray aloud:

> Lord, I agree that I have been deceived in the area of
> _____. Thank You for forgiving me. I commit
> myself to know and follow Your truth. Amen.

Choosing the truth may be difficult if you have been living a lie (been deceived) for many years. You may need to seek professional help to weed out the defense mechanisms you have depended upon to survive. The Christian needs only one defense—Jesus. Knowing that you are forgiven and accepted as God's child is what sets you free to face reality and declare your dependence on Him.

Faith is the biblical response to the truth, and believing the truth is a choice. When someone says, "I want to believe God, but I just can't," he or she is being deceived. Of course you can believe God. Faith is something you decide to do, not something you feel like doing. Believing the truth doesn't make it true. It's true; therefore we believe it. The New Age movement is distorting the truth by saying we create reality through what we believe. We can't create reality with our minds; we face reality. It's what or who you believe in that counts. Everybody believes in something, and everybody walks by faith according to what he or she believes. But if what you believe isn't true, then how you live (walk by faith) won't be right.

Historically, the Church has found great value in publicly declaring its beliefs. The Apostles' Creed and the Nicene Creed have been recited for centuries. Read aloud the following affirmation of faith, and do so again as often as necessary to renew your mind. Read it daily for several weeks.

DOCTRINAL AFFIRMATION

I recognize that there is only one true and living God (Exod. 20:2,3) who exists as the Father, Son and Holy Spirit, and that He is worthy of all honor, praise and glory as the Creator, Sustainer and Beginning and End of all things (Rev. 4:11; 5:9,10; Isa. 43:1,7,21).

I recognize Jesus Christ as the Messiah, the Word who became flesh and dwelt among us (John 1:1,14). I believe that He came to destroy the works of Satan (1 John 3:8), that He disarmed the rulers and authorities and made a public display of them, having triumphed over them (Col. 2:15).

I believe that God has proven His love for me because when I was still a sinner, Christ died for me (Rom. 5:8). I believe that He delivered me from the domain of darkness and transferred me to His kingdom, and in Him I have redemption, the forgiveness of sins (Col. 1:13,14).

I believe that I am now a child of God (1 John 3:1-3) and that I am seated with Christ in the heavenlies (Eph. 2:6). I believe that I was saved by the grace of God through faith, that it was a gift and not the result of any works on my part (Eph. 2:8).

I choose to be strong in the Lord and in the strength of His might (Eph. 6:10). I put no confidence in the flesh (Phil. 3:3) for the weapons of warfare are not of the flesh (2 Cor. 10:4). I put on the whole armor of God (Eph. 6:10-20), and I resolve to stand firm in my faith and resist the evil one.

I believe that apart from Christ I can do nothing (John 15:5), so I declare myself dependent on Him. I choose to abide in Christ in order to bear much fruit and glorify the Lord (John 15:8). I announce to Satan that Jesus is my Lord (1 Cor. 12:3), and I reject any counterfeit gifts or works of Satan in my life.

I believe that the truth will set me free (John 8:32) and that walking in the light is the only path of fellowship (1 John 1:7). Therefore, I stand against Satan's deception by taking every thought captive in obedience to Christ (2 Cor. 10:5). I declare that the Bible is the only authoritative standard (2 Tim. 3:15,16). I choose to speak the truth in love (Eph. 4:15).

I choose to present my body as an instrument of righteousness, a living and holy sacrifice, and I renew my mind by the living Word of God in order that I may prove that the will of God is good, acceptable and perfect (Rom. 6:13; 12:1,2). I put off the old self with its evil practices and put on the new self (Col. 3:9,10), and I declare myself to be a new creature in Christ (2 Cor. 5:17).

I ask my heavenly Father to fill me with His Holy Spirit (Eph. 5:18), lead me into all truth (John 16:13), and empower my life that I may live above sin and not carry out the desires of the flesh (Gal. 5:16). I crucify the flesh (Gal. 5:24) and choose to walk by the Spirit.

I renounce all selfish goals and choose the ultimate goal of love (1 Tim. 1:5). I choose to obey the two greatest commandments; to love the Lord my God with all my heart, soul and mind, and to love my neighbor as myself (Matt. 22:37-39).

I believe that Jesus has all authority in heaven and on earth (Matt. 28:18) and that He is the head over all rule and authority (Col. 2:10). I believe that Satan and his demons are subject to me in Christ since I am a member of Christ's Body (Eph. 1:19-23). Therefore, I obey the command to submit to God and to resist the devil (Jas. 4:7), and I command Satan in the name of Christ to leave my presence.

Step 3: Bitterness Versus Forgiveness

We need to forgive others so that Satan cannot take advantage of us (see 2 Cor. 2:10,11). We are to be merciful just as our heavenly Father is merciful (see Luke 6:36). We are to forgive as we have been forgiven (see Eph. 4:31,32). Ask God to bring to mind the names of those people you need to forgive by expressing the following prayer aloud:

> Dear heavenly Father,
> I thank You for the riches of Your kindness, forbearance and patience, knowing that Your kindness has led me to repentance (Rom. 2:4). I confess that I have not extended that same patience and kindness toward others who have offended me, but instead I have harbored bitterness and resentment. I pray that during this time of self-examination You would bring to my mind those people that I have not forgiven in order that I may do so (Matt. 18:35). I ask this in the precious name of Jesus. Amen.

As names come to mind, make a list of only the names.

At the end of your list, write "myself." Forgiving yourself is accepting God's cleansing and forgiveness. Also, write "thoughts against God." Thoughts raised up against the knowledge of God will usually result in angry feelings toward Him. Technically, we don't forgive God, because He cannot commit any sin of commission or omission. But you need to specifically renounce false expectations and thoughts about God and agree to release any anger you have toward Him.

Before you pray to forgive those people, stop and consider what forgiveness is and what it is not, what decision you will be making, and what the consequences will be.

Forgiveness is not forgetting. People who try to forget find they cannot. God says He will remember our sins "no more" (Heb. 10:17), but God, being omniscient, cannot forget. Remember our sins "no more" means that God will never use the past against us (see Ps. 103:12). Forgetting may be the result of forgiveness, but it is never the means of forgiveness. When we bring up the past against others, we are saying we haven't forgiven them.

Forgiveness is a choice, a crisis of the will. Since God requires us to forgive, it is something we can do. But forgiveness is difficult for us because it pulls against our concept of justice. We want revenge for offenses suffered. But we are told never to take our own revenge (see Rom. 12:19). You say,

"Why should I let them off the hook?" That is precisely the problem. You are still hooked to them, still bound by your past. You will let them off your hook, but they are never off God's. He will deal with them fairly—something we cannot do.

You say, "You don't understand how much this person hurt me!" But don't you see, they are still hurting you? How do you stop the pain? You don't forgive someone for their sake; you do it for your sake, so you can be free. Your need to forgive isn't an issue between you and the offender; it's between you and God.

Forgiveness is agreeing to live with the consequences of another person's sin. Forgiveness is costly. You pay the price of the evil you forgive. You're going to live with those consequences whether you want to or not; your only choice is whether you will do so in the bitterness of unforgiveness or the freedom of forgiveness. Jesus took the consequences of your sin upon Himself. All true forgiveness is substitutionary, because no one really forgives without bearing the consequences of the other person's sin. God the Father "made Him who knew no sin to be sin on our behalf, that we might become the righteousness of God in Him" (2 Cor. 5:21). Where is the justice? It is the Cross that makes forgiveness legally and morally right: "For the death that He died, He died to sin once for all" (Rom. 6:10, NKJV).

How do you forgive from your heart? You acknowledge the hurt and the hate. If your forgiveness doesn't visit the emotional core of your life, it will be incomplete. Many feel the pain of interpersonal offenses, but they won't or don't know how to acknowledge it. Let God bring the pain to the surface so He can deal with it. This is where the healing takes place.

Decide that you will bear the burden of their offenses by not using that information against them in the future. This doesn't mean that you must tolerate sin; you must always take a stand against sin.

Don't wait to forgive until you feel like forgiving; you will never get there. Feelings take time to heal after the choice to forgive is made and Satan has lost his place (Eph. 4:26,27). Freedom is what will be gained, not a feeling.

As you pray, God may bring to mind offending people and experiences you have totally forgotten. Let Him do it even if it is painful. Remember, you are doing this for your sake; God wants you to be free. Don't rationalize or explain the offender's behavior. Forgiveness is dealing with your pain and leaving the other person to God. Positive feelings will follow in time; freeing yourself from the past is the critical issue right now.

Don't say, "Lord, please help me to forgive," because He is already helping you. Don't say, "Lord, I want to forgive," because you are bypassing the hard-core choice to forgive, which is your responsibility. Stay with each person until you are sure you have dealt with all the remembered pain—what they did, how they hurt you, how they made you feel (rejected, unloved, unworthy, dirty).

You are now ready to forgive the people on your list so that you can be free in Christ; those people no longer have any control over you. For each person on your list, pray aloud:

> Lord, I forgive (name) for (specifically identify all offenses and painful memories or feelings).

Step 4: Rebellion Versus Submission

We live in a rebellious generation. Many believe it is their right to sit in judgment of those in authority over them. Rebelling against God and His authority gives Satan an opportunity to attack. As our commanding general, the Lord says, "Get into ranks and follow Me. I will not lead you into temptation, but I will deliver you from evil" (see Matt. 6:13).

We have two biblical responsibilities in regard to authority figures: Pray for them and submit to them. The only time God permits us to disobey earthly leaders is when they require us to do something morally wrong before God or attempt to rule outside the realm of their authority. Pray the following prayer:

> Dear heavenly Father,
> You have said that rebellion is as the sin of witchcraft and "insubordination is as iniquity and idolatry" (1 Sam. 15:23). I know that in action and attitude I have sinned against You with a rebellious heart. I ask Your forgiveness for my rebellion and pray that by the shed blood of the Lord Jesus Christ all ground gained by evil spirits because of my rebelliousness would be cancelled. I pray that You will shed light on all my ways that I may know the full extent of my rebelliousness. I now choose to adopt a submissive spirit and a servant's heart. Amen.

Being under authority is an act of faith. You are trusting God to work through His established lines of authority. There are times when employers, parents and husbands are violating the laws of civil government, which is ordained by God to protect innocent people against abuse. In those cases, you need to appeal to the state for your protection. In many states the law requires such abuse to be reported.

In difficult cases such as continuing abuse at home, further counseling help may be needed. And, in some cases, when earthly authorities have abused their positions and are requiring disobedience to God or a compromise in your commitment to Him, you need to obey God not man.

We are all admonished to submit to one another as equals in Christ (see Eph. 5:21). However, there are specific lines of authority in Scripture for the purpose of accomplishing common goals.

Civil government	Husband (see 1 Pet. 3:1-4)
(see Rom. 13:1-7; 1 Tim.	Employer (see 1 Pet. 2:18-23)
2:1-4; 1 Pet. 2:13-17)	Church leaders (see Heb. 13:17)
Parents (see Eph. 6:1-3)	God (see Dan. 9:5,9)

Examine each area and ask God to forgive you for those times you have not been submissive, and pray:

Lord, I agree I have been rebellious toward_____.
Please forgive me for this rebellion. I choose to be submissive
and obedient to Your Word. In Jesus' name. Amen.

STEP 5: PRIDE VERSUS HUMILITY

Pride is a killer. Pride says, "I can do it! I can get myself out of this mess without God or anyone else's help." Oh no we can't! We absolutely need God, and we desperately need each other. Paul wrote: "We...worship in the Spirit of God and glory in Christ Jesus and put no confidence in the flesh" (Phil. 3:3). Humility is confidence properly placed. We are to be "strong in the Lord, and in the strength of His might" (Eph. 6:10). James 4:6-10 and 1 Peter 5:1-10 reveal that spiritual conflict follows pride. Use the following prayer to express your commitment to live humbly before God:

Dear heavenly Father,
You have said that pride goes before destruction and an arrogant spirit before stumbling (Prov. 16:18). I confess that I have lived independently and have not denied myself, picked up my

cross daily, and followed You (Matt. 16:24). In so doing, I have given ground to the enemy in my life. I have believed that I could be successful and live victoriously by my own strength and resources.

I now confess that I have sinned against You by placing my will before Yours and by centering my life around self instead of You. I now renounce the self-life and by so doing cancel all the ground that has been gained in my members by the enemies of the Lord Jesus Christ. I pray that You will guide me so that I will do nothing from selfishness or empty conceit, but with humility of mind I will regard others as more important than myself (Phil. 2:3). Enable me through love to serve others and in honor prefer others (Rom. 12:10). I ask this in the name of Christ Jesus my Lord. Amen.

Having made that commitment, now allow God to show you any specific areas of your life where you have been prideful, such as:

___ Stronger desire to do my will than God's will
___ More dependent upon my strengths and resources than God's
___ Sometimes believe that my ideas and opinions are better than others'
___ More concerned about controlling others than developing self-control
___ Sometimes consider myself more important than others
___ Tendency to think that I have no needs
___ Find it difficult to admit that I was wrong
___ Tendency to be more of a people pleaser than a God pleaser
___ Overly concerned about getting the credit I deserve
___ Driven to obtain the recognition that comes from degrees, titles, positions
___ Often think I am more humble than others
___ Other ways that you may have thought more highly of yourself than you should

For each of these that has been true in your life, pray aloud:

Lord, I agree I have been prideful in the area of_____.
Please forgive me for this pridefulness. I choose to humble myself and place all my confidence in You. Amen.

STEP 6: BONDAGE VERSUS FREEDOM

The next step to freedom deals with habitual sin. People who have been caught in the trap of sin-confess-sin-confess may need to follow the instructions of James 5:16, "Confess your sins to one another, and pray for one another, so that you may be healed. The effective prayer of a righteous man can accomplish much." Seek out a righteous person who will hold you up in prayer and to whom you can be accountable. Others may only need the assurance of 1 John 1:9: "If we confess our sins, He is faithful and righteous to forgive us our sins and to cleanse us from all unrighteousness." Confession is not saying "I'm sorry"; it is saying "I did it." Whether you need the help of others or just the accountability of God, pray the following prayer:

> Dear heavenly Father,
>   You have told us to "put on the Lord Jesus Christ, and make no provision for the flesh in regard to its lusts" (Rom. 13:14). I acknowledge that I have given in to fleshly lusts that wage war against my soul (1 Pet. 2:11). I thank You that in Christ my sins are forgiven, but I have transgressed Your holy law and given the enemy an opportunity to wage war in my members (Rom. 6:12,13; Jas. 4:1; 1 Pet. 5:8). I come before Your presence to acknowledge these sins and to seek Your cleansing (1 John 1:9) that I may be freed from the bondage of sin. I now ask You to reveal to my mind the ways that I have transgressed Your moral law and grieved the Holy Spirit. In Jesus' precious name I pray. Amen.

The deeds of the flesh are numerous. You may want to open your Bible to Galatians 5:19-21 and pray through the verses, asking the Lord to reveal the ways you have specifically sinned.

It is our responsibility to not allow sin to reign in our mortal bodies by not using our bodies as instruments of unrighteousness (see Rom. 6:12,13). If you are struggling with habitual sexual sins (pornography, masturbation, sexual promiscuity) or experiencing sexual difficulty and intimacy in your marriage, pray as follows:

> Lord, I ask You to reveal to my mind every sexual use of my body as an instrument of unrighteousness. In Jesus' precious name I pray. Amen.

As the Lord brings to your mind every sexual use of your body, whether it was done to you (rape, incest or any sexual molestation) or willingly by you, renounce every occasion:

> Lord, I renounce (name the specific use of your body) with (name the person) and ask You to break that bond.

Now commit your body to the Lord by praying:

> Lord, I renounce all these uses of my body as an instrument of unrighteousness and by so doing ask You to break all bondages Satan has brought into my life through that involvement. I confess my participation. I now present my body to You as a living sacrifice, holy and acceptable unto You, and I reserve the sexual use of my body only for marriage. I renounce the lie of Satan that my body is not clean, that it is dirty or in any way unacceptable as a result of my past sexual experiences. Lord, I thank You that You have totally cleansed and forgiven me, that You love and accept me unconditionally. Therefore, I can accept myself. And I choose to do so, to accept myself and my body as cleansed. In Jesus' name. Amen.

SPECIAL PRAYERS FOR SPECIFIC NEEDS

Homosexuality
Lord, I renounce the lie that You have created me or anyone else to be homosexual, and I affirm that You clearly forbid homosexual behavior. I accept myself as a child of God and declare that You created me a man (or woman). I renounce any bondages of Satan that have perverted my relationships with others. I announce that I am free to relate to the opposite sex in the way that You intended. In Jesus' name. Amen.

Abortion
Lord, I confess that I did not assume stewardship of the life You entrusted to me, and I ask your forgiveness. I choose to accept Your forgiveness by forgiving myself, and I now commit that child to You for Your care in eternity. In Jesus' name. Amen.

Suicidal Tendencies
Lord, I renounce the lie that I can find peace and freedom by taking my own

life. Satan is a thief, and he comes to steal, kill and destroy. I choose life in Christ who said He came to give me life and to give it abundantly.

Eating Disorders, or Cutting on Yourself

Lord, I renounce the lie that my worthiness is dependent upon my appearance or performance. I renounce cutting myself, purging or defecating as a means of cleansing myself of evil, and I announce that only the blood of the Lord Jesus Christ can cleanse me from my sin. I accept the reality that there may be sin present in me because of the lies I have believed and the wrongful use of my body, but I renounce the lie that I am evil or that any part of my body is evil. I announce the truth that I am totally accepted by Christ just as I am.

Substance Abuse

Lord, I confess that I have misused substances (alcohol, tobacco, food, prescription or street drugs) for the purpose of pleasure, to escape reality, or to cope with difficult situations, resulting in the abuse of my body, the harmful programming of my mind and the quenching of the Holy Spirit. I ask Your forgiveness, and I renounce any satanic connection or influence in my life through my misuse of chemicals or food. I cast my anxiety onto Christ who loves me, and I commit myself to no longer yielding to substance abuse, but to the Holy Spirit. I ask You, heavenly Father, to fill me with Your Holy Spirit. In Jesus' name. Amen.

After you have confessed all known sin, pray:

> I now confess these sins to You and claim through the blood of the Lord Jesus Christ my forgiveness and cleansing. I cancel all ground that evil spirits have gained through my willful involvement in sin. I ask this in the wonderful name of my Lord and Savior Jesus Christ. Amen.

STEP 7: ACQUIESCENCE VERSUS RENUNCIATION

Acquiescence is passively giving in or agreeing without consent. The last step to freedom is to renounce the sins of your ancestors and any curses that may have been placed on you. In giving the Ten Commandments God said:

"You shall not make for yourself an idol, or any likeness of what is in heaven above or on the earth beneath or in the water under the earth. You shall not worship them or serve them; for I, the Lord your God, am a jealous God, visiting the iniquity of the fathers on the children, on the third and the fourth generations of those who hate Me" (Exod. 20:4,5).

Familiar spirits can be passed on from one generation to the next if not renounced and your new spiritual heritage in Christ is not proclaimed. You are not guilty for the sin of any ancestor, but because of their sin, Satan has gained access to your family. This is not to deny that many problems are transmitted genetically or acquired from an immoral atmosphere. All three conditions can predispose a person to a particular sin. In addition, deceived people may try to curse you, or satanic groups may try to target you. You have all the authority and protection you need in Christ to stand against such curses and assignments.

In order to walk free from past influences, read the following declaration and prayer to yourself first so that you know exactly what you are declaring and asking. Then claim your position and protection in Christ by making the declaration verbally and humbling yourself before God in prayer.

DECLARATION

I here and now reject and disown all the sins of my ancestors. As one who has been delivered from the power of darkness and translated into the Kingdom of God's dear Son, I cancel out all demonic working that has been passed on to me from my ancestors.

As one who has been crucified and raised with Jesus Christ and who sits with Him in heavenly places, I renounce all satanic assignments that are directed toward me and my ministry, and I cancel every curse that Satan and his workers have put on me. I announce to Satan and all his forces that Christ became a curse for me (Gal. 3:13) when He died for my sins on the cross. I reject any and every way in which Satan may claim ownership of me.

I belong to the Lord Jesus Christ who purchased me with His own blood. I reject all other blood sacrifices whereby Satan may claim ownership of me. I declare myself to be eternally and completely signed over and committed to the Lord Jesus Christ. By the authority that I have in Jesus Christ, I now command every familiar spirit and every enemy of the Lord Jesus Christ that is in or around me to leave my presence. I commit myself to my heavenly Father, to do His will from this day forward.

PRAYER

Dear heavenly Father,

I come to You as Your child, purchased by the blood of the Lord Jesus Christ. You are the Lord of the universe and the Lord of my life. I submit my body to You as an instrument of righteousness, a living sacrifice, that I may glorify You in my body. I now ask You to fill me with Your Holy Spirit. I commit myself to the renewing of my mind in order to prove that Your will is good, perfect and acceptable for me. All this I do in the name and authority of the Lord Jesus Christ. Amen.

Once you have secured your freedom by going through these seven Steps, you may find demonic influences attempting reentry days or even months later. One person shared that she heard a spirit say to her mind, "I'm back," two days after she had been set free. "No you're not!" she proclaimed aloud. The attack ceased immediately.

One victory does not constitute winning the war. Freedom must be maintained. After completing these Steps, one jubilant lady asked, "Will I always be like this?" I told her that she would stay free as long as she remained in right relationship with God. "Even if you slip and fall," I encouraged, "you know how to get right with God again."

One victim of incredible atrocities shared this illustration: "It's like being forced to play a game with an ugly stranger in my own home. I kept losing and wanted to quit, but the ugly stranger wouldn't let me. Finally I called the police (a higher authority), and they came and escorted the stranger out. He knocked on the door trying to regain entry, but this time I recognized his voice and didn't let him in."

What a beautiful illustration of gaining freedom in Christ. We call upon Jesus, the ultimate authority, and He escorts the enemy out of our lives. Know the truth, stand firm and resist the evil one. Seek out good Christian fellowship and commit yourself to regular times of Bible study and prayer God loves you and will never leave or forsake you.

AFTER CARE

Freedom must be maintained. You have won a very important battle in an ongoing war. Freedom is yours as long as you keep choosing truth and standing firm in the strength of the Lord. If new memories should surface or if you become aware of "lies" that you have believed or other non-Christian experiences you have had, renounce them and choose the truth. Some have found it helpful to go through the steps again. As you do, read the instructions carefully.

You should read *Victory over the Darkness, The Bondage Breaker, Released from Bondage* and *Living Free in Christ.* If you are a parent, read *The Seduction of Our Children. Walking Through the Darkness* was written to help people understand God's guidance and discern counterfeit guidance.

Also, to maintain your freedom, we suggest the following:

1. Seek legitimate Christian fellowship where you can walk in the light and speak the truth in love.
2. Study your Bible daily. Memorize key verses. You may want to express the Doctrinal Affirmation daily and look up the accompanying verses.
3. Take every thought captive to the obedience of Christ. Assume responsibility for your thought life, reject the lie, choose the truth and stand firm in your position in Christ.
4. Don't drift away! It is very easy to get lazy in your thoughts and revert back to old habit patterns of thinking. Share your struggles openly with a trusted friend. You need at least one friend who will stand with you.
5. Don't expect another person to fight your battle for you. Others can help but they can't think, pray, read the Bible or choose the truth for you.
6. Commit yourself to daily prayer. You can pray these suggested prayers often and with confidence:

DAILY PRAYER

Dear heavenly Father,

I honor You as my sovereign Lord. I acknowledge that You are always present with me. You are the only all-powerful and only wise God. You are kind and loving in all Your ways. I love You and I thank You that I am united with Christ and spiritually alive in Him. I choose not to love the world, and I crucify the flesh and all its passions.

I thank You for the life that I now have in Christ, and I ask You to fill me with Your Holy Spirit that I may live my life free from sin. I declare my dependence upon You, and I take my stand against Satan and all his lying ways. I choose to believe the truth, and I refuse to be discouraged. You are the God of all hope, and I am confident that You will meet my needs as I seek to live according to Your Word. I express with confidence that I can live a responsible life through Christ who strengthens me.

I now take my stand against Satan and command him and all his evil spirits to depart from me. I put on the whole armor of God. I submit my body as a living sacrifice and renew my mind by the living Word of God in order that I may prove that the will of God is good, acceptable and perfect. I ask these things in the precious name of my Lord and Savior, Jesus Christ. Amen.

BEDTIME PRAYER

Thank You, Lord, that You have brought me into Your family and have blessed me with every spiritual blessing in the heavenly realms in Christ. Thank You for providing this time of renewal through sleep. I accept it as part of Your perfect plan for Your children, and I trust You to guard my mind and my body during my sleep. As I have meditated on You and Your truth during this day, I choose to let these thoughts continue in my mind while I am asleep. I commit myself to You for Your protection from every attempt of Satan or his emissaries to attack me during sleep. I commit myself to You as my rock, my fortress and my resting place. I pray in the strong name of the Lord Jesus Christ. Amen.

CLEANSING HOME/APARTMENT

After removing all articles of false worship from home/apartment, pray aloud in every room if necessary.

Dear heavenly Father,

We acknowledge that You are Lord of heaven and earth. In Your sovereign power and love, You have given us all things richly to enjoy. Thank You for this place to live. We claim this home for our family as a place of spiritual safety and protection from all the attacks of the enemy. As children of God seated with Christ in the heavenly realm, we command every evil spirit, claiming ground in the structures and furnishings of this place based on the activities of previous occupants, to leave and never to return. We renounce all curses and spells utilized against this place. We ask You, heavenly Father, to post guardian angels around this home (apartment, condo, room, etc.) to guard it from attempts of the enemy to enter and disturb Your purposes for us. We thank You, Lord, for doing this, and pray in the name of the Lord Jesus Christ. Amen.

LIVING IN A NON-CHRISTIAN ENVIRONMENT

After removing all articles of false worship from your room, pray aloud in the space allotted to you.

Thank You, heavenly Father, for a place to live and to be renewed by sleep. I ask You to set aside my room (or portion of a room) as a place of spiritual safety for me. I renounce any allegiance given to false gods or spirits by other occupants, and I renounce any claim to this room (space) by Satan based on activities of past occupants or myself. On the basis of my position as a child of God and a joint-heir with Christ who has all the authority in heaven and on earth, I command all evil spirits to leave this place and never to return. I ask You, heavenly Father, to appoint guardian angels to protect me while I live here. I pray this in the name of the Lord Jesus Christ. Amen.

Continue to seek your identity and sense of worth in Christ. Read the book *Living Free in Christ.* Renew your mind with the truth that your acceptance, security and significance is in Christ by saturating your mind with the truths from the "Who I Am in Christ" list on the last page of this book. Read the entire list aloud morning and evening over the next several weeks. You may want to remove the list and carry it with you throughout the day.

Freedom in Christ

Conducts Conferences!

Freedom in Christ Ministries is an interdenominational, international, Bible-teaching church ministry that exists to glorify God by equipping churches and mission groups, enabling them to fulfill their mission of establishing people free in Christ. Thousands have found their freedom in Christ; your group can too! Here are some conferences your community can host that would be led by Freedom in Christ staff:

Resolving Personal and Spiritual Conflicts

(A seven-day Bible conference on living free in Christ)

Spiritual Conflicts and Counseling

(A two-day advanced seminar on helping others find freedom in Christ)

Setting Your Church Free

(A leadership conference on corporate freedom for churches, ministries, and mission groups)

Stomping Out the Darkness

(A youth conference for parents, youth workers, and young people)

Setting Your Youth Free

(An advanced seminar for youth pastors, youth workers, and parents)

Setting Your Kids Free

(A seminar for parents and children's workers wanting to train children free in Christ)

Resolving Spiritual Conflicts and Cross-Cultural Ministry

(A conference for leaders, missionaries, and all believers desiring to
see the Great Commission fulfilled)

The above conferences are also available on video and audio cassettes. To order these and other resources, write or call us.

To host a conference, write or call us at:

Freedom in Christ Ministries • 491 East Lambert Road • La Habra, CA 90631
Phone: (310) 691-9128 • Fax: (310) 691-4035

More resources from Neil Anderson and Freedom in Christ Ministries
to help you and those you love find freedom in Christ.

Books

Regal Books
Victory over the Darkness
Living Free in Christ
Stomping Out the Darkness
(Youth)
Setting Your Church Free
*Helping Others Find Freedom
in Christ*

Harvest House Publishers
The Bondage Breaker
The Seduction of Our Children
Winning Spiritual Warfare
Daily in Christ
The Bondage Breaker Youth Edition
A Way of Escape
To My Dear Slimeball
(Richard Miller)

Thomas Nelson Publishers
Released from Bondage
Walking in the Light

Crossway Books
Spiritual Warfare
(Timothy M. Warner)

Personal Study Guides

Regal Books
*Victory over the Darkness
Study Guide*
*Stomping Out the Darkness
Study Guide*

Harvest House
The Bondage Breaker Study Guide
*The Bondage Breaker Youth Edition
Study Guide*

Teaching Study Guides

Regal Books
*Breaking Through to Spiritual
Maturity* (Group Study)
Busting Free
(Youth Study Guide)

Who I Am in Christ

I Am Accepted in Christ

John 1:12	I am God's child
John 15:15	I am Christ's friend
Romans 5:1	I have been justified
1 Corinthians 6:17	I am united with the Lord and one with Him in spirit
1 Corinthians 6:20	I have been bought with a price; I belong to God
1 Corinthians 12:27	I am a member of Christ's Body
Ephesians 1:1	I am a saint
Ephesians 1:5	I have been adopted as God's child
Ephesians 2:18	I have direct access to God through the Holy Spirit
Colossians 1:14	I have been redeemed and forgiven of all my sins
Colossians 2:10	I am complete in Christ

I Am Secure in Christ

Romans 8:1,2	I am free forever from condemnation
Romans 8:28	I am assured that all things work together for good
Romans 8:33,34	I am free from any condemning charges against me
Romans 8:35	I cannot be separated from the love of God
2 Corinthians 1:21	I have been established, anointed and sealed by God
Colossians 3:3	I am hidden with Christ in God
Philippians 1:6	I am confident that the good work God has begun in me will be perfected
Philippians 3:20	I am a citizen of heaven
2 Timothy 1:7	I have not been given a spirit of fear, but of power, love and a sound mind
Hebrews 4:16	I can find grace and mercy in time of need
1 John 5:18	I am born of God and the evil one cannot touch me

I Am Significant in Christ

Matthew 5:13,14	I am the salt and light of the earth
John 15:1,5	I am a branch of the true vine, a channel of His life
John 15:16	I have been chosen and appointed to bear fruit
Acts 1:8	I am a personal witness of Christ's
1 Corinthians 3:16	I am God's temple
2 Corinthians 5:17-20	I am a minister of reconciliation
2 Corinthians 6:1	I am God's coworker
Ephesians 2:6	I am seated with Christ in the heavenly realm
Ephesians 2:10	I am God's workmanship
Ephesians 3:12	I may approach God with freedom and confidence
Philippians 4:13	I can do all things through Christ who strengthens me

Taken from *Living Free in Christ*, by Neil Anderson. © 1993, Regal Books.